G000273875

NED KELLY: AUSTRALIAN SON

When a nation has bestowed upon a man the highest tribute in its power to give in the phrase, "Game as Ned Kelly," what remains to be said?

Clive Turnbull

In the Kellian country there were not the facilities for a Charlemagne, nor the need for a Washington; but Providence assigned to our *General* the task of resisting that low estimation the European placed upon the native born, and to affirm that we have an individuality of our own making that is not to be trifled with . . . No matter what his faults were, he is the father of our national courage and the heart of our literature.

Robitt Jon Clow

The old story that we don't look too closely into our ancestors for fear of finding a horse-thief is commonplace, of course. Indeed, wouldn't it be shameful to find one of our grandpaws doing such a petty theft? Who could be proud of a great-grand-daddy with ambition no higher than stealing a horse? B'gad, we Americans go in for big stuff. Steal a horse? No! But steal a continent, a nation; steal the lives and labour of thousands of black men and women in slavery; steal the wages of underpaid workers; steal a railroad, a bank, a million dollars — oh, boy, now you're talking! That's real class! Those are the ancestors America's blue-bloods worship. But steal a horse — aw, heck, the guy might have been hanged for that!

Don West

Side by side with the unhappy figure of Faust stands another character also known to every nation. In Italy he is Pulcinello, in England, Punch, in Turkey Karapet, in our country Petruska. He is the invincible hero of the puppet show. He defeats everyone and everybody — the police, the clergy — even death and the devil — while he himself remains immortal. In this crude and naive image the working people incarnated their own selves and their firm belief that in the long run it will be they who will defeat and overcome everything and everybody.

Maxim Gorky

By the same author
Wild Turkey
The Jimberi Track
The Black Eureka

AUSTRALIAN CLASSICS

NED KELLY: AUSTRALIAN SON

3597238

ANGUS & ROBERTSON PUBLISHERS

ANGUS & ROBERTSON PUBLISHERS
London • Sydney • Melbourne • Singapore • Manila

*This book is copyright. Apart from any fair dealing for the
purposes of private study, research, criticism or review, as
permitted under the Copyright Act, no part may be reproduced
by any process without written permission. Inquiries should
be addressed to the publishers.*

First published as *Australian Son*, 1948
This revised Australian Classics edition published
by Angus & Robertson Publishers, Australia, 1981

© Max Brown 1948, 1980

National Library of Australia
Cataloguing-in-publication data.

Brown, Maxwell MacAlister
  Ned Kelly, Australian son.

  (Australian classics (Angus & Robertson))
  Previously published: Melbourne: Georgian House, 1948
  as: Australian son.
  Includes index
  ISBN 0 207 14421 4

  1. Kelly, Ned, 1855-1880. 2. Bush-rangers — Biography.
  I. Title. II. Title: Australian son. (Series)

364.1'55'0924

Printed in Hong Kong

Contents

3597238
IR-364·1550924

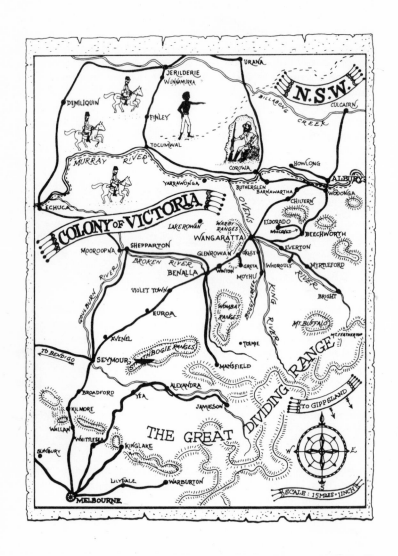

Foreword

I CANNOT REMEMBER when I first heard of Ned Kelly and the youths who were his comrades who flamed along these sombre hills towards the south-east corner of the Australian continent in the days of the lion rampant. I can imagine that good Queen Victoria — assured, satisfied, and with a tendency towards obesity, yet at the summit of her age — was the perfect emblem of the dominant, middle-aged, middle-class, righteous British Empire of the loud steam age in which they lived. Amid the huzzahs of petty wars for the enlargement of Empire, fought to the accompaniment of music-hall ditties, her plump hand never trembled, her name remained virtue.

Yet I suspect that behind the name of evil given these young men was a certain worth little understood then or now, which, in a perverse way, put the seal of manhood on the young Australian nation; and that their fame, which made the bushland ring, will therefore never cease to ring in Australian hearts.

Strange that four such young men, born of poor selector families, educated by few books, but by the deeds of men and the signs of earth, should live so briefly and be remembered so long in spite of the fiercest campaign of calumny the young colony had witnessed.

People are not remembered for nothing; and Kelly, over seventy years dead, his own defence for long denied a hearing, will not lie down. Why, otherwise, should I add to the packed shelf of Kellyana?

Was it the Second World War which gave me a realisation of the validity of my own country? Was it that in the men with whom I lived I found a certain unique Australian character — a promise and a threat, which had found expression in the life of Kelly many years before?

On my way north in 1945 in sound of Sydney surf, I idly bought a cheap, brightly coloured booklet which I read in the shadow of the Black Stump. Not knowing, and scarcely caring what else had been written, I decided, when I returned to Melbourne in peace, to take a year off to write a book on the Kelly gang.

In a year I have been to many strange places following chance or deliberate word.

In the Melbourne Public Library and Mitchell Collection, I have read every line I could find which dealt with the gang, and much about the life of their time. I have visited many of the old haunts, travelled across their country, spoken with old people who remember them. I have seen evidence of the time in the opulent cornices and enduring workmanship of private mansions and public buildings, and in the squat homes of the common people. I have narrowed my eyes in the twilight of scarred clearings and imagined the roaring days of the golden plague. On some farm I have come across an old toolshed built of slabs — once the home of a settler in the days of the pit saw. I have pulled the bootlace latch as so many before me, and entering the gloom, have noted the broad hearth and rusted camp oven, and up against the wall a rough-hewn stool; and it has not been so difficult to hear again the voices of the selector and his wife, and the chatter of the barefoot children. I have asked the old man who showed me around: "Did you work hard in the old days?" and with the ghost of a hearty laugh, he has replied: "Work hard? Why, they used to put a bag over the sun so we wouldn't see it go down."

Out of the rain or sun in spacious stables dead with the smell of dust and sump oil, and incongruous with sleek, beetle-shaped automobiles, I have seen the wooden stalls as they were, each with its mount. I have heard them whinny and champ in the night. I have smelt whiffs of hay and horses and the ripe tang of manure. I have seen again the days when the iron horse was advancing, but still the horse was king, when benzine was hay, the service station the farrier's forge, the days when the flasher your horse and the flasher your gear, the damn sight flasher you were.

But, dream as I can in the shadow of the Alps where these four young bushmen rode, I shall never savour the tang of their voices, hear them laugh or curse, feel with my hand against their hearts, the impact of the first great disaster — of their summer triumphs when the telegraph flung their deeds across the world, of the days of waiting and boredom towards the end, and of their final ill-starred attempt to come to terms with the police and officials they never ceased to contend had harried them without just cause.

In books old and new, in old documents and official reports, in the stained files of newspapers, in the dumb evidence of trees and rocks and old buildings, in the quavering voices and still bright eyes of old folk who knew them, but are soon to die, I have read something. Sometimes I felt I had moments of insight into the enigma of their leader who has been described as low thief and murderer, and again as "the father of our national courage — our General — our King — whose mystical presence is still growing about us, never to die". Other times I have felt it futile that I — insecure and living in these days of judgement — should ever try to concentrate my gaze to see behind these words and stones, and have hoped for the day when a bolder and freer wit would write down that which I could not.

We have never known or have forgotten already. Hunted, tracked and spied on, and with a price on their heads, they themselves in statements which they tried to bring to the attention of the people and government of the time, likely enough distorted the truth to justify themselves or put the police off the scent. How could they be expected to tell even close friends what they were up to when each had £2000 on his head? What little the gang told was to an inner circle of relatives who stood by them to the end. These are dead; but even while they lived they said little, and had nothing but contempt for the tribe of hacks, who, they said, were out to make blood money from heroes.

Many writers have recorded many views and are praised or scorned according to prejudice, class interest or their ability to write conventional English. As Kelly himself said, we must all one day be judged according to our mercy and our deeds; and anyone wishing to find how poorly most have done the job need refer little further than Kelly's own statements and the 700-page Police Commission Report of 1881.

As for this work, suffice that I, setting out in January 1946, with the tattered remnants of youthful idealism, declared to myself that I would leave no stone unturned, and that three months later, I tramped along a track near Greta bitterly disappointed, aware already of a great limitation placed on my aim, muttering to myself the first line of a preface I would one day write: This is the story of failure; but from the ashes rises some achievement!

The hands of the dead had reached out to keep the silence. Already I knew there were gaps in the Kelly history I could not mend, as well as major issues concerning which accounts were opposed. Time, class interest and perversity had done their job so that no effort of mine nor the readily extended assistance of almost everyone to whom I went could solve these contradictions. I realised, finally, that the truth I once regarded as absolute was largely relative — in the eye of many beholders, as well as running its course in an earlier age — and that I was indebted to erring men for every record of Kelly and his times.

Nevertheless, in the processes of work, many details fell into place to be supported by other evidence and point to conclusions, which in turn received support, so that what emerged assumed a strength and validity I could not have imagined earlier. Incomplete, erroneous in some details, and ill-conceived as this account may be, I believe it will, nevertheless, do some justice to a man, who, in his day, appeared to many not as a blackhearted murderer, but as a new messiah of Australian democracy.

The legend says that when the die was cast and Kelly was fated to follow the course to inevitable eclipse, he approached his mate, Joe Byrne, like Christ summoning his disciples, and said: "What about it, Joe?"—to which the latter replied: "I'll tell you what I'll do; I'll hit the earth with this stick and if it breaks I'm with you." Whereupon, he picked up a stick and smashed it on a granite outcrop at his feet, laughed, tossed the stump away, jumped on his horse, and rode off with his mate into the ranges.

It says also that when Ned approached Steve Hart as he chopped wood on his father's land, Steve laughed also, tossed his axe on the heap, said: "Here's to a short life and a merry one!" and went off to saddle his nag.

It declared that in the hour of his capture, the police took from Kelly's pocket a declaration for a Republic of North-Eastern Victoria!

It is not legend—it is truth—that in this hour, bleeding from his many wounds and staggering under his fifty kilograms of ploughshares through the mist and half-light of the morning to join his mates, Kelly actually did assume supernatural proportions in the eyes of the troopers, who cried out to each other: "It's the bunyip! It's the devil himself!"

Likewise, it was sober fact when Judge Sir Redmond Barry passed sentence and concluded with the words, "May the Lord have mercy on your soul!" Kelly replied: "Yes, I will meet you there!"—and that twelve days after Kelly was hanged, the honourable judge was killed no less effectively by a common ailment of the flesh.

Flowers open to the sun and close to the night. In the shadow of death through which he stalked for twenty months, Ned Kelly summoned up such aspects of heroism, dormant in all but a few of us, that some who have known the commoner rut say this man was approaching the stature of god or devil. So does the myth become greater than reality to react upon reality!

1. Old Melbourne Town

THE DATE WAS 18 JULY 1841, the day brisk, and the barque *England,* arriving in Hobson's Bay in the south-east corner of this Australian continent, hove to off the flat shore of a place appropriately named Sandridge. Finally at peace after a stormy voyage from Liverpool in which sixteen children and two adults had died of whooping cough, she dropped anchor and swung into the wind within sight of the southern extremity of a rough settlement known to the few thousand people on earth who had heard of it, as Melbourne.

The *England* was a former convict transport, built near the Forest of Dean in the war against Napoleon thirty years before, and recently modified to carry the bounty immigrants who now crowded the decks. Not that Merry England had contributed the bounty to get rid of them; the £15 per head paid to the shipowners was met from land sales in the new colony. Mostly poor families who had been a burden on English parishes or Irish landlords, the immigrants included some Scots pushed off their crofts to make way for sheep in the latest series of Highland clearances.

The newcomers were cheap labour, shipped out to become servants and shepherds in this most recent annexation to the Imperial Crown, the Port Phillip District of New South Wales. Who of them had more cause to celebrate is unclear—the English to have fled their factory hells or the Scots and Irish their impoverished farms—but among the Irish, relieved at the bright vision of a beach with timber jetty and hotel bearing the sign Liardets, was a family called Quinn from the neighbourhood of Belfast, County Antrim.

Thus, in the morning of Victoria's brief history, at a spot later to be known as Port Melbourne beach, landed James and Mary Quinn and their six children from a ship's boat. Of these our story is particularly to concern a nine-year-old girl named Ellen who was to live across a century to the year 1923 when the T-model Ford and bitumen road, the prophets said, were preparing the golden age of industrialism. By that conjunction of forces which we, after the event, term fate, Ellen Quinn was to become concerned in deeds written no less indelibly in the memory of this young nation than on this page.

The first thing the passengers saw ashore was a canvas booth used in promoting land sales and a pile of empty champagne bottles nearby. It being Sunday, when Liardets' horse omnibus was otherwise employed, they made their own way several

1

kilometres through the ti trees and erected tents against a large encampment where people were cooking on open fires amid the tinkle of sheep-bells. Sheep were pastured in the bush to right and left and at night were enclosed for safety within portable fences made of rough timber hurdles.

After trying whaling, sandalwooding and various other industries in its early life, the infant Australian colony based on Sydney had hit upon wool as an export staple. The English mills could not get enough of it, and the Port Phillip pioneers who had crossed from Launceston five years before were still bringing sheep across the strait from Van Diemen's Land. Through the eucalypts and she-oaks could be seen a fine river and a variety of small ships, while on the northern bank rose yards and sheds, a Customs House and the assorted buildings of a growing town. Melbourne had thrived from the start, and — following the visit of Governor Bourke from Sydney — now had its own administrator, Mr Latrobe, and a town plan which provided for a business district of one mile square.

Mr Latrobe, in fact, had brought with him a chalet which he had erected upstream on a gentle rise which his Swiss wife called Jolimont. This served as the social centre of the colony, while a brand new set of offices at the foot of Queen Street provided the administrative centre.

James Quinn started work at once. His job as porter took him from the quagmire at the riverfront to all parts where he had occasion to meet the motley collection of Vandemonians and Sydneysiders whose sweat was transforming this Australia Felix that the explorer Mitchell had described as ready for the immediate use of civilised man. The Vandemonians had scarcely landed when Mitchell opened the way for the Sydneysiders driving stock overland.

Melbourne's infant years had seen the growth of a motley assortment of buildings of slab, wattle and daub, weatherboard and brick, mostly within the area bounded by William, Lonsdale and Swanston streets, some one to an allotment, others two, some set against the street alignment, others well back, all made homely by a variety of stumps and an occasional tree still holding full sway. The streets were bogs in winter and dust-tracks in summer, while, with any fall of rain, Williams Creek poured down Elizabeth Street and cut the town in two.

In the central area, especially in Collins Street, were many new businesses — including emporiums, insurance houses, steam-packet companies and banking-chambers — while west of these stood the government block and barracks, and west again around John Batman's hill an assortment of slaughterhouses, boiling-down works and other manufactories to supply meat, soap, hide and candles to the rapidly growing populace. John Pascoe Fawkner, the town's other founder, had a family hotel in Swanston Street where all the latest magazines and intelligence were available.

What struck the newcomer at once was the scarcity of elderly folk, women and the dark dress of the old world, and the abundance of land sales and auctions, often conducted with the aid of free champagne. The assorted males sported an extraordinary variety of dress and uniforms in which straw hats and stovepipes distinguished the gentry and land speculators come down by coasting schooner from Sydney from the ruck of bush-dwellers who wore broad felt, or cabbage-tree, hats.

The Sydney road was the main route to the bush, which was why the Catholic church, named for St Francis, was sited up Elizabeth Street. As the foundation stone of a new permanent church was laid soon after the Quinn family's arrival and new parties of Irish immigrants were arriving weekly, it is likely that they attended the ceremony and heard reports of mass meetings in Ireland and new threats to imprison the Irish leader, Daniel O'Connell. No doubt too, with the eyes of one who knew the wrongs done Ireland, James Quinn noted the timber gibbet thrusting into the sky up Russell Street, the treadmill taking shape at the new brick gaol near the barracks, and nearby the triangles where convict servants and shepherds who had still time to do were given the lash.

Melbourne had been without crime for three or four years until brawls involving women and drunken shepherds down from the bush had led to the establishment of a gaol, police force and judiciary, not to mention an active temperance movement. Mostly time-expired convicts or ticket-of-leave convicts freed on condition they serve out their time, these bush bachelors were in the habit of entrusting their wage cheques to one or another publican, and then spent their leave "knocking" the cheques over.

The squatters were in colourful contrast to both the men they employed and the officials who modelled their life on the sedate English pattern. Likely enough Quinn had opportunity to see them at the Melbourne Club where they went to dicker over brandy and cigars with the Commissioners of Crown Lands. Yes, they were all in favour of dropping the military trappings which held Sydney back, but they could not run their properties with immigrant labour; they wanted a continuance of transportation. On occasions they could be seen riding into town to set out demands for political rights for Port Phillip and for security of tenure for the lands they had seized.

They looked like an army of buccaneers. Whiskers on chest, locks flowing over their red and blue serge coats, wide black belts hitching their moleskins, pistol on saddle and muzzle-loader on back, they walked their horses under flying pennants to the skirl of a Highland piper at the head. They came from Corio Bay, Gippsland, the Goulburn Valley and points west and north, or from further out — from the frontier of burned stockyards and killed and stolen stock, where the Aborigines were fighting desperately to keep what remained of their hunting grounds and their dreamings.

A generation before, the governors in Sydney had awarded huge tracts to almost any individual "of good family", and a few score had established their herds and homesteads inland from Port Jackson with the aid of short-sentence convicts, while iron-gangs under the military built a system of roads and stockades.

For a time, efforts were made to confine settlement to an area which could be controlled from Sydney. However, the rising demand for wool had prompted these same gentlemen — joined by anyone else with money enough.— to push inland and squat on one tribal territory after another; soon a few hundred squatters, with the aid of several thousand convicts, had occupied pasturelands the size of France or Spain and won legal right.

Land was not so easily come by for those outside the club — and that covered almost all the Irish. Nevertheless, Port Phillip District offered many opportunities to anyone who had the help of a woman. And so James Quinn, by saving his shillings, was able to rent some land to the north at Brunswick where he cultivated part of his holding and kept some cows, between times carting timber. In Melbourne, butter in the hogshead was assured of a ready sale.

As the children became more useful, the Quinns were able to shift to a larger property at Broadmeadows, and north again to a rented block at Wallan near the Great Dividing Range. Up range was a pass which travellers called Pretty Sally for its first sight of Melbourne and promised joys, and beyond — like a sentinel — stood Kilmore, marking the spot where the original overlanders who had followed the wheeltracks of Mitchell's drays from the Sydney side found the Launceston men in occupation in 1837.

Large squatting runs lay all around. However, the Kilmore estate, including several hectares of rich, volcanic soil, had been subdivided and sold or rented to small farmers, mostly Irish. So

Kilmore was Irish by name and Irish by nature, the town where you stopped if you preferred the sound of the brogue. But it was also where the bush began, and a place too where many an Irish new chum met Irishmen of the older colonial school who had felt the lash or had bloodhounds on their tracks and knew the tricks of the trade.

The farmers had the saying that every new bun-in-the-oven was better than £100 in the bank. Four more children were born to the Quinns — William, Mary, Margaret and Grace — and before long Patrick and John, the elder boys, were able to take the teams in hand, and carry on the carting side of the business.

Around 1849, James Quinn made the acquaintance of a young countryman with reddish hair, John Kelly, who was splitting and fencing along Merri Creek. Red Kelly, as he was known, had completed a seven-year sentence in Van Diemen's Land. Born in County Tipperary, he had worked as a ranger on Lord Ormonde's Killarney estate until transported for stealing two pigs — a typical offence since eight of every ten Irish convicts were transported for larceny of an animal.

Known variously as His Lordship (because the landlord was English), or Georgie (after the profligate George IV), the pig was more commonly called 'the gentleman who pays the rent' because he made all the difference between solvency and beggary. Red Kelly had made the voyage to the Derwent in the barque *Prince Regent* and served time with the bushranger William Westwood — better known as Jacky Jacky — who had finally been hanged with ten others on Norfolk Island for organising a mutiny. Like Kelly himself, Westwood had been a harmless short-sentence man before absconding from a sheep station south of Sydney.

In spite of such horrors, transportation was no longer quite the punishment intended, especially if an assigned man found himself in the rich Port Phillip District which was resolutely opposed to transportation and looked to the wage system as its basis for the future. Long though the labour might have been, the horizons of this new world were expanding, and the one-time convict — if he was young and had a mind to it — now had more to look forward to than the solace of his pipe and the company of his dog.

Red Kelly, aged twenty-nine, soon paid court to Ellen, now a petite seventeen-year-old; but Quinn did not favour the alliance, maybe because Kelly was unassertive and seemed unlikely to make much of a mark on the world.

The Quinns were dealt a blow that year by the drowning of their son, Patrick, who had taken a bullock wagon to Echuca; but if they lost one son, they gained another — Red and Ellen eloped and were married in St Francis Church, on Monday, 18 November 1850, the celebrant being Father Gerald Ward, himself barely arrived from Ireland. Melburnians, who had been petitioning London for independence from New South Wales, happened to be in gay mood, for the British Parliament had passed a bill to separate Port Phillip District into a colony in its own right to be named after the Queen, and with Mr Latrobe elevated to Governor.

The records show Kelly to have been well behaved as a prisoner; he seems to have been a peacemaker and to have had a strong hatred of injustice which prompted him to take the part of anyone who was badly used. Although he could read and sign his name like most of his peers, it is doubtful it he could write much, which is not surprising since what few common schools Ireland had were conducted illegally under hedgerows.

At any rate, he was able to win himself a young attractive wife at a period when the plainest spinster was plagued by a dozen suitors. All her life, Ellen Kelly was proud of Red Kelly, which suggests that the match was a good one. Moreover, his eldest son, whom this story specially concerns and whose voice will be heard when others fail, spoke of his father with pride.

The young couple found accommodation about five kilometres from Wallan at Mercer Vale, later to be called Beveridge after a Scots family which kept a local inn. Red split logs and erected a slab hut a short distance from the Sydney road, and here they lived along with a few cows while he earned a wage by axe and adze putting up sheds and yards or simply knocking together hurdles for the sheep men.

2. *The Roaring Fifties*

DURING Victoria's first fifteen years, settlers both free and tied continued to arrive, and by 1850 the population scattered south of the Murray exceeded 70 000, two-thirds of them male. Workers in the wool industry for the most part, they looked forward to years of toil and perhaps even to buying a property. So they made the best of it, and when loneliness became too bitter, drowned their sorrows in spirits or sleep. Who would have thought this wide and peaceful land was on the brink of a revolution?

As far back as 1814, and then again in 1823 and 1825, gold had been discovered near Bathurst, but each time the authorities suppressed news of the discovery. In 1839, the Polish explorer,

Count Strzelecki, made a find west of Sydney near Hartley, and two years later a Rev. W. B. Clarke found gold in the same spot. What effect would news of easy-to-win riches have on the iron-gangs at work on the Bathurst road or even on the redcoats guarding them? "Put it away Mr Clarke, or we shall all have our throats cut," remarked Governor Gipps when shown a sample. In Victoria, finds were made on the Ovens in 1845 and in the Pyrenees in 1848.

By 1848, when Prince von Metternich was at his wit's end to hold the lid on insurgent capitalist Europe, the New South Wales establishment was equally hard put to conceal the fact that gold was to be found in many parts of the colony; but neither in the old world nor the new could the tide of history be halted. Edward Hargraves, a forty-niner returned from a gold strike in the Sierra Nevada near San Francisco, demonstrated the existence of a large field near Bathurst in February 1851 and—as a stream of gold-seekers packed their bags for New South Wales—Melbourne took fright and offered £200 reward to someone who could make a strike south of the Murray.

Within weeks, finds quite eclipsing those in New South Wales were made at Clunes, Burnbank, Buninyong, Ballarat, Mt Alexander and a dozen other spots, and soon the news had spread the other side of sundown. Artisans and clerks picked up their coats and walked off the job. Crews tied up their ships, left a man in charge and took to the road. The Masters and Servants Act was pitched out the window. Panic spread among the squatters and gentry as servants and shepherds disappeared, wages and prices soared and the order of privilege based on the lash and noose was dealt a blow from which it would never recover.

Meanwhile streams of men pushing wheelbarrows and driving carts and canvas-tilted bullock drays packed with bags of flour, cases of food, bedding, pots, tin dishes, buckets, iron kettles, picks, shovels and tools struck in from the seaboard to the El Dorados of Ballarat, Bendigo, Creswick, Clunes, Talbot, Castlemaine and the Ovens diggings. The military had to be summoned from Van Diemen's Land to deal with bushrangers on the Mt Alexander road.

"Within three weeks, Melbourne and Geelong have been almost emptied of many classes of inhabitants," wrote Governor Latrobe in October. "In some of the suburbs not a man is left, and the women for protection group together to keep house . . . It really becomes a question of how the more sober operations of society, and even the functions of Government, may be carried on."

Then in 1852, as the clipper ships driven by the gales of the high latitudes carried the news to America and Europe, came the first wash of the flood of immigrants, which within ten years was to raise the population of Victoria to more than half a million. Came adventurers, gamblers, mountebanks, Californian wildcatters, the oppressed and impoverished of a score of European countries.

Many in the rush were refugees from Ireland. Following the failure of the potato crop in 1847, and while exports of food continued as usual under the guns of English troops, one out of every four people died of starvation. Revolt rumbled, guns barked behind hedgerows, shillelaghs struck in the night, but the colonial safety valve was turned on full cock and thousands were ferried out of the Emerald Isle.

Poorer and less literate than their English and Scottish equivalents, yet with a powerful rebel spirit forged in oppression, the Irish soon comprised a significant part of the population of the diggings.

Thus, with an energy unsurpassed in history, peasants, scholars, ship captains, ex-convicts, Yankees, Polish and Irish rebels — people of all sorts, clad in fustian, red and blue Crimean shirts, jumpers in flaming colours, oddments of uniform and genteel dress — toiled and sang along the creeks amid the gums, and towns of ten thousand tents, bark humpies and slab huts sprang up overnight to wax and wane on the golden tide.

In Melbourne, wharves, warehouses and shops imitating Bond Street shot up and diggers were known to light their pipes with banknotes. The town became a playland for diggers on a bender — a place of paradox where men of birth and education worked as menials in the kitchen, and roughnecks, drunk with champagne, drove through the streets in landaus, caressed by ladies easily won with jewels and excitement. And yet many a man whom fortune had spurned and driven to some trivial offence was dragged to the lock-up, handcuffed to a police stirrup-iron — past wealth and fashion, the gold coaches with their escorts from the interior and bullock wagons groaning with imports bound for the golden hinterland.

From the start, the authorities sought means to force workers back on to the sheep runs. Following the New South Wales example, Governor Latrobe decreed that diggers must buy a licence to be produced on demand, but as the fee of 30s a month was equal to one week's wage in four, they evaded payment by joining any new rush, and then by passing licences from hand to hand. It became a common sight to see strings of men marched off in irons.

Society was in the melting pot. The question was asked: who

gave themselves the right to imprison others? If it came to cases, not a few diggers were as well-connected as their gaolers, and soon the cry, "No taxation without representation!" coined in the Reform Bill agitation in the British Isles, rang out along the clearings.

Ugly incidents occurred, including official protection for a murderer, and the new Governor marched a force to Ballarat, leading to a pitched battle with the diggers on the Eureka claim.

As the roll of the dead was called — thirty diggers and four soldiers — there echoed a growl which swept the goldfields from end to end and re-echoed from Melbourne; and the colony's sole lawmaker, the Legislative Council, finding the people had a pistol at its head, refused funds to impress London with the urgency of a new constitution.

When the diggers' leaders appeared on charges of high treason, the juries found them not guilty amid public rejoicing. Then a new constitution providing two elective chambers was proclaimed, and before the singing of Auld Lang Syne that year, gallant Governor Hotham, aged forty-nine years, was dead of a cerebral haemorrhage brought on by worry.

Before gold, the Sydney road had been little more than a bush track linking the station properties and river crossings, and its traffic had consisted mainly of bullock wagons hauling flour and stores up country, or wool to Williamstown and Geelong for export. Jimmy Quinn had rapidly identified with the basic Australia — that undeclared confederacy of one-time Irish farm labourers, London pickpockets, assorted bankrupts and alcoholics that had begun to take shape before the First Fleet cleared the English Channel. The Quinns had burned off, established pasture and followed their teams like the rest, with little to disturb them save an occasional traveller.

Then, when thousands of hungry gold-seekers suddenly descended on central Victoria, Kilmore and district became the focus of a roaring trade in cattle-on-the-hoof, and the Quinns joined with the rest in the game of catch and grab that went on day and night in the unfenced ranges. The police were no problem; they could be found nightly drinking and gambling till all hours, and supplied a bed for a price or for nothing at all if you could show them where to get some colours.

And so with enhanced prices for everything and the thriving cattle trade, Jimmy Quinn was able to buy 284 hectares from the Crown and build a substantial stone and timber dwelling from materials at hand.

Respectability, so to speak, had caught up with him, while Mrs

Quinn, in particular, was kindness itself, renowned far and wide for her hospitality, not only to friends, but to perfect strangers off the road. Kate and Jane, meanwhile, had married two brothers, Jack and Tom Lloyd, and the clan included a brace of tallish young Australians who spoke a tongue rather different to the brogue of their parents.

Down the road, Red Kelly had written home telling his young brother James about the rich, southern land where people were demanding "a vote, a rifle and a farm". Beveridge had grown vastly. Opposite the Kellys' hut had been built the Inverlochy Castle Hotel, a regular coach change for Cobb and Co. With its extensive stables, feed loft, and its spelling paddocks which always had upwards of fifty animals, it could be seen for miles.

Bullock wagons, passenger coaches and gold coaches with their uniformed escorts lumbered downhill to Melbourne, or uphill to the Goulburn Valley and the Ovens. Cavalcades of horsemen trotted by — bushmen, shearers, diggers, squatters, troopers — and strings of Chinese wearing pigtails and bearing baskets suspended from wooden yokes — all bound one way or another. How many travellers called in for fodder or for water, or to yarn over a kettle of tea? What tales were told of gold nuggets, of the Irish famine, the exodus to New York, of the revolution in Germany or battles on the diggings, of treeless plains on the overland and lush valleys in the Great Divide where 10 000 cattle might tread?

In the early fifties when the rushes were at their height, Red too yielded briefly to the call of gold, joining the stampede to the find at nearby Deep Creek. The arrival of a baby girl whom they named Ann helped the couple to recover from the death of their first-born, Mary Jane; and here in the winter of 1855, within sight and sound of the cracking of whips and the great concourse of men and of animals, was born Ellen Kelly's first son, Edward, whom history remembers.

3.   To Avenel

ALTHOUGH theft and highway robbery were endemic in the fifties — some days the *Argus* published twelve columns of stolen horses — the Quinns managed to keep out of trouble; but, as the sixties approached, they had their first brush with the law.

The action, which stemmed from a £50 reward offered by the lessee of Tallarook station, attempted to show that the sixteen-year-old James Quinn had been involved with cattle duffers, and was followed in 1860 by stock-theft charges brought against both James junior and his older brother, John. In the same year, charges of brawling were brought against James junior and John Lloyd, and old Jimmy Quinn was awarded £150 plus costs for a road deviation through his property.

Two facts are evident—one, that society was taking organised shape, and secondly, that the Quinns, as small freeholders who had links with the "fence" for strayed and stolen stock, could expect more trouble from the squatters, particularly as Victoria was entering a new era.

In the tumultuous gold centres, the surface gold was giving out. The wealthier diggers clubbed together, bought machinery, dug deeper into the leads and crushed the quartz. Mining was becoming a capitalist industry in which Jack worked underground for his old mate, Bill—not so maty now—who sat in the office, or perhaps drew dividends in Melbourne or London. And Charlie, they said, had bought into the squatting business, and Mick set himself up in a pub.

As for the poorer ones—some who could not resist the call followed the gold to New South Wales or across the Tasman. Others went into commerce, and more again went to the towns to construct wharves, buildings and roads and continue the works of the prison gangs—the bluestone courtyards, alleys and floodwater channels which would mark the land for centuries to come. Many who had worked before on the runs returned to find that the squatter had replaced shepherds and hurdles with brush or split-rail fences and boundary riders.

But these represented a drop in the bucket. The thousands who remained looked out at the squatter's lands stretching horizonless and virgin, and demanded the right to settle and farm.

Thus, the crowds of the gold centres, which so shortly before had won representation, now issued orders to their M.P.s to start them on the land and introduce tariffs so that native industries could make ploughs, reapers, wagons and all else needed for the progress of the colony and the employment of its people. In Melbourne demonstrators packed the top of Bourke Street opposite Parliament House, and Collins Street at election time was black with crowds outside the newspaper offices.

From the start, the strong-armed first-comers, entrenched behind law-and-order, were committed to yield ground, for arrayed against them were not only the diggers, who comprised the bulk of the population, but the traders and workers of the cities who looked to the new markets and employment that would be opened up by closer settlement. But from the start, also, the

11

squatters fought blindly and bitterly. They complained: "No sooner is all fear of the blacks dispatched, than the whites become almost as great a nuisance, sending in applications and petitions for portions of our runs."

The Government was forced rapidly to pass acts throwing open millions of hectares, but giving the squatter in each case his pre-emptive right, equivalent to first option on up to one square mile containing his homestead and major improvements. Now the carts set out for the bush as a few years before they had made for the diggings, and the squatter pulled down the brim of his hat and watched the digger families invade his land, look over and select parts of his run and bid at the land sales.

From the first, no love was lost. To the squatter, the newcomers appeared a rough and lawless lot. To the selectors, the squatter and the police troopers represented the old-world landlord and his bailiffs. So the squatter got in first and bought up the best portions of the run. Or he packed the land sales with his agents, bribed the auctioneer, elbowed the selectors out, bought up the water frontages through dummies and so made the intermediate areas valueless. This was known as "peacocking". But, like an advancing army, the selectors got a toehold, brought up their reserves, fanned out, and sat on their bare selections around the squatter's dwindling yet still vast domains. Just as he had a generation before, they built their huts, felled the trees and burned a few acres. Where he had established sheep and cattle, they set out to plough the land.

No one threatened old Jimmy's few hundred hectares, all he knew was that civilisation was coming to the bush and showed the same ugly Anglo-Saxon face to which he had thumbed good riddance when leaving the Mersey. Like many another Irishman, he dreamed of a larger spread further out, where there were fewer traps and fine manners; but it was Red Kelly who made a first move. In or about 1860, Red and Ellen sold out at Beveridge and arranged to lease a farm up the Sydney road at Avenel.

The rental was £14 a year for sixteen hectares on Hughes Creek. Red could have obtained land on better terms, but Avenel had an inexpensive school to which he could send the children. Since he was an old lag and could ill afford to become involved in police action, the move was also dictated by the need to put some distance between his familly and the duffing trade in which the Quinns were involved. Barely arrived from the Emerald Isle, his own brother, Tipperary Jim as they called him, was already up to his neck in it.

Next year, the Kellys shifted up over Pretty Sally and the

Goulburn, a four-day drive with stock, although a first-class horseman could do it overnight. Avenel was an ideal spot for the barefoot children who now numbered Annie eight years, Ned six, Margaret four and Jim two. Situated near the creek crossing where the original squatter, Henry Kent Hughes, had established his headquarters in 1838, it had found a lively trade in the Ovens diggings traffic and grown into a sizable village scattered around a handsome stone bridge and tollhouse. The farms were mainly along the creek, lined with gum trees lofty and thick through the butt, which also dotted the rolling countryside as in a park.

Although new land was being selected nearby, the Kelly block — next to the Morgans and about two kilometres downstream — was freehold bought by the original blacksmith William Mutton in the early fifties, the rent being payable to his widow. Red Kelly, therefore, was in much the same position as an Irish or Scots tenant farmer, although land was going begging in Australia, they said.

He chose an elevated position within sight of the Morgans and about 150 metres from the creek, and again put axe and adze to work to build a slab hut. The design was more or less standard — broad chimney one end, veranda in front, skillion and water butt at the rear and earthen floor. Then he fenced in the home paddock and put up a shed or so.

The pioneer settlers along the creek had had it hard at the start, clearing big timber, burning it, or dragging it to the sides of the fields and then grubbing before the ground could be ploughed; but they had gradually prospered. Red's work settled down to putting in post-and-rail fences for selectors and others who had the problem of keeping cattle out of the crops. He ran no more than a few cows, a few poddy calves and as many horses. Flour was cheap enough and game of all sorts plentiful, so although he seldom killed a beast, the children were well fed. When he did kill, he was required by law to retain the skin and the brand.

For their first few months in Avenel, Annie and Ned attended the Church of England school near the bridge where the pupils paid a shilling each Monday. However, as public opinion favoured a free and secular system, a school board was set up and the old bark structure replaced by the Common School built of slabs further up the creek.

The pupils numbered more than thirty first generation Victorians — including Muttons, Chappells, Campions, Burrows, Vearings and Sheltons — mostly from English, Welsh and Cornish parents, and Anglicans or Methodists, and, as everyone remarked, all rather tall, happier and better looking than children

13

in the Old Country. The teachers were Mr James Irving, and later Mr E. Lewis who owned an orchard near the town.

In the mornings the Shelton children, who lived about a kilometre to the west, crossed the creek on a fallen tree near the Kelly home, and often a half dozen or more children made their way to school together — sometimes walking, sometimes riding bareback two or three together. The Sheltons had a weatherboard general store and butcher's shop opposite the Royal Mail Hotel and toll gate at the Seymour entrance to town. Most of the town lay over the bridge, with the Avenel Arms on the right, and beyond that, some distance back, the police reserve and barracks. The Avenel Arms was a coach change and both it and the police had spelling paddocks for the teams.

Besides Shelton's, Avenel had two general stores — one run by the postmaster who was also registrar of births and deaths — as well as two blacksmiths, a feed store, a bakery, a saddlery, a shoemaker and a wine shanty. About half the buildings were of slabs, some with separate kitchen and stables. The rest were of brick, palings or bark. To the rear of the police barracks were a red brick courthouse and the cemetery.

Avenel had everything for a good life for children. Their chores were to round up the cows, feed the chooks, pen the calves, fetch firewood and water and look after the younger members of the family; and when that was done they had a world of nature riding in the hills around and along the creek. Upstream past the school was a large camp of Aborigines with boomerangs, spears and bull-roarers. Downstream were Chinese market gardens with watermelons and firecrackers. Further downstream again, Hughes Creek joined the Goulburn on its long trip to the Murray and past the junction were the Tabilk vineyards and grapes.

Young Ned was mad about horses, but that was not remarkable since everybody who was anybody in Australia had a horse.

4.   Schooldays

THE GREATEST SIGHT in Avenel, of course, was the Sydney road. Bullock wagons, horse wagons, carts, coaches, jinkers, Chinese at the trot — as well as drovers with their mobs — were always moving up and down between the trees. The Overland Mail came through regularly. The passenger coaches were regular too, both Crawford's and Cobb's, but it was hard to guess when the gold escorts from the Chiltern, Buckland and Ovens diggings would turn up, for the police didn't want to oblige bushrangers.

Dan Morgan was at large in the Riverina, while further north, Frank Gardiner and Ben Hall, operating from hideouts in the Weddin Range, had such immunity from arrest that anyone who wanted to suggest you were stupid, simply remarked: "Why, even blind Freddie could see that!" the reference being to police chief Sir Frederick Pottinger. A straw effigy of Pottinger had been burnt in Forbes before 5000 people.

Invariably the gold coach came in sight at a fast clip, the escort in blue and white uniforms, swords rattling in scabbards, sometimes in front, sometimes in the rear. Sometimes too, the coach was followed by a cart carrying boxes of bullion driven by a goldbuyer unwilling to go to the cost of hiring an escort.

Without slackening pace, the coach entered the police yard, and with a "Whoa there!" suddenly stopped. In half an hour or half a day, but generally next morning, a fresh team was yoked into the shafts and the cavalcade disappeared just as smartly, again with a flea on its tail.

The children knew the coaches, the drivers and many of the passengers. They also knew most of the troopers and some of the horses. They were inclined to giggle when the lunatic van from the Beechworth Asylum pulled in, but when it was the prison coach from the diggings, they watched with awe as, fetters rattling, the prisoners stepped from behind bars to enter the lock-up for the night. Sometimes the prisoners could be heard singing.

The Kellys had not been long in Avenel when Mrs Kelly gave birth to a boy whom they named Dan. Then, the following year, she paid a visit to Wallan to have a baby daughter called Kate. She found her sisters with new babies also and her brother Jimmy not long out of gaol, having served four months for using a neighbour's horse, while her father had sold part of his land to be used for a station on the projected Melbourne—Wodonga railway. Inside the next two years, Quinn junior collected twelve months for horse stealing, while Tipperary Jim got three years for cattle stealing. Meanwhile, old Quinn had sold out and bought part of the former Glenmore run in the hill country behind Mansfield; and there he shifted in 1864 with his tribe of sons and daughters, their wives, husbands and grandchildren, no doubt expecting a return to the free and easy life he had once known around Kilmore.

Local tradition has it that Ned attended school for close on seven years and goes no further than that. But he was always ready for a lark, and the chances are he helped the family exchequer from time to time by working for stockmen and others — both goodies and baddies — who made their living on Tabilk, Mangalore, Tallarook and various other Goulburn Valley sheep stations.

Outside the farming areas, the valley was a spacious sheep walk without fence or impediment, where flocks and herds, attended by shepherds or stockmen, fed at leisure on the abundant grass. At the same time, drovers and boundary riders tailed stock here and there, the general movement being from the great sheep factory of the Riverina, up the valley to the fattening areas near the southern markets. Paid a pound a week and kept in stores, these men camped out on the job, since the cattle in particular were fair game for rival squatters and duffing gangs on the lookout for cash on the hoof. Once stolen, the stock would be rapidly driven off and disappear through a network of staging points and blinds.

It was in search of such a blind, situated close to the valley and about thirty kilometres from Avenel, that a pioneer carter, Charles McAlister, formerly of Strathaird station, Goulburn, New South Wales, had this to say:

> Presently, near a bush track leading towards the Plenty River Ranges, I came across a rough, slab hut, near which two sturdy boys were clearing and stacking timber for a man named Gleeson, so they said. I have ever believed the younger . . . to have been the afterwards notorious outlaw, Ned Kelly . . . he being at the the time . . . about eight or nine years old.
>
> . . . By the direction of the boys I shortly took a track which led towards the Ovens. I camped that night in the scrub, and next day came to a small public house on the Kilmore — Murchison road. I there learned that the mysterious "pound" was fifteen miles further away on the Murchison. Soon after nightfall, following the gleam of a camp fire, I arrived at a shearing shed about 200 yards away from the river bank.
>
> Two men were sitting by the fire after supper. In answer to my greeting, one of them, a sturdy, bearded man, well up in years, sang out, "Hello, Mac! How are they all over on the Goulburn side?" Surprised at this unexpected recognition, I sought to learn the name of my unknown acquaintance, but without avail. "Oh, never mind that," he said roughly "but you'll camp here tonight; there's some tucker in the box near the fire and you'll find a bunk in that tent over there." And at

the words, my good Samaritan, after saying something in a low voice to his mate, walked away to his camp.

The other man, who remained smoking at the fire, surprised me by saying that the horse I was after was "in the pound up the creek", and gave me bearings of the locality. But he was as close as his mate regarding their identities, and seven years passed by ere I discovered the "lineage"of my good friends of that night. One of them was Joe Green, the convict who ran away from Strathaird in 1845 . . . and the other was an escaped Tasmanian convict . . .

When I reached the pound next morning, a slatternly woman came from a bark hut near the yard and told me nothing had been impounded for a week, but I decided to take a survey of the "premises", and with success, as in a long gully a mile away I came across a black boy minding several horses — my good hack amongst them . . .

New Zealand in those times was a great horse market, and thousands of stolen horses were shipped away to that country . . . Many a poor man went looking in vain for his lost horse through the bush, while the animal was in the hold of a ship . . . bound with a freight of 500 or 600 equines for Auckland or some other port of Maoriland. Little weeds of scrubbers that couldn't be given away for boiling . . . were shipped and sold to the Maoris at prices ranging from £5 to £50.

The year 1865 saw a series of events which served to remind the Kelly children what it meant to be poor. Dan Morgan emerged from his hideout in the Galore scrub early in the year and set to work robbing travellers up the Sydney road. As they said, he had enough hide to stock a tanyard. He had tied up the squatter on Mittagong Station while he feasted the shearers and had the habit of ordering drinks on the house whenever he called at an inn. In April, Morgan was shot dead at Peechelba Station out of Wangaratta, and his head with beard scalped off — packed in a box addressed to a phrenologist at Melbourne University — was carted through Avenel to the disgust of people along the road.

The scandal had barely subsided when one Saturday in May, Constable Doxcy of the Avenel police searched the Kelly home and arrested Red Kelly on charges of cattle stealing and illegal possession of a hide belonging to his neighbour Morgan. On the Monday, Philip Morgan gave evidence that he had seen the hindquarters of a heifer on a hook in the yard and Constable Doxcy said he had found a hide with brand removed in the house.

17

The local bench, Messrs J. E. Blake, J.P. and C. Summiss, J.P., dismissed the theft charge, but imposed a fine of £25 on the second count, and in default six months hard labour at Kilmore. The sentence meant the collapse of hopes for Red, in gaol for stealing bread for his children — that crime for which so many thousands of his countrymen had been transported.

However, the matter went largely unnoticed, for Avenel was excited by a sensational event. Across the border in New South Wales Ben Hall had been betrayed, tracked to his camp amid the gums and blasted with a hail of lead. Thirty-two bullet holes had been counted in his body. The police had roped the bloody corpse on to the back of Ben's own mount and led it through Forbes to appease their wounded vanity.

Barely ten, the young Ned Kelly had few doubts about the police as he cantered to and from the town carrying messages for his mother; he had seen the way they pushed the prisoners around. It would take a lot of post-and-rail to pay back £25.

When at last the money was raised and Red came home from gaol, Mrs Kelly had a baby girl they named Grace, and in October came news from Beechworth that John Lloyd and Tom Lloyd had been given five years for cattle stealing.

All along the creek and in the valley the gums were an axe handle through the butt. It was all hard work with crosscut saw, hammer and wedge. The slabs had to be dragged by sled and lifted; digging the postholes was the easiest bit. In the winter of 1866, Red became ill. Christmas day saw him confined to bed with dropsy; and two days later, while Avenel was agog at the arrest at the race ball of a bushranger said to be Harry Power, Red passed away.

Some of the local folk came to the rescue. A coffin was knocked together, a grave dug, and the mortal remains of John Kelly, aged forty-seven, were laid without headstone in Avenel Cemetery, directly opposite the Courthouse where he had been tried, the service being read by a resident, John Brady. In due course, it was given to Ned to fill out the death certificate with these details: Mary Jane (dec.), Ann 13, Edward 11½, Margaret 9, James 7, Daniel 5, Catherine 4, Grace 1½; the addition of the six months in each instance possibly being a reaction to his failure previously in an arithmetic exam.

The grief of this warm Irish-Australian family went unrecorded, but Ned was to write in stern years to come of "the flag and nation" that had "destroyed, massacred and murdered" his forefathers — "all of true blood, bone and beauty" — and transported them "to Van Diemen's Land to pine their young lives away in starvation and misery among tyrants worse than the promised hell itself".

Five months after Red's death, Ellen Kelly got some of her feelings off her chest by abusing the Morgans and was hauled into court and fined £2, the shoemaker, William Austin, and James Smith, a vegetable grower, going surety for her. The fact was that Ellen's life at Avenel was over and the time had come to move on. Various Land Acts had been passed with the avowed purpose of putting the small man on the land, her relatives were taking up selections and she might as well do the same.

After the Kellys had left Avenel, the local folk remembered Mrs Kelly as a neighbour who could be depended on in need and as a great horsewoman, and Ned as something of a hero for rescuing the eight-year-old Richard Shelton from the creek. Ned later wore a green and gold sash presented by the Shelton family under his armour at Glenrowan, as if to indicate, if the battle went against him, that it was not as a bushranger but as a friend and neighbour that he wished to be remembered.

5. Eleven Mile Creek

IN THE AUTUMN of 1867, Ellen Kelly and her family set out for the fertile north-eastern lands towards the Ovens diggings. Their effects piled on the back of a wagon, driving the stock in front, they crawled up the dusty coach road which followed the track Hume and Hovell had blazed forty-three years before. Now and then they saw a selector's hut or the weatherboard homestead of a squatter. Every twenty or thirty kilometres they passed through a primitive township with its rows of slab dwellings and few verandaed single-storey buildings of weatherboard or hand-made brick — the general store, the smithy, the pub.

After Longwood came Euroa and Violet Town, with the low Strathbogie Ranges on the right; and then the Broken River and Benalla, where they met some of the Quinns and selected a 36 hectare block with slab hut eighteen kilometres further on towards Wangaratta. Situated on green and wooded land near a creek, the hut had an earthen floor, slab sides, a broad chimney and hessian draped from the rafters dividing it into rooms. The busy road offered ample opportunity for business.

The land was pleasant, undulating to the west. The single line of the Warby Ranges ran north past Wangaratta. The flat and well-watered Oxley Plains stretched thirty kilometres or more to the Beechworth hills in the east; while directly to the south, the foothills of the Wombat Ranges rose to join the alpine barrier in the distance. The Alps, in fact, swung in a great arc around the entire southern and eastern horizon, embracing Mansfield and Beechworth in their foothills, and giving rise to the Ovens and King rivers which straddled the Oxley Plains and joined the Murray to the north early in its long westward trek.

Eleven Mile Creek, as the Kellys' place became known, was at the very hub of this arc and joined directly to it by the steps of the Wombat Ranges. It and the green lands surrounding were eternally in the presence of these mountains which shuddered in the liquid air of summer days, and flashed with the white of snow across the winter distance.

The Quinns had shown good judgement. Here was country which the overlanders had acclaimed "a land, the glory of all lands". The overlanders had followed the Ovens from its junction with the Murray, and, never questioning their right, built their huts on tribal grounds. When the Aborigines drove off stock, they sent out armed bands and shot them down. They divided the land into provinces, each comprising 50 to more than 500 square kilometres of territory, gradually extended their flocks and herds, built substantial homesteads, bred fine horses and established their law and culture in the English pattern.

They had scarcely settled on the Oxley Plains when the first traders set up business where Major Mitchell had crossed the Ovens. The Oxley Plains proved such wonderful cattle country that by 1850, Ovens Crossing—or Wangaratta as it came to be called—was a thriving one-pub town which staged its own race meetings and fist-fights. But in 1851 with the discovery of gold around Ballarat, it became almost denuded of male population. Then gold was found on Woorajay Station and the tide recoiled eastward and poured up into the Ovens and Buckland River diggings. Within a year, scores of thousands were earning rich rewards from the easily worked alluvial beds, while many Chinese worked Reedy Creek in the narrow funnel of the Woolshed. As for the squatters, they put the best of the land to crop after the initial panic and were soon able to add to the wool cheque the proceeds from foodstuffs sold to the new market at the diggings.

Vanishing rapidly, meanwhile, were the days of the bullock wagon, slab hut, the camp oven, the hand gristmill and wholemeal bread. Steam flourmills, bakehouses, breweries, slaughteryards, sawmills, brick-kilns came into being. Scores of inns with accommodation for men and horses sprang up. On the bar counter, somewhat tipped in favour of the publican, were gold-scales for the convenience of the heavy-pocketed diggers. In Beechworth, rows of tents gave way to streets of weatherboard, brick and stone. In 1857, when the fields began to show signs of depletion and a few miners drifted off to buy land at auction, the citizenry were so prosperous that they rejected the Government's offer to lay the railway to Sydney through the town.

In the sixties, however, the gold dwindled further, and scores of diggers began to take up blocks each month, only to find that the squatters had the inside running. Each time a new Land Act was introduced the squatter-dominated Legislative Council managed to nullify its purpose. Not only had the squatter secured the best of the farming lands, but by his influence in local government and business he virtually controlled all the grazing lands. The selector might allow a couple of cows to stray on to the road and then find at the end of a day's work that he had to travel in to the pound and pay a stiff fee to have them released. In the event of illness, bushfire or any other natural disaster, he was forced to go cap in hand to the money-lender, or perhaps the squatter himself, for assistance. Short of tools and seed, his wife too often bent with work and child-bearing, the children growing up shy and illiterate, himself feeding on worry while waiting for the crop to grow, it was little wonder that he sometimes entered the rich man's fence at night and killed a ewe for meat. Next day, the squatter came down — with or without his thoroughbred and troopers — and the selector found cattle in his crop, the creek fenced off or his credit stopped at the bank.

The night forays, these covert acts in a great yet almost imperceptible economic revolution, clouded by many side issues, the squatter lumped together under the one word "lawlessness". Fortunately or otherwise, the "lawless", inarticulate and unable to counter the spate of morality which issued from press and pulpit, seldom understood that their "lawlessness" was a necessary part in the development of Australia from a giant sheep paddock into a nation where a wide variety of products was drawn from the soil. Thus, while southern areas were settling down to a steadier pulse as women arrived, children were born, kitchen gardens bloomed, and work and the seasons transformed the stark clearings, the North-East with its areas of extreme poverty was headed for trouble.

There is little doubt where the Kellys stood — they were at the bottom of the social ladder. Unable to work her land, Ellen Kelly set out to provide meals and accommodation to the diggers, shearers and landless travelling up and down to Beechworth, and as they often liked a glass of brandy when they came off the road, she learned to keep a bottle and gained a reputation with some folk for running a shanty house. For security, she took in regulars too — young ex-diggers including William Skillion who was a teamster's son, Bricky Williamson, an Englishman, and Alec Gunn, a Scot who began to take an interest in Annie, now sixteen. All held blocks nearby and got a bit of ready cash by shearing in the Riverina in the season.

Old Jimmy Quinn — as at Wallan — stood somewhere between the extremes of wealth. The Glenmore run, situated in the wild country towards the headwaters of the King, had been abandoned twice, originally because of Aborigines and dingoes; nonetheless, he managed to make a living by running cattle and rounding up scrubbers and brumbies in the ranges. But Glenmore could not support all the growing clan and some drifted off to take up selections, particularly along Fifteen Mile Creek and Boggy Creek, and at Greta, which was about seven kilometres from the Kelly property. This was the country, rising towards Glenmore and the mountain barrier, where the young Ned began his working life and which he soon learned to cross on horseback by night and day.

The life was rough and tumble in more ways than one — not least inside the clan itself, where the menfolk were in gaol from time to time or away doing seasonal work, and the women had to club together to feed and clothe their large families. In 1868, for instance, Tipperary Jim tried to seduce Mrs Kelly, and then in a fit of drunken rage set fire to Kate Lloyd's where Mrs Kelly had taken shelter with her family for the night. The incident may have been in the nature of a family quarrel; nevertheless the justice on the case, Judge Sir Redmond Barry, brought in the death sentence and Tipperary Jim went through several gruelling weeks in the death cells before the Executive Council commuted the sentence to fifteen years imprisonment.

Ned's rapscallion uncle had been in Pentridge no more than a few months when Harry Power, the bushranger said to have been captured at the Avenel race ball a few years before, made his escape in the gaol rubbish cart and drifted up country to the North-East. It is doubtful if the Kellys realised quite what was at stake when Power turned up at the Eleven Mile and entertained them with a description of his latest coup — he had robbed the Mansfield — Jamieson coach twice in one week. Humorous and genial although he had spent most of his life in prison, he explained that it was getting harder than ever to operate. Morgan had never had less than four telegraphs to scout for him, but he didn't even have someone to hold his horse; he would look a terrible fool if his horse strayed off. Chiefly he needed a place where he could lay off without the perpetual fear of being jumped, so he was headed for a spot on Glenmore of which the Lloyd brothers had told him. After reaching an understanding with Ned, Power moved on to set up camp near the Quinn homestead overlooking the King Valley.

Until now, the criminal record of the Quinn-Kelly clan had been unexceptional considering the times and the fact that they had been in the stock business for twenty-eight years. Certainly some of them had been gaoled for brawling in pubs and stealing cattle, but such crimes were common; it was not unknown for whole mobs of cattle to disappear from one colony and turn up in another. However, the arrival of Power close to the mountain routes where the Omeo butcher, Bogong Jack, and his gang of duffers had operated in the fifties, put the clan—and in fact the North-East itself—in the spotlight, particularly as it coincided with the death of old Jimmy Quinn. The squatters in the Mansfield district immediately petitioned the authorities to prevent the transfer of the lease to John Quinn, no doubt because a man called Lewis had his eye on Glenmore.

In the meantime, Ned found himself hauled into court at Benalla, charged with attacking and robbing a Chinese digger named Ah Fook. Ah Fook said he had called in at Eleven Mile Creek and asked one of the Kelly girls for a glass of water, and that subsequently a youth—whom he described as 5 feet 8 inches, wearing moleskins and a straw hat with black band—had beaten him across the shins and taken ten shillings from his purse. He was annoyed because the water in the glass was dirty, no doubt meaning the drink was short on brandy.

Chief witness for the defence was Annie—now Mrs Gunn—whose husband Alex was away droving. She claimed Ah Fook had done the attacking, and William Skillion, who lodged with Mrs Kelly, gave evidence in support, as did William Grey. As Ah Fook admitted having £25 in his purse at the time the ten shillings was stolen, the case was dismissed; the real nature of the incident was apparently an attempt to get at Mrs Kelly for sly-grogging.

According to the reporters, Ned gave a broad smile as he stepped down from his first brush with the law; if so the smile was beside the point. He had yet to learn that any offence becomes magnified and immune to normal morality when recorded in an official system; the old saying "give a dog a bad name" did not express half of it.

6. Harry Power

IN THE DAYS when New South Wales served as Britannia's rubbish bin, bushrangers were either old lags dehumanised in the iron-gangs, or ticket-of-leave men driven by injustice to desperate resort. In Van Diemen's Land, where penal conditions were the worst, they committed the worst crimes. Called bolters because they fled, they were often poor bushmen and were rapidly hunted down. Bold Jack Donohue, the wild colonial boy from Dublin, who could vault a horse and led a gang on a four-year career, was an exception; but none of them could have operated without the sympathetic support of servants, ex-convicts and the dungaree farmers (dungaree — later known as denim — being the cheapest cloth available in the colony).

But the discovery of gold and the gradual emergence of a society in which wage-labour replaced forced labour saw the arrival of a different brand of bushranger — a horseman, often native-born, interested in getting his share of riches the easy way, or alternatively, a cattle duffer who used weapons in an emergency. In a land without roads, rail or telegraph, and in which police and governmental administration lagged behind the needs of expanding enterprise, the man of daring could do as he wished, provided he had a head for tactics and a fast horse. Some worked in large gangs and waylaid the gold coaches. Sooner or later they miscalculated and had to fight it out. Most worked in small gangs, relieving the pockets of travellers along the narrow bush tracks. Some robbed without respect of person, but many were courteous, particularly to women, and a few operated with such flair and humour that their victims felt they had had their money's worth. Then, as the gold dwindled, communications improved and the authorities became better organised, the trade grew less profitable and those who hadn't been hanged or shot took up selections or jobs.

So when a bushranger was taken, a jury could rarely be found in his own district to convict him, and he was conveyed to Darlinghurst or Melbourne where many a hard-eyed outlaw went to his death shaking hands with the hangman and shouting forgiveness to witnesses, having played the Australian game and known the inequality of its rules. Truly it was said that a bushranger had a short life and a merry one. Johnny Dunne was nineteen when hanged, John Lynch twenty-nine, and the Clarke brothers twenty-six and twenty-four. Fred Lowry, who had taken to the saddle for a joke, was shot dead at twenty-seven. Shot dead—that was how John O'Meally, aged twenty-two, ended, Johnny Gilbert, twenty-five, Ben Hall, twenty-seven, and many others—most of them native-born Australians of a generation which preferred the road and the bush to buckling under to the antique arrogance of the New South Wales authorities who could not get it into their heads that the convict days were dead and gone.

In central New South Wales, where the cockies were particularly impoverished and the over-populated Lachlan goldfields were surrounded by wealthy estates, the Gardiner and Ben Hall gangs engineered a redivision of wealth with a finesse and on a scale Australia had not witnessed before. Before the gold escort robbery at Eugowra Rocks in 1862, they rode from farm to farm outlining their plans and calling for volunteers, and were farewelled like soldiers to the wars.

By contrast, Harry Power was little more than a petty thief on horseback who will-o'-the-wisped around the bush, although the *Argus*, which spoke for the squatters, described him as a scoundrel who raided settled districts to return "like a hunted dog" to the ranges, and raised an agitation for a special act of parliament against any who aided him. Ned's association with Power began in that year 1870 when blood-and-iron Bismarck was welding together the German states into a power soon to challenge the ascendancy of Old Mother England.

In March, Power stuck up and robbed Robert McBean on Kilfera Station, sixteen kilometres from Benalla. McBean, one of the Mansfield squatters who had been pressing for action against the Quinns, knew the Kelly family; he had tried to buy their block, originally part of the Kilfera run. Power's accomplice, it was recorded, was a youth on a brown horse, swag on pommel, who remained in the background. McBean did not so much mind the loss of his horse and wallet, but sent Power word—per medium of John Lloyd who had at last been released from Pentridge—that he wanted his watch back, to which Power sent the rude reply that McBean could have it for £15. McBean raised the matter with the Chief Commissioner of Police, Captain Standish, at the Melbourne Club, with the result that a £500 reward was offered for information leading to Power's arrest.

The next appearance was at Mt Battery Station, near Mansfield, where the lessee, Dr J. P. Rowe, was brought word that Power and a companion were lying on the hill over the horse paddock. Seizing a rifle, the doctor made use of cover, got within range and managed to knock some gravel into their faces. Not discouraged, Power waylaid a traveller near Kyneton.

25

The police, in the meantime, had caught up with their paper work, and Ned awoke one dawn to find the house surrounded by armed police and himself under arrest as Power's accomplice and for highway robbery under arms. According to the local paper, he waved to acquaintances as the police escorted him through Benalla, but appeared exhausted, as well he might since the poundkeeper at Moyhu had caught him driving some of the Quinns' stock out the gate and given him a thrashing. While in the lock-up, "this junior highwayman", as the *Benalla Ensign* termed him, "sang like a bird and cracked jokes with the warders".

The McBean case on 5 May naturally attracted a large crowd. Entering the dock, Kelly seemed indifferent to the danger of his position, nodded to his relatives and smiled. "This misguided youth, to judge by his jaunty air, considers himself a character to be admired," the reporter recorded, echoing a line of comment favoured by leader-writers and others who looked on this new generation of Victorians with disapproval, especially for a certain flashness shown in their dress and their penchant for sharing each other's horses and money.

The case was put back, and when it came to court, McBean appeared torn between pocket and his conscience, and — in the crunch — refused to identify Kelly positively. The main witness in the second matter could not be found, so the police introduced a new charge related to the Kyneton hold-up.

Ned signed the property book at Kyneton for "one knife, two spurs and one handkerchief". According to the local paper, the police were favourably impressed by his appearance and behaviour in the lock-up, but this may have been because Superintendent Nicolson, who was up from Melbourne and hoping to get information of Power's whereabouts, had offered him a job in the Riverina. However, Ned had no intention of leading Nicolson to Power. He appeared in Kyneton Court on 17 May, but was remanded. The press, at first, was hoping to see him sent to prison, but after another four weeks began to talk of "scandalous interference with the liberty of the subject".

Following the dismissal of yet another charge stemming from a reported appearance of Power near Geelong, Ned returned home to find that his mother, during his absence, had narrowly escaped conviction for sly-grogging, identification being once more the problem.

In contrast to Superintendent Nicolson who had kept up the pressure on Ned for almost two months and generally made life difficult for anyone he dealt with, Power was an entertainment.

He continued his small forays, appearing here there and

everywhere, always gallant to the ladies and firm with the men. On the one day he was reported from points hundreds of kilometres apart; as the Beechworth paper put it: "The Power of the imagination is such that this bushranger can show up in a dozen places at once."

But Power's scorn of the authorities had created a political scandal and he was due for retirement. The police, having finally established a station at Glenmore and made things uncomfortable for the Quinns, got McBean to put them in touch with John Lloyd and offered him the £500 reward to lead them to Power. So, one night in June, a party of troopers led by Sergeant Montfort who had arrested Lloyd five years before, and accompanied by Superintendent Nicolson and another equally ambitious officer from Melbourne, Superintendent Hare, set out to make the final assault on Power's eyrie above the King valley.

Power slept content in the knowledge that the track to his hideout passed within a few metres of the Quinn homestead where a peacock served as watchdog. However, a deluge of rain enabled the party to creep past without an alarm and Nicolson and Hare were able to drag the bushranger from his small shelter at dawn. Power was upset, and particularly ashamed he should be caught asleep. "That bloody bird!" he remarked. "Well, well, they've got old Harry at last!" Whereupon he boiled the billy and cracked jokes with Superintendent Hare about his height. Hare, who had been born in South Africa, was so big, said Power, that his horse would back away in fright.

The police party returned to Wangaratta on the Sunday while numbers of people were out for their evening ramble. A cry went up and the congregations flooded from the churches. Seated in the springcart, the bushranger waved to the crowd and cried: "They've caught poor old Harry Power; but they caught him asleep!" Next morning, when cart and escort continued on their way, he stood up, bade the folk good day and hoped he would meet them again in his professional capacity. People were out all along the route to Beechworth. As the police party approached Newtown Bridge which spans the gorge at the entry to town, an array of people in buggies, springcarts, wagons and on horseback was seen approaching, and fearing he might not be recognised, Power jumped to his feet and waved his handcuffs above his head.

The Beechworth folk, in fact, were out to meet him, and a cheer went up. They turned around, and an imposing cavalcade crossed the bridge and moved up the rise into Ford Street. Power bowed regally to right and left amid shouts and laughter, constantly repeating that he had been caught asleep. On arrival at the gaol at the far end of town, he greeted the officer in charge as an old friend and expressed the hope that they would never fall out. Thereupon, he turned around, thanked the police publicly for the considerate manner in which he had been treated, and explained finally that they would never have caught him had he not been asleep. A voice from the crowd shouted: "You should have slept with one eye open, Harry!"

Power appeared in court a hale and hearty middle-aged man with grizzled hair and beard. It was apparent he had taken great care over his toilet. His tall, solid figure was clad in neat and somewhat modish garb. The ladies remarked he was hardly what one might expect a bushranger to be. Obviously in his element, he leaned over the dock, and in a friendly, free and easy manner told witnesses not to be frightened but to speak up. A whole array of evidence was brought against him, but he had never killed a soul and invariably been courteous to his victims.

Before sentencing him to ten years imprisonment, the judge gave him an opportunity to say a few words. "It is too bad, altogether too bad," said Power. "Not content with trying to make me out a pitiful pilferer instead of the bold highwayman I actually was, some of these rags they call newspapers are actually endeavouring to decry my personal appearance. I am willing to bet the £15 the police took out of my pockets, and leave the decision to the ladies of Beechworth, that I am a better looking man than the whole lot of the reporters present in this court today."

So ended the life on the road of Harry Power, alias Henry Johnston, one time of Waterford, Ireland, and of Van Diemen's Land, and lately Ned Kelly's professor in bushranging. After some years in Pentridge, he was released, and went to work as a gardener for two middle-aged spinsters he had once charmed and robbed many years before. His imprisonment had the effect of illustrating just how the Quinn threat had been magnified beyond reality, for Captain Standish wrote to his officers in the North-East: "I hope every exertion will be made to apprehend Quinn. He is not unlikely to take to the bush, and will be a far more dangerous criminal than Power ever was."

The truth of the matter was that Jimmy Quinn's roistering days were over; still a bachelor and given to the bottle, he began to hang around the Kelly home for want of anything better. The real situation was set out by Montfort when he had become Inspector Montfort: "A great deal of the difficulty with these men would be got over if they felt they were treated with equal justice — that there was no down on them."

7. Pentridge Gaol

POWER was a selfish old bachelor who might have made a name in the circus had he not drifted into bushranging, No doubt Ned found it exciting riding around the country watching the old man at work, and no doubt his young head swelled at the thought that he was Power's associate; but the experience was to cost him dearly since it brought him squarely under the attention of the authorities. And yet, in a way, this was inevitable, if only because of the challenging quality of this fifteen-year-old, already possessed of a courage and competence many fail to achieve in manhood.

Ned found himself in trouble again when two hawkers became bogged near Greta, and one of them, finding himself unjustly accused of borrowing the other's horse to pull his wagon out of the mud, got Ned to hand him an insulting note wrapped up with a pair of calf's testicles. The butt of the joke was Jeremiah McCormack, whose wife happened to be childless; and the next time Kelly visited Greta a brawl developed which led to McCormack laying a complaint with Senior Constable Hall, recently transferred from Glenmore where he had been watching the Quinns.

McCormack told the court in Wangaratta that Kelly had threatened to shoot him so that he had been forced to sit up until midnight with a loaded pistol, and Ned was sentenced to three months gaol for offensive behaviour and fined £10 (in default three months gaol) for assault. This virtually meant six months in Beechworth since he could not pay the fine. In addition, he was bound over on securities to keep the peace for twelve months.

While Ned did his first spell in gaol, horse stealing continued unabated in the North-East. The continual effort of squatter and selector to control the grazing lands was no more than the central theme of the general push and grab in which frequently no motive was apparent or excuse of unjust treatment given. Thus horses disappeared out of spite, as a practical joke, or merely because someone wanted to get home in a hurry. This was commonly regarded as slickness — all right if you could get away with it. Yet, because society was authoritarian, the penalties were sometimes as heavy as those awarded for manslaughter in this century.

Ned came out of Beechworth in March to find Alex Gunn at Eleven Mile Creek in the company of a tall, softly-spoken horsebreaker who proved to be Isaiah Wright, of Mansfield. Wright was in a fix because his chestnut mare had strayed, so Ned loaned him a mount. The mare was of distinctive appearance with white blaze and docked tail. Ned found her, rode her into Wangaratta and loaned her to the publican's daughters to ride around the town; and this, he suggested, was proof enough he had no knowledge Wright had shaken the mare from Maindample Park Station.

Unfortunately for Ned, Senior Constable Hall had read the mare's description in the *Police Gazette* and attempted to arrest him the next time he appeared in Greta. Although he was an extremely big man, Hall must have been nervous of the teenager for he admitted in his official report that he tried to shoot him after failing to unseat him. He claimed that Kelly had made for some bushes across the street, then halted and cried, "Shoot and be damned!" Ned said that had he known he was to be arrested, he would have quietly ridden off; however, Hall invited him to the barracks to sign some bail bonds, so he stopped. Kelly said:

> I was getting off when Hall caught hold of me and thought to throw me, but made a mistake and came on the broad of his back, himself in the dust. The mare galloped away, and instead of me putting my foot on Hall's neck and taking his revolver and putting him in the lock-up, I tried to catch the mare. Hall got up and snapped three or four caps at me and would have shot me but the Colt's patent refused.
>
> This is well known in Greta. Hall never told me he wanted to arrest me until after he tried to shoot me.
>
> When I heard the caps snapping, I stood until Hall came close. He had me covered and was shaking with fear, and I knew he would pull the trigger before he would be game to put his hand on me. So I duped and jumped at him, caught the revolver with one hand and Hall by the collar with the other.
>
> I dare not strike him, or my sureties would lose the bond money. I used to trip him and let him take a mouthful of dust now and then, as he was helpless as a big goanna after leaving a dead bullock or horse.
>
> I kept throwing him in the dust until I got him across the street—the very spot where Mrs O'Brien's hotel stands now. The cellar was just dug then. There was some brush fencing where the post-and-rail was taken down; and on this I threw the big, cowardly Hall on his belly. I straddled him and rooted with both spurs into his thighs. He roared like a big calf attacked by dogs and shifted several yards of fence. I got his hands at the back of his neck and tried to make him let the revolver go, but he stuck to it like grim death to a dead

volunteer. He called for assistance to men named Cohen, Barnett, Lewis, Thompson, Jewitt, and two blacksmiths looking on. I dare not strike any of them, as I was bound to keep the peace, or I could have spread those curs like dung in a paddock.

They got ropes, tied my hands and feet, and Hall beat me over the head with his six-chambered Colt's revolver. Nine stitches were put in some of the cuts by Dr Hastings. And when Wild Wright and my mother came, they could trace us across the street by the blood in the dust and which spoiled the lustre of the paint on the gatepost of the barracks.

Hall, in his account of the matter, claimed he struck Kelly on the head four or five times with "all his might", so as to leave part of Kelly's head "a mass of raw and bleeding flesh".

In the lock-up, Constable Arthur—later to be dismissed from the force for declaring that police treatment made the Kellys what they were "whether they were guilty or not"—asked Ned why he didn't surrender peaceably, and Ned is supposed to have replied: "There are two ways of taking a man!"

That night an angry crowd gathered outside the barracks, and next day, when placed under escort to Wangaratta, Ned was handcuffed and roped to the seat of the cart. "Hall was frightened I would throw him out of the cart, so he tied me, whilst Constable Arthur laughed at his cowardice," he wrote later.

Hall's frank admission at the preliminary hearing that he had beaten Kelly with his revolver did not encourage the police to persist with an assault charge, but Kelly was refused bail.

Next, Wild Wright was arrested, then Alec Gunn; then—as Kelly had been in gaol when the mare disappeared—the theft charge was changed to one of receiving. Finally, the case came up at the Beechworth assizes in August, with the offending chestnut tied up outside the courthouse. The main witnesses were Hall himself and one of the Kellys' neighbours, a James Murdoch who alleged Ned had invited him to go horse stealing. However, Murdoch had served a term for possessing stolen meat. Bricky Williamson gave evidence that Wright had told Kelly, "If you find the mare, stick to her."

Despite Ned's assurance that he had intended nothing to imperil the money of those who had gone surety for him, he was sentenced to three years hard labour. Wild Wright, on the other hand, was able to show that despite a reputation for borrowing horses, he was well-regarded in Mansfield, and received the lesser sentence of eighteen months for the more serious offence. Gunn received three years for stealing another horse from around Maindample.

Here too, Kelly, who admitted having stolen many horses, was to have the last word. He stated that Hall received a cash reward which amounted to bribery of the law from "persons with too much money round Greta", and used £20 of it—equivalent to two months' wages—to buy the evidence of Murdoch. "It is a credit to a policeman to convict an innocent man, but any mutt can pot a guilty one. There never was such a thing as justice in English laws, but any amount of injustice to be had."

So Edward Kelly, aged sixteen, said goodbye to the beat of his steed's hoofs across a brave land—and like all who grow older—to these so proud, so reckless, so uncompromising days of his adolescence, no doubt wondering whether it paid to be braver than heroes, and stiffer than the martyrs of his own race, whose story he had heard too often but had yet to understand too late.

On 2nd August 1871, he again entered Beechworth Gaol. His particulars were entered in the records: Height 5 feet 10 inches, weight 11 stone 4 pounds, sallow complexion, hazel eyes, dark brown hair, broad visage, low forehead, eyebrows meeting—the last two items being adduced, no doubt, in support of the theory that criminals were closer to the apes than the rest of the community. A list of nine scars on his head and hands bore witness to the rough and tumble which had conditioned a courage already remarkable. A photograph revealed a well-built young man showing the first wisps of beard, clad in loose gaol clothes and calmly regarding the camera.

For eighteen months, Ned worked in the gangs which daily marched to and from work within the rim of the May Day Hills. Then in February 1873, he set off in irons like the prisoners he had watched as a boy, for Pentridge Stockade, near where his grandfather, Quinn, had first taken up land thirty years before. In midwinter he was transferred to the prison hulk *Sacramento* anchored in Hobsons Bay off Point Gellibrand, and in the spring to the hulk *Battery* nearby. These vessels, painted a dismal yellow and patrolled by sentries, fair weather and foul, were remnants of the portable convict labour force which did the hard and dirty work keeping the British Navy afloat around the globe. During these months he rowed ashore daily with the gangs which laboured in the Newport quarries and built roads and the stone facings of the piers.

Ned and Alec Gunn were scarcely inside Pentridge when Jimmy Quinn was given three months for threatening Senior Constable Hall and three months for assault. Hall had potted four of the clan's breadwinners when he was dismounted for being overweight and transferred to Geelong. His successor, Constable Flood, set out to pot the women and children, starting with the twelve-year-old Jim, who was working for a hawker, and his young brother Dan, still going to school in Greta. The boys were caught "illegally using" the hawker's horse and locked up for two days. Flood then tried to get Mrs Kelly and William Skillion for "furious riding", but this charge was dismissed too.

Thus, at Christmas 1871, the women and children at Eleven Mile Creek had little to celebrate, especially as Uncle Jimmy, just out of Beechworth, made a pass at a Miss Brown who was staying at the house and attacked an elderly man who came to the door asking questions. The net result was that Jimmy was put away again for assault, and what was worse, their friend and neighbour Bricky Williamson was given eighteen months as an accessory.

In November 1872, Flood tried again to get Mrs Kelly — this time for stealing a saddle — but failed. Then three months later, John Lloyd — the same who had put Power away — was convicted of maliciously killing a horse, and his son, Tom Lloyd, in an attempt to raise money for his father's defence, got Jim Kelly, aged fourteen, and a sixteen-year-old called Williams to sell some cows picked up on the road, as a result of which both were gaoled for five years.

Two and a half years after his entry into Beechworth, Kelly was set free. Seven days had been added to his sentence for handing tobacco to a fellow prisoner aboard *Sacramento*, but in recognition of good behaviour he had received two-thirds of the maximum remission of sentence. He came out having learned self-discipline and endurance, and of the depths of bitterness experienced by his fellows who had carved into the oaken beams of the hulks the two words which expressed everything — Mad dog, read in reverse as God dam. Yet two and a half years had been torn out of his life.

While Ned had chewed things over in Pentridge, the pace of Victoria's adolescent growth scarcely slackened. Outside its ports and mining centres lay tiny rural communities connected by bush tracks. This was Victoria — a land heartily and crudely alive in its self-centred cells, but less unified than the ancient Egyptian or Roman civilisations. The bottleneck was transport — principally the lumbering bullock wagon. The vast growth of population cried out for the improvement of roads and the introduction of waterworks, sewerage, the telegraph and railways to hasten the turgid flow of imports and exports. The sixties had seen the start of an orgy of overseas borrowing, but private enterprise found so many profitable fields for investment that it was left to the governments belatedly to pioneer grander enterprises such as the railways. Borrowing here too! From the London banks came the money, from the English and Scots ironmasters, the rails and rolling stock. The backbone of Victoria's future railway system was laid in a great burst of activity, and in 1873 the Governor, Sir George Bowen, opened the last section of the north-eastern railway, which struck up from Melbourne to reach the Murray at Wodonga.

Thus Ned came home in February 1874, to find a railway and new, direct road to Wangaratta a few kilometres west of the old home which was more run down than ever. It was a house of women. His horses were gone; Flood had been selling ungazetted strays to navvies on the line and been transferred to Yandoit on the complaint of Brown, the Laceby squatter. No doubt Flood had taken his horses; he had certainly locked away enough members of the family. His mother was living with a young man, George King by name, who had been born in California. Still, all was not bad — Alec Gunn was back with Annie, Maggie and Bill Skillion had been married in St Pat's, Wangaratta, Kate and Grace would soon be in their teens, and Dan, although quiet, had plenty of schoolmates and was already showing a good wrist in the saddle.

Already 1.8 metres tall, Ned was powerful, yet lithe and well-proportioned. His brow was wide and surmounted by dark curly hair which grew well forward giving it a somewhat shallow appearance. His complexion was fresh, his jaw powerful, and his chin sprouted a dark reddish beard. He was not an extremely big man, but standing or moving he gave the impression of being bigger than he was. He had a presence, and his hazel almond-shaped eyes were direct examining the worth of a man.

Three years of rough treatment in which he mixed daily with the toughest criminals in the colony had given him time and cause to reflect. He was now mature enough to realise that to pursue the course of his youthful days could only lead to sharper struggles with authority, one result of which he had seen in the lives of his gaolmates at Pentridge. He now had a fuller understanding of how other men lived, a sense that the traditions of his clan were not those of all the world, and that tradition itself must always be interpreted anew in a world that is always renewing itself. It was not that he was less uncompromising than before, but his self-discipline had grown and much of his adolescent braggadocio had disappeared. He realised he had little chance of making a fresh start among the old influences. He announced, "I would rather face the gallows than go to gaol again."

34

8. Duffing Days

ELLEN KELLY and George King were married in Benalla on 19 February according to the rites of the Primitive Methodists, the practitioner being the Rev. William Gould and the witnesses Ned and Bill Skillion. Soon after, Ned left Eleven Mile Creek and took a job as faller for Saunders and Rule who held a sleeper contract for the Beechworth branch line. Later in the year, he joined another sawmiller, Heach and Dockendorf, in the Mansfield district.

He earned good money—never less than £2 10s a week—and for the first time in his life began to enjoy himself. Various pictures survive showing him smartly dressed in strapped riding breeches and tweed jacket, generally holding the reins of a thoroughbred with which he appeared as a trick rider at shows and sports meetings in the North-East. He also fought and beat Wild Wright in a twenty round bare knuckle contest staged in the yard of one of the pubs at Beechworth.

The following year, he rejoined Saunders and Rule as overseer at Bourkes Waterhole sawmill in Benalla district; then, as the sleeper contract cut out, he went prospecting with his stepfather up the headwaters of the King. They soon found payable gold on Bullock Creek and added to their income by rounding up scrubbers and brumbies in the ranges as the Quinns had done. Lewis had the Glenmore lease now, and with the Quinns gone, the police took the squatter McBean's suggestion and closed the Glenmore police station.

Ned soon found people had long memories for such as he. He ran in a wild bull in the ranges and heard that a squatter on the King, James Whitty, had accused him of stealing it, so he stopped Whitty on Oxley racecourse and asked for an explanation. It must have been with some discomfiture that Whitty was forced to admit that his son-in-law, Farrell, had fed him the rumour, and that, in fact, the animal he was missing had turned up.

By means of an elaborate peacocking system, the Whitty, Blackwood, Lewis and Byrne families controlled almost all the land along King River and Boggy Creek above Oxley. Whitty held frontages on both streams, while the Byrnes held an area ten kilometres wide straddling the King. It was common complaint that these men between them rented large unoccupied areas held by the banks, and in addition, by virtue of certificate granted by the Lands Department inspector at nominal fee, held sole grazing rights to comparable areas of crown land.

Whitty and Byrne, declared Kelly, impounded every beast they could get, even off government roads: "If a poor man happened to leave his horse or a bit of a poddy calf outside his paddock they would be impounded. I have known over sixty head of cattle impounded in one day—all belonging to poor farmers. They would have to leave their ploughing or harvest and other employment to go to Oxley; and then perhaps not have money enough to release them, and have to give a bill of sale or borrow the money, which is no easy matter."

The bull incident was still fresh when Farrell took a horse belonging to George King and spread the report that Kelly had stolen some of Whitty's calves. Kelly said: "I began to think they wanted me to give them something to talk about; therefore I started wholesale and retail horse and cattle dealing."

Such was his only excuse for entering the dangerous duffing trade to which the hard economic circumstances of his life were pushing him, but there must have been more to it. True, he had worked for wages for two years or more, most of the time cut off from the people and roaming life he loved. Had he met the girl of his heart he might have settled down to the good and staid life. Perhaps, because he had been shown so much that was unjust, he demanded more than this—a faith to live by which would enable him to participate in the creation of a better world. Yet who were the prophets of his day? They were sharp businessmen who employed missionaries, soldiers and trade representatives to subjugate the world to their will. The bravest of them could watch the Union Jack flutter to the breeze in some foreign land with tears in their eyes, or march with fire and sword through Africa without a tremor, for they believed in the machine and their mission to turn unhappy mankind into a herd of milch cows.

But Kelly was not of them and had no sympathy for them for he knew only too well what they had done to his own family, and blood and bone he was of the Australia that had shown its true colours at Eureka and was carrying on as best it knew the age-old struggle waged against the princes of Europe.

Yet again came the thoughts that would not let him go—of Jim gaoled at fourteen for the crime of helping his cousin, of his father gaoled, of his uncles, of his mother forced to run a shanty house but with more courage than the greatest in the land, of the cocky farmers ground under by poverty and the eternal pin-pricking of the authorities, of Pentridge and the hulks—and of the opportunities to make a rise for himself and his family that the return to his old haunts placed in his path.

Back came the spirit that had characterised Ireland from the days when its chieftains had refused to knuckle under to English power and Cromwell had distributed 4.45 million hectares of its best land amongst his soldiers — of hatred for authority, of fear and contempt for its traitors, of suspicion of strange people, strange thoughts and change itself. And yet of generous love for its martyrs, its wit and laughter and the gay and reckless warmth of the small clan living close together and believing that to close the doors and windows only made the world brighter inside.

At dinner one day in a hotel at Oxley, a certain Mrs Woods remarked it was a pity that such a strapping young fellow should have become a horse thief, and Ned replied weightily, "Madam, what is a man's lot cannot be blotted out."

So after two years of steady work, Kelly took up life where he had left it off five years earlier and opened large-scale war on the wealthy stock-owners of the North-East, bringing to it a bold and clever hand.

Before long the numbers of disappearing horses and cattle began to rise. Eleven horses disappeared from Whitty's paddocks. The Dockers lost two thoroughbreds from the Ovens. Two mounts unable to make the pace in midnight journeys were found between Wangaratta and the Murray, one strangled and the other with its throat cut; they had not been shot for the reports might have alerted the police. Bones and hides of cattle were recovered from creeks and old mine shafts as selectors and prospectors joined in the offensive. Nothing like it had occurred since the days of Bogong Jack. Bogong Jack had collected the best from the Gippsland studs and driven them north through the passes into inaccessible valleys where he had changed the brands. When the sores had healed and the mob was in good condition from the mountain pastures, he drove them down the slopes to sell them in the Riverina. Then he stole from Riverina squatters in turn, and set off back home to the safety of the high blue ranges across the plain.

Kelly realised that now, with closer settlement and improved communications — the telegraph in particular — the game demanded a quicker turnover. In the old days the duffers had burnt out the old brand with an iron pan and branded the animals anew with a bit of old hoop iron twisted into a suitable shape. But all that took too much time — an A could be made into AB, a P into a B or a C into an O simply by plucking the hairs and pricking the skin with iodine, and the new brand was presentable within a few days.

This land of crop and pasture with its humble selectors' huts, occasional homesteads, its clay roads and tracks, its bearded rough-clad men toiling over the earth, looked peaceful by day, but many a sign was passed and quietly spoken word dropped of swift sallies after dark. Kelly wrote later that in eighteen months of 1876 and 1877, he and his accomplices stole 200 head of horses. The brands were changed in the foothills up the King or in the Strathbogies. Some were trucked direct to Melbourne; others sold through agents in Benalla, Melbourne and New South Wales.

That the injustice done to Jim would not be repeated became evident when Dan — following a trip into Benalla with some of his teenage mates — was arrested for stealing a saddle and bridle. Ned hired a lawyer this time, and — with the help of a receipt and the support of his mates — Dan was acquitted. The lift given to the selectors' sons living around Eleven Mile Creek and Greta was considerable. The new spirit in the air gave rise to what became known as the Greta Mob and became evident in their horsemanship and riding dress — in particular, their high-heeled boots and hat worn with chin-strap.

Months passed before the authorities formed any suspicion that Kelly was behind the new spate of horse stealing, and as the police were desperate for evidence, twenty-seven squatters on the Oxley Plains formed the North Eastern Stock Protection Society and offered cash rewards for information leading to arrests. Such rewards, Kelly argued, gave the police incentive to "go whacks with men to steal horses". "It would be far better for them to subscribe a sum and give it to the poor of their district," he said. "Then there would be no fear of anyone stealing their property, for no man could steal horses without the knowledge of the poor." To clinch the argument, he pointed out that of all the animals he had stolen, only eight head of culls had been recovered, and not one person had come forward of all those who could have given evidence against him.

With the rewards going begging, more active police measures were inevitable, and so the Chief Commissioner, Captain Standish, sent his deputy, Superintendent Nicolson, on an inspection of the North-East. Nicolson was a puritan and a martinet, and as usual, all ranks copped it, including Constable Thom, of Greta, whom he found beard untrimmed and wearing dirty breeches.

"I visited the notorious Mrs Kelly's house on the road from Wangaratta to Benalla," Nicolson reported to Standish. "She lived on a piece of cleared and partly cultivated land on the roadside in an old wooden hut with a large bark roof. The dwelling was divided into five compartments by partitions of blanketing, rugs, etc. There were no men in the house, only women and two girls about fourteen, said to be her daughters. They all appeared to be existing in poverty and squalor. She said her sons were out at work, but didn't say where, and that their relatives seldom came near them. However, their communications with each other were well known to the police. Until the gang referred to is rooted out of the neighbourhood, one of the most experienced and successful mounted constables in the district will be required in charge of Greta. I do not think the existing arrangements are sufficient . . . At the same time, some of the offenders may commit themselves foolishly one day and may be apprehended and convicted in a very ordinary manner."

To Constable Hays, who had accompanied him to the Kelly home, Nicolson issued instructions to be conveyed to Constable Thom: "Never go near that house alone; always have a second constable with you!" And to Inspector Brooke Smith, in charge at Wangaratta, he wrote: "Without oppressing the people or worrying them in any way, you should endeavour, whenever the Kellys commit any paltry crime, to bring them to justice and send them to Pentridge even on a paltry sentence."

Nicolson's statement is remarkable in view of two circumstances — the first, that what he was advocating, his men had been doing all along, and secondly, that the police at the time had no knowledge or suspicion that Kelly was responsible for the new spate of duffing in the North-East. It would appear that what upset Nicolson just as much as the frigid reception from Mrs Kelly was the flashness apparent in the district; it was evidence of a generation without education who imagined all they had to do in life was ride from place to place and enjoy themselves. His aim was to "take the flashness out of the Kellys" and rob them of the prestige he considered held them together — which, in the mind of the ranks, meant lagging Ned himself, since every schoolboy knew him.

Nicolson's report had barely been tabled when Jim came out of Beechworth gaol, having been given one year's remission of sentence for good behaviour. Now eighteen and as tall as Ned himself, he soon cleared out with some of his mates to earn a cheque in the Riverina sheds.

9.   The Fitzpatrick Affair

IN SEPTEMBER, Ned was arrested for riding across a footpath when drunk and taken over the Broken River to the Benalla police barracks where Sergeant Whelan, who remembered him from the Ah Fook matter, was in charge. When he came to, he claimed the publican had hocussed his liquor, so it was little wonder Whelan took three troopers along next morning to escort him to court — Constables O'Dea and Lonigan and a hefty young recruit from Richmond Depot named Fitzpatrick who impressed Kelly as "rather genteel, more fit to be a starcher to a laundress".

The party turned out of the Sydney road and was crossing the street, when — in accordance with the police practice of getting the new chum to do the dirty work — Fitzpatrick set out to handcuff the prisoner. Kelly hit out and ran back into a bootmaker's shop, only to find, before he knew it, that Fitzpatrick had him by the throat and Lonigan by the testicles. He hit out again, and the police were preparing for another sally when the local flourmiller, Mr McInnes, J.P., entered the shop, took the handcuffs and said, "Come on Ned, this is the only way out!"

As usual, Ned responded to a friendly approach and the miller locked the handcuffs on him; but, as the myth has it, he turned as he left the shop and remarked, "Well, Lonigan, I never shot a man yet; but if I ever do, so help me God, you'll be the first!"

McInnes accompanied Kelly to court. In the dock, Ned vehemently contended his liquor had been hocussed and so dominated proceedings that despite Whelan's demand that the prisoner be committed for trial the magistrates let him off with fines and costs totalling £4 6s.

Ned and George King had gone unscathed in 18 months of horse stealing and it would have been too much to expect them to keep it up indefinitely; yet the significance of the police breakthrough, when it came, was not immediately apparent. Two hard-working German settlers, William and Gustave Baumgarten, who farmed land near Barnawartha in a spot well suited to moving stock across the Murray, got a rude shock in October, 1877, when several of Whitty's horses were recovered from Howlong, New South Wales, and they found themselves arrested along with three other men, William Cook, Samuel Kennedy and Thomas Studders. Seven warrants had been issued, including one for a man called Thompson who could not be found.

So began an interminable series of hearings in Beechworth, with Sergeant Steele of Wangaratta police, who had arrested the Baumgartens, well to the fore. In the event, Cook was convicted, Gustave Baumgarten and Studders were discharged and the cases against William Baumgarten and Kennedy were adjourned. Thompson remained at large.

Meanwhile, following a lark in a store at Winton, three members of the Greta Mob—Dan and his cousins Tom and Jack Lloyd—were arraigned on multiple charges involving unlawful entry, theft and damage to property—and in the case of Tom Lloyd—of assault with intent to rape the storekeeper's wife.

Having been outpointed in the bootmaker's shop, Sergeant Whelan went into court determined to make the most of his chance, but once again Ned had hired a lawyer for the defence. Mr McLeary argued successfully that unlawful entry could not be sustained since the shop was open to the public; moreover nothing had been stolen. However, the wilful damage charge was sustained and the magistrate sentenced the trio to three months in Beechworth, plus restitution of £2 10s each, in default another month. In the graver matter, Tom Lloyd was remanded to Beechworth where the rape charge was dropped for one of indecent assault and he was given an extra three months.

The case had several odd sequels; for instance, Goodman, the storekeeper, was later gaoled for perjury. But all such matters were pushed into the background on Black Wednesday, 9 January, when the police force narrowly escaped disbandment at the hands of the newly elected Berry Government. In the event, 200 high public servants were sacked and all police magistrates suspended, with the result that Superintendent Nicolson, frustrated at every turn by his superior officer, Captain Standish, felt impelled to create a diversion, which, at one blow, would advance his own career, serve his squatter friends and prove to Berry and his rabble that they could never do without the police.

The Baumgarten proceedings had led to a veritable bog of complications, but in March he saw his opportunity when the mysterious Thompson was found to be Ned Kelly himself. Parties of police armed with a warrant and led by Sergeant Steele of Wangaratta and Senior Constable Strahan of Greta searched Eleven Mile Creek and district night and day for almost three weeks, but again found themselves cheated. All they could report was that the Kelly family had shifted into a new house, and that Dan and Jack Lloyd were around again, having completed their stint in Beechworth. There was no sign of either Ned or his father-in-law. George King, as events proved, had abandoned his wife and two infants and disappeared into the blue, never to be heard of again.

Ned said later he had given his connections instructions for the sale of some horses at grass near Lake Rowan and set out as "a rambling gambler" to see the country along the Lachlan. He and his stepfather had stolen all the Baumgartens' horses, but the

Baumgartens had not known they were stolen. Innocent men were being arrested and convicted on false witness because the police were out to get the rewards offered by the Stock Protection Society, but it suited the police to pot innocent men; if they took the guilty ones they would go out of business.

Meanwhile, to keep the pot on the boil, Steele fitted Dan Kelly and Jack Lloyd to a description of some youths reported with horses near Chiltern and issued two more warrants which were duly notified in the *Police Gazette*. This new opportunity was good enough for Nicolson, who had learned in the detective force that a sprat can be used to catch a mackerel. Service of the warrants was delayed for ten days, and then on 15 April, by which time Nicolson had arrived in Wangaratta, the raw and inexperienced Fitzpatrick, carrying a telegram from Chiltern and under the general instruction to relieve Senior Constable Strahan at Greta, was sent to Eleven Mile Creek to arrest Dan Kelly, aged seventeen.

For many years, people in the North-East contended that the ensuing disaster which gave the Kelly name nationwide currency for the first time sprang from an attempt by Fitzpatrick to pull Kate onto his knee, but although Kate was sixteen and pretty enough, the myth does not fit the evidence.

Fitzpatrick admitted calling at Lindsay's shanty on the Sydney road after leaving Benalla; and, although he did not say so, he no doubt drank something there to quieten a bad attack of nerves. When he first inquired at the Kelly home he got no satisfaction, he said, so he followed the sound of chopping to the creek where a selector named Williamson was splitting rails; and he was about to continue on his way to the Greta barracks when someone entered the sliprails near the old home. Going over, he found William Skillion holding Dan Kelly's horse, so he rode up to the house where Dan appeared knife and fork in hand.

Fitzpatrick said in court that when he told Dan he was under arrest, Dan replied, "Very well, but you'll let me have something to eat before you take me." Two girls stood beside the fire inside the house. Mrs Kelly immediately began to abuse him; then Ned Kelly rushed in crying, "Out of this, you bastard!" and fired two shots at him, while Mrs Kelly seized a shovel from the hearth and knocked his helmet over his eyes. He reached for his revolver, but Dan had taken it. Meanwhile Ned had fired again. He then found Williamson and Skillion had him covered. Ned said, "That'll do boys!" and he had fainted.

Finally, he described how he came to and found a ball in his wrist, and how Ned insisted on prising it out with a penknife despite his protests that he wanted it attended to in Benalla. He was allowed to leave about 11 p.m., he said, after agreeing under duress to say nothing about the incident.

Ned's account of the incident was quite different. He claimed he was 300 kilometres away at the time. The fracas began, he said, when Fitzpatrick produced a telegram from Chiltern instead of a warrant. Mrs Kelly ordered him off the premises. The trooper had then drawn his revolver which had prompted Mrs Kelly to retort, "It's just as well Ned is not home or he would ram that down your throat!" This had given Dan the opportunity to cry, "Ned is coming now!" and to clap a wrestling hold on him.

Although Kelly claimed to have been out of the colony, the evidence suggests he was intent on scraping together as much ready cash as possible, and did, in fact, arrive home that night with Bill Skillion, some horses and his cousin, Joseph Ryan, who had bought one of them. What part Ned played is unclear, but it seems that he and Dan packed some supplies soon after and rode off into the night with a friend called Joe Byrne — probably to Bullock Creek where he had been panning for gold with George King.

Whatever the facts, Fitzpatrick — after visiting the shanty at Winton again — got back to barracks about 2 a.m. with a story melodramatic enough to send Sergeant Whelan and all hands off to the Eleven Mile at the gallop. But Whelan went about matters circumspectly, questioning him and assembling particulars which he commenced to telegraph to Wangaratta when the post office opened for business. On Fitzpatrick's information, it appeared there was a case against Ned and Dan for wounding with intent to murder, and against Ellen Kelly, William Williamson and William Skillion for aiding and abetting. Meanwhile, Fitzpatrick had his wound dressed by Dr John Nicholson who stated that one of them "might have been produced by a bullet", and added, "There was a smell of brandy on him."

If Fitzpatrick's lone visit to the Eleven Mile had been irregular by police standards, then what happened in Wangaratta was routine. Nicolson was well apprised of the Baumgarten ramifications thanks to Detective Ward, his master spy in the North-East who had gathered the information for swearing the warrant against Ned. He read the telegrams. His officer-in-charge, Inspector Brooke Smith, was next to useless, but he had Sergeant Steele, an eager Englishman who had pushed the Baumgarten business, and he had precise local knowledge in

Senior Constable Strahan, of Greta. With care and a little persistence, he thought, it should be possible to pull off an outstanding coup in the North-East.

Around noon, Steele and Strahan, accompanied by Ward's assistant, Detective Constable Brown, set off from Wangaratta with the job of arresting four members of the Kelly family and Bricky Williamson. As the party approached the Eleven Mile, Steele was annoyed to see some children spot them and immediately run off to the Kelly home. That put Mrs Kelly's arrest off the agenda for the meantime, so Steele sent Strahan on to prepare the lock-up at Greta and took cover with Brown above the creek to spy out the land.

As expected, there was no sign of Ned or Dan, so they arrested Williamson, who lived by himself, about 9 p.m., and soon after midnight walked in on Skillion and his wife, Margaret. No weapons were found in either place. Around dawn, they arrested Mrs Kelly and took her babe-in-arms to the Greta lock-up. Meanwhile Senior Constable Strahan arrested young Jack Lloyd, partner with Dan in the supposed Chiltern sighting.

A newspaper of the day recorded: "Constable Fitzpatrick has been laid up, and is still in great pain though recovering slowly. Three of the parties who aided and abetted have been arrested . . . Troopers are scouring the country, and, if possible, they will capture these two ruffians, when, we trust, they will receive their due punishment."

After spending a month in prison, Mrs Kelly appeared before her old enemy, the squatter McBean, J. P., and was remanded on £200 bail. That such a large sum was forthcoming says as much for her neighbours as against a bench that set such an outrageous sum. No bail was awarded Williamson or Skillion who had another five months to go before trial.

Severe flooding occurred that winter, and when the trial took place in October, the court list was the heaviest in years, sure evidence if any were needed of bad times in the North-East. Fitzpatrick told his story in detail and a half-hearted defence by a local lawyer named Bowman attempted to discredit it by proving an alibi for Skillion. Fitzpatrick caught his wrist on the door latch, Mrs Kelly said.

Addressing the jury, Justice Sir Redmond Barry, having put on weight and a second knighthood since the time he had sentenced Tipperary Jim to death, is reputed to have said, "You all know this man Kelly. If he were here I would give him fifteen years."

So Ellen Kelly, mother of ten, was sentenced to three years hard labour in Pentridge, while Skillion and Williamson were each given six years — all on the evidence of a single witness who a year or so later was to be cashiered from the force — in the words of Chief Commissioner Standish — "as a liar and a larrikin".

When the case concerning the reported Chiltern sighting came up, no one appeared to notice that the police withdrew the horse stealing charge against the teenage John Lloyd or draw the necessary conclusion that Dan was also innocent and that the Fitzpatrick episode and all to follow were the result of a concocted charge and Nicolson's policy of gaoling the Kellys on any pretext.

The recruit from Richmond Depot had been a dupe from the start and for the next hundred years would prove to be a scapegoat for the Victorian police. Even Ned was taken in.

Regarding Fitzpatrick, he wrote:

> He said we were good friends and even swore it; but he was the biggest enemy I had in the country, with the exception of Lonigan; and he can be thankful I was not there when he took a revolver and threatened to shoot my mother in her own house. It is not true I fired three shots and missed him at a yard and a half.
>
> I don't think I would use a revolver to shoot a man like him when I was within a yard and a half of him or attempt to fire into a house where my mother, brothers and sisters were, according to Fitzpatrick's account, all around him. A man who is such a bad shot as to miss a man three times at a yard and a half, would never attempt to fire into a house full of women and children, while I had a pair of arms and a bunch of fives at the end of them that never failed me at anything they came in contact with. And Fitzpatrick knew the weight of one of them only too well, as it ran up against him once in Benalla. . . .

It is said that when Ned was told his mother was sentenced to Pentridge, he swore he would take vengeance that would make his name ring down the generations.

This is no doubt near the truth, for shortly afterwards he wrote:

> When I hear a picked jury, amongst which was a retired sergeant of police, was empanelled on the trial, and that David Lindsay, who gave evidence for the Crown, is a shanty keeper having no licence and is liable to a heavy fine, and keeps a book of information for the police, and his character needs no comment, for he is capable of rendering Fitzpatrick any assistance he required for conviction, as he could be broke any time Fitzpatrick cared to inform on him, I am really astonished to see members of the Legislative Assembly led astray . . . The witness which can prove Fitzpatrick's falsehood

can be found by advertising, and if this is not done immediately, horrible disasters will follow. Fitzpatrick shall be the cause of greater slaughter to the rising generation than St Patrick was to the snakes and toads of Ireland — for had I robbed, plundered, ravished and murdered everything I met, my character could not be painted blacker than it is at present; but, thank God, my conscience is as clear as the snow in Peru . . . If I get justice, I will cry a go, for I need no lead or powder to revenge my cause . . .

Meanwhile, a certain quiet middle-aged gentleman, Alfred Wyatt, Police Magistrate at Benalla, of speculative turn of mind, whom later events would suggest as possessing the most acumen of any of the official gentry concerned with the Kelly trouble, was approached by one of the Quinns who stated Ned and Dan would give themselves up if their mother were released. Wyatt reported the matter to Whelan, at Benalla, and expressed the opinion that the brothers could not hold out and the situation would become worse the longer they kept from justice.

But no action was taken or likely to be taken, for Nicolson's "send them to Pentridge" policy was showing results and satisfaction was high at the Melbourne Club.

10. Washing for Gold

WHILE DAN was hiding out at Bullock Creek and his mother and brother-in-law were facing trial, Ned had no alternative but to remain in the North-East and play his part in organising support for them, legal and otherwise. If, on the other hand, we accept his statement that he was 650 kilometres away when he heard that the Government had offered £100 reward for his arrest and the Stock Protection Society another £100 to anyone who could prove a conviction of horse stealing, then he returned to Bullock Creek already a virtual outlaw and believing he would get no justice if he gave himself up.

I came back, [wrote Kelly] with the full intention of working a still to make whisky, as it was the quickest means to obtain money to procure a new trial for my mother. I tried every legal means to obtain justice, therefore, you see, it never crossed my mind for revenge . . . We had a house, two miles of fencing, 20 acres of ground cleared for the purpose of growing mangleworsels and barley for the purpose of distilling whisky.

We were also digging for gold. We had tools and sluice bores and everything requisite for the work. We had a place erected close to the house for the purpose of erecting a small distill, so if anyone informed on us, they would not get the most valuable or main distill that was further down the creek with the sugar and other requisitions.

The "we" in Kelly's account included two or three mates he and Dan had made in Beechworth Gaol and elsewhere. A bridle path led over the hills towards Greta, and along this came supplies and regular news of police movements brought by Tom Lloyd or some other trusted member of the Greta Mob.

I heard, [records Kelly] how the police used to be blowing that they would shoot me first, then cry surrender — how they used to come to the house when there was no one there but women, and how Inspector Brooke-Smith used to say, "See all the men I have out today. I will have as many more tomorrow, and blow him to pieces as small as paper that is in our guns," and they used to repeatedly rush into the house, revolver in hand, and upset milk dishes and empty the flour out on the ground, and break tins of eggs, and throw the meat out of the cask on to the floor, and dirty and destroy all the provisions — which can be proved — and shove the girls in front of them into the rooms like dogs and abuse and insult them. Detective Ward and Constable Hayes took their revolvers and threatened to shoot the girls and children whilst Mrs Skillion was absent, the eldest being with her.

The greatest murderers and ruffians would not be guilty of such an action. This sort of cruelty and disgraceful conduct to my brothers and sisters, who had no protection, coupled with the conviction of my mother and those innocent men, certainly made my blood boil, as I don't think there is a man living could have the patience to suffer what I did.

Such matters, then, gave Kelly and his mates food for thought as they worked steadily in their peaceful valley. An enterprising reporter, who made a trip there after it so dramatically came into the public eye, described it in these words:

The hut was situated on a rise in the middle of a basin bounded east by Ryan's Creek, west by high, steep mountains of the Wombat Ranges, north by a small creek flowing down between ranges, and south by a ridge. Reigning in my horse on the crest of this ridge, I could not but be struck with wonderment that such a perfect settlement should have existed so long within half a dozen miles of selections without being discovered. Farmer Jebb within four miles, and Harrison within six, assert they were not even aware the Kellys were in the vicinity, although the basin was so improved, they must have lived there many months. The basin contains 70 acres fenced in by sapling, dogleg and brush fences, the west side needing no fencing because of the steepness of the hill.

Twenty acres immediately around the hut are cleared, the trees are ringed, and the timber — mainly swamp gum and peppermint — is placed in heaps ready for burning. The ground had even been raked so as to give every chance for the grass to grow. Bark had been removed from peppermints for the roof. In the creek to the north, there had been gold-digging mainly by sluicing. From appearances, there had been gold in payable quantities, the workings were of extent that four men must have worked for several months.

The hut was erected of bullet-proof logs, fully two feet in diameter, one on top of the other, crossed at ends. The door was six feet high by two feet six inches wide, made of stiff slabs and plated with iron nearly a quarter of an inch in thickness, which was loop-holed to fire through. The door is on the north side, opposite the gold workings in the creek, and a well-built log chimney occupies the greater part of the west end of the hut. Such was the home of the Kelly gang for some months before the police murders. Its interior was fitted up just as substantially as its exterior, and in a manner calculated to stand a long siege, there having been every provision made for the storage of flour, beef, tea, sugar, and other necessaries of life. To show that in fresh meat, at least, they were not wanting, we discovered portions of several carcases, together with seven or eight heads of cattle, with bullet holes in the centre of the forehead, lying outside. These may have belonged to either "scrubbers" out of the ranges, or the fat bullocks of some not far distant squatter or farmer, but most probably the latter. Empty jam and sardine tins, old powder flasks, cap boxes, broken shovels, old billy cans, glass bottles, door hinges, and a great variety of other articles were to be seen all round the hut.

But the crowning wonder of all was the evident pains taken by the Kellys to improve themselves as marksmen. In every direction — taking the hut as a standing-point — we saw trees which were marked with bullets, from five to fifty having been fired into each, at ranges varying from twenty to 400 yards. The bullets, being afterwards chopped out, were melted down and converted again into their former state. On one small tree, a circle of charcoal six inches in diameter had been traced, and into this two or three revolver bullets had been fired, one striking the black dot meant to represent the bull's eye in the centre, and the other two being close to it. Some of the bullets had gone to a depth of four inches in the trees, and consequently, a great deal of chopping had to be done to get them out. There was abundant evidence, too, to prove that the more practice the outlaws had, the more they improved in the use of the rifle and revolver, the shooting at some marks on the trees being very wide, and on others remarkably straight and dead into the bull's eye.

So then, in days to come, wrote a reporter, eyes widened and gaze directed by terrible events. Meanwhile, Ned and his brother worked away in their silent little valley with several mates, two of whom — Joe Byrne and Steve Hart — would be fated to stick by them till the end.

Steve Hart, whom events would prove to be Dan's particular mate, was at this time approaching his nineteenth birthday. Born in 1859 at Beechworth, he grew up on his father's eighty hectare selection at the back of Wangaratta racecourse, and after a year or so at school went to work as a butcher's boy at Milawa. The Harts were of Irish origin, decent people and popular with their class. They enjoyed a drink, a practical joke and a brawl now and then.

Steve was a slim jockey type of average height who wore strapped moleskins and high-heeled riding boots and sometimes sported a bright silk sash. His face was smooth and regular, set off by dark eyebrows and hair brushed back and parted in the middle. One thing about him stood out — he was a horseman and as lithe, fit and devil-may-care as this active life made him. One of the chief things people remember about him in later years was the way he cleared the railway gates riding to and from Wangaratta. Like many horsy youths, he had a facility for picking up and dropping other people's mounts at his own convenience; but when Sergeant Steele was posted to Wangaratta, this finally got him into trouble.

Steele's predecessor, Sergeant Cuddin, had been easy going concerning himself only with the graver crimes of the district. But Steele, who boasted propertied English connections — he was named Loftus and Maul after two members of the aristocracy — proceeded to enforce the letter of the law. He met up with Steve in the Warby Ranges not far from the Kelly home, and asked him where he got the mare he was riding. "Oh, I got a lend of it from a bloke back in town," replied Hart. "What bloke?"

asked Steele. Hart replied, "Have you got a warrant for me? I'll give you no bloody information unless you have."

In January 1877, Steve was sentenced to twelve months in Beechworth for illegally using horses, and during his spell of road-making met Dan, in for skylarking at Winton.

Joe Byrne came from the Woolshed where Reedy Creek, a few miles north of Beechworth, tumbles down between granite boulders and chatters towards Wangaratta. Towards the western end of this long fertile valley stood the Byrne home in a tiny half-acre clearing up against a steep corner of the southern flank of hills. A typical slab hut, lined with hessian and paper, it was about six metres long by four metres wide, with a broad chimney of granite boulders across one end and a tiny bedroom and skillion adjoining the kitchen.

Pat, the father, had been a teamster and a miner, and had died thirteen years after Joe was born in 1857. The mother, with her four girls and two boys, struggled along, growing a few vegetables, drawing water from a spring which welled up a few metres from the door, and cooking over the broad hearth with its camp oven, three-legged pots and iron kettles. Luckily her brother helped her to buy a few clothes and other necessities.

The Byrnes were a nice looking family, Mrs Byrne a quiet, active woman, the girls pretty, and Joe an intelligent, lithe youngster, clean and tidy in his habits and a little old-fashioned and grave in his ways. The children attended the Woolshed Common School with its teacher, pupil teacher and fifty young scholars.

The Woolshed diggings was one place where the small man without machinery could still win a living. Hundreds of miners' huts followed the white and yellow coach-road down the valley, and although thousands of diggers had moved on, thousands of others including Chinese, panned and sluiced beside the lively, shallow stream. Chinese workings lay opposite the Byrne home, the Chinese diggers had a joss house in the valley and at Easter staged a spectacular dragon procession up the hill into Beechworth.

Despite the Buckland riots of some years before, the Chinese were well-liked, and Joe had learned enough Chinese to make himself understood. He caught their horses for them, ran their errands and sometimes played practical jokes on them in fashion with a time which patronised Chinese with such ridiculous names as Hoo Flung Dung.

When he left school, he took up odd jobs, fossicked along the river and roamed among the scrub gums, dwarf pines and moss-covered outcrops of the hillsides, hunting for rabbits and foxes. His passions were books and horses. His best friend was an old schoolmate, Aaron Sherritt, who lived just over the range towards Beechworth, and whose father was frequently before the Beechworth Court for non-payment of rates and similar offences. On one occasion he was fined for whipping a horse which was already bleeding where the collar was chafing it. He had been in the Royal Irish Constabulary and was a fanatical Queen's man.

Aaron too, had been fined for brutally using a horse, yet he was a fine horseman and had a vitality and wayward charm which made him good company. His main ambition was to follow his whims and ride fine horses.

By the time Joe was twenty, he was a handsome young man of more than medium height, with light, wavy hair, regular features and a fine brow. Dressed in the trousers and jacket of the sober citizen of the day, he made no attempt to ape the larrikins and the gentry with their strapped trousers and bright waistcoats. In company, he was quiet and well-behaved; yet he could express himself aptly if he wanted.

Times were leisurely and food was simple and plentiful. He roamed the district on horseback, stopping with friends wherever he happened to be. If Joe liked to stop the night, he was welcome. If he didn't take to work—well, what man with spirit didn't sow his wild oats before he took a wife and settled down?

And so Joe came and went—frequently on other men's horses borrowed for twenty-four hours, never imagining in those carefree days that seventy years later, an old lady approaching death would rise from her bed in an old weatherboard house in Beechworth specially to speak of him. Reaching down tremblingly into the well of years to the time when she was a girl of fourteen and he a handsome youth of eighteen, she recited some songs he wrote.

There was no harm in Joe. He was a nice boy. He brought me two young curlews, but the mother bird followed them down, and when it came night, they commenced to squeal, so we let them go. Then he brought me a lamb. You never knew where he got it; and it followed us round for years, even after he himself was dead. He was a nice, quiet boy—not flash—and a fine horseman. He would come in at any old hour to stay for the night, and my father would say, "Whose horse have you got tonight?" and Joe would tell him. He probably did a bit of cattle-duffing—just kill a cow where it stood for the meat—but that was no great crime, unless you were caught. A lot of people did it and had good reason. He got in with Sherritt, and that was when the trouble began.

After spending six months of 1876 in Beechworth for possessing stolen meat, Joe and Aaron were charged the following January with injuring a Chinese digger who had found them diving into a dam near his camp and ordered them off. Aaron had thrown a rock at him and he had been admitted to the Ovens District Hospital.

Joe's young sister appeared in court for the defence. The Beechworth paper commented:

> It was painful to hear such an intelligent looking little girl of twelve repeating word for word to the Crown Prosecutor what she had already told to Mr Brown for the defence — just as if she were repeating a lesson. The defence was utterly improbable. Chinamen are not in the habit of pursuing and assaulting Europeans without provocation, but merely for amusement, as our larrikins are in the habit of treating them. We would just remind these two strapping lads of the fate of Smith and Brady, who commenced life like them and ended on the gallows.

So Ned and Dan spent one long winter based on Bullock Creek, working at their various enterprises, slaughtering an occasional beast, sharing their grub with various mates who came and went and preparing for the day a police party might ride in and try to bring them to justice — in which case they were inclined to make a break for the border.

Meanwhile the police followed rumour after rumour as their spies gave them contradictory reports, some fed to them by the Kelly relatives who were becoming increasingly bitter. Casual remarks were seized by listening ears, watchful eyes noted police comings and goings, and fast horses relayed vital news to an inner circle at Greta which kept in touch with Ned and Dan. So began the bush telegraph which was soon to expand into a network spread over a district 200 kilometres across and fed by hundreds of relatives and sympathisers.

After some months of fruitless search in which Detective Ward declared the brothers' were not in the colony, Sergeant Kennedy, stationed at Mansfield, discovered that some gold dust had been sold locally and guessed they were hiding out in the area Power had frequented, an opinion supported by Power himself who had been told by his warders in Pentridge that Ned had betrayed him eight years before. Kennedy suggested the formation of a well-armed party to search the Wombat Ranges, and Superintendent Sadleir, who had been placed in charge of the newly created North-Eastern Police District, decided to mount a pincer operation with one party to patrol south from Greta and the other to search north from Mansfield, the two to meet on the upper King at Edi.

Born in Westmeath, Ireland, Sergeant Michael Kennedy had been a wild young man, but had married a Mansfield girl, joined the Rechabites and now had five children. An efficient policeman and good bushman, he made a reconnaissance of the largely unsettled and sometimes impenetrable country towards the King and proposed to establish an outpost on Stringybark Creek and systematically search the heart of the Wombat area. Both he and Sadleir in Benalla had had numerous conversations with various spies as well as Wild Wright and Tom Lloyd senior; at any rate the spot chosen was to prove perilously close to the Kelly hideout.

Kennedy took care in organising his party. He chose Mounted Constable Michael Scanlon, a crack shot and former prospector who knew the Mansfield country, and Scanlon was temporarily relieved of his responsibilities at Mooroopna. Constable Lonigan, of Violet Town, who had clashed with Ned in the bootmaker's was included because he knew both Ned and Dan. The fourth member of the party was Constable McIntyre, a reliable Orangeman who had a reputation as a camp cook. With considerable secrecy, the party set out from Mansfield on Friday morning, 25 October, disguised as prospectors. Each man carried a service revolver in his belt. In addition, Scanlon carried a brand new Spencer revolving rifle and McIntyre a double-barrelled shotgun, borrowed at the last moment in Mansfield. They also led two packhorses loaded with a small tent and two weeks' provisions.

That day they toiled over ridge and gully. The last inhabited point was a sawmill twenty kilometres out owned by a man called Monk. They reached their objective thirty-two kilometres from Mansfield on nightfall and erected the tent beside Stringybark Creek near a broken-down shingle hut, where some years before, diggers had lived and washed for gold.

Kennedy and Scanlon were old comrades and no doubt had decided the reward money looked better split two ways, for they said nothing of any plan, but instead, left camp at six next morning, leaving Lonigan and McIntyre behind to keep camp and stop the horses from straying in the thick timber.

It was quiet among these remote hills. The murmur of the creek, the sigh of the wind in the branches, the chatter of small birds, the occasional screech of a parrot or bleak cry of the jay—bird of desolate places—must have emphasised the entire lack of human sound in the tangled bush surrounding the small clearing with its tent and decayed hut, so that at lunch time, when

Lonigan and McIntyre heard a noise down the creek, they put down the fresh bread they were eating and went downstream to investigate. They found nothing and came to the conclusion it had been caused by a wombat.

In the afternoon, McIntyre took the shotgun, wandered about the creek and shot a couple of parrots. As the sun sank towards the hills and the cold began to rise from the ground, the two men collected deadwood from the tangled wattles and scrub gum and built a fire to guide Kennedy and Scanlon back to camp. Perhaps they heaped more logs on to the blaze to exorcise their loneliness. For a time, they sat on the fallen tree gazing into the flames. Then McIntyre picked up a shotgun while Lonigan hobbled the horses.

The tale goes that when Lonigan left some days beforehand, he remembered that Ned had once said, "If I ever shoot a man, it'll be you, Lonigan," and returned twice to bid his wife farewell. Perhaps Scanlon, too, had forebodings, for people say he called out to the wardsman of the hospital at Mooroopna, "If I don't come back, you can take my dog."

But now Lonigan and McIntyre were electrified by a voice which rang with authority through the small clearing: "Bail up! Hold up your hands!"

11. Stringybark Creek

IT IS SAID that Sergeant Kennedy had dealings with an agent who told him where the gang was hiding, and that when the police party left secretly, the agent became panicky and rode to square himself with the Kellys. Was this the same swift messenger of death who later galloped towards Benalla shouting out to selectors as he passed, so that news of the disaster became common knowledge while the sole police survivor of the battle was still fleeing from the wrath behind him?

Following the trial in Beechworth, Ned returned to Bullock Creek to find Joe Byrne and Steve Hart sharing the hut with Dan and Tom Floyd. Tom, who had lately arrived from Greta to deliver stores and pick up gold dust, announced that police parties were out from Greta and Mansfield; and late the same day Ned came upon tracks making for the shingle hut about two kilometres distant on Stringybark Creek.

Overnight, the mates took turns standing sentry on a small rise outside. Next morning Ned and Dan reconnoitred and found a tent and two troopers dressed as prospectors near the shingle hut and fresh horse tracks disappearing downstream.

Ned wrote:

> . . . I knew the other party of police would soon join them and if they came on us . . . they would shoot us like dogs at our work. As we had only two guns, we thought it best to try and bail them up, take their firearms and ammunition and horses, and we would [then] stand a chance with the rest.

In the afternoon, Ned sent Tom to watch downstream, while he and Dan, using the sassafras scrub and speargrass as cover, approached as close as they could get to the police camp which stood across a space of clear ground in the battery of logs. Steve and Joe made up the rear. They noted two men at the logs. In Kelly's words:

> They got up, and one took a double-barrel fowling piece and one drove the horses down and hobbled them against the tent, and we thought there were more men asleep in the tent, those being sentry. We could have shot those two men without speaking, but not wishing to take life, we waited. McIntyre laid his gun against a stump and Lonigan sat on the log. I advanced, my brother Dan keeping McIntyre covered. I called on them to throw up their hands.

Although the account of what occurred gains support from Kelly, it depends mainly on McIntyre who later made several contradictory statements. McIntyre raised his arms in surrender. Lonigan, however, ran to the cover of a log, but had no sooner raised his head to fire when a bullet from Ned's rifle hit him in the temple. As Ned and Dan advanced at the run, Lonigan cried, "Oh, Christ, I'm shot!" jumped to his feet, raised his arms in surrender, staggered a few metres and fell.

Ned seized McIntyre's shotgun from the log. "Where's your revolver?"

"At the tent!"

"Keep him covered lads!"

As Dan secured Lonigan's revolver, Ned entered the tent. He reappeared as the last echoes of the gunshots faded and the silence bore down on them. "Dear, dear, what a pity the bastard tried to run," he said.

Steve and Joe were examining Lonigan; he was already dead.

"Who is that man?" Ned asked McIntyre.

"Lonigan."

"Oh, I'm glad it's Lonigan; that bugger gave me curry in Benalla one day." Ned was under the impression the dead man was Senior Constable Strahan who had boasted to the Quinns how he would shoot him on sight like a dog.

"Did you see how he caught at his revolver?" said Dan, moving his hand across his hip.

"Plucky fellow," said Byrne.

Ned joined McIntyre near the fire and reloaded.

"He'll lock no more poor buggers up," remarked Dan as he bent down and removed a set of handcuffs from the dead man's pocket. "Put these on that bastard," he said, indicating McIntyre.

"What can I do when you are armed?" the trooper objected.

"You bastards would soon handcuff us if you had us."

Ned thought for a second, then tapped his rifle. "All right, I've got something better here. Don't try to run or I'll track you to Mansfield and shoot you at the police station. Where are your mates?"

"They went down the creek."

"When will they be back?"

"I don't think they'll be back tonight."

Byrne took the billy off the fire, poured a pannikin of tea and handed it to McIntyre. "Is there any poison about?" he asked.

"No, why should we have poison?"

McIntyre drank and returned the billy; and while the others ate bread and ham at the fire, Ned checked the ammunition from the tent and replaced the shot in a couple of cartridges with bullets from his pocket. When he had reloaded McIntyre's shotgun, he handed it to Dan.

"Do you smoke?" Byrne asked McIntyre.

"Yes."

Byrne, McIntyre and then Ned filled their pipes and smoked for several minutes. Ned lifted the battered, short-barrelled rifle with which he had killed Lonigan and laid it across his knees.

"This is a curious weapon with which to travel the country."

"Perhaps it is better than it looks."

"I can shoot a roo at a hundred yards."

Ned knocked out his pipe and rose. "That'll do, lads. Dan, you take a look over that rise. You two better go back to see the police haven't found the camp."

As the trio filed out into the quiet afternoon, Ned motioned to a log near the fire and said to McIntyre, "Go and sit there and mind you give no alarm or I'll put a hole through you."

When the constable had done as instructed, he lay down behind the log, his two old guns beside him. "Who showed you this place?" he asked.

"No one. We were on the beat at Mansfield. We crossed Hollands Creek and followed the blazed line."

"Who are you and what brought you here?"

"You know very well who we are."

"I suppose you came after me?"

"No."

"Well, you came after Ned Kelly."

"Yes, we came after Ned."

"And you buggers would shoot us, I suppose?"

"No, we came to apprehend you."

Kelly knew that whatever McIntyre's personal intentions, countless lawbreakers had been shot on sight, not least the bushranger Midnight who had killed a Sergeant Wallings near Dubbo and himself been killed by police two weeks before "while attempting to escape" as the newspapers said.

"Why did you bring so much firearms and ammunition?"

Kelly had found three dozen revolver cartridges, three dozen shotgun shells and 21 rifle cartridges in the tent.

"We only brought powder to shoot kangaroos."

"Don't give me such rubbish," said Kelly. "Why was that shooting down the creek today?"

"I was shooting parrots."

"That's very strange. Didn't you know we were here?"

"No, we didn't know you were within ten miles." He pointed towards Glenmore. "We thought you were over there."

"When do you expect the others home?"

"I don't think they'll be home; I think they must have got bushed."

"What direction did they go?"

"Over there." McIntyre pointed in the direction of Benalla.

"Well, that's very strange. Perhaps they'll never come back — there's a good man down the creek if they fall in with him. What's their name and station?"

"Sergeant Kennedy and Constable Scanlon. What do you intend doing? Surely you wouldn't shoot them down in cold blood?"

"I'll shoot no man who holds up his hands."

"What do you intend doing with me? Are you going to shoot me?"

Kelly regarded him scornfully. "I could have shot you half an hour ago at this log if I had wanted to. I thought at the time you were Flood. It's a good job for you, or I would have roasted you on that fire. There are men in the force, if I lay my hands on them, I'll roast them—Fitzpatrick, Flood, Steele, Strahan and Strong—all blowing about how they would take me single-handed . . . How are these men armed?"

"In the usual way—revolvers."

"Have they got a rifle with them?"

McIntyre hesitated.

"Come on, tell me the truth. You lie, and I'll put a hole through you."

"Yes, they've got a rifle."

"A breech-loader?"

"Yes."

"For kangaroos, you say?" said Kelly with scorn. "Do you know what happened to the man who shot Sergeant Wallings two weeks back?"

"Yes, the police shot him."

"The police gave him no chance to surrender and for all we know they might have shot the wrong man," cried Kelly.

"The police have got their duty to do."

"The police are not ordered to go around the country shooting people," replied Kelly angrily. "That bloody Fitzpatrick was the cause of all this. The people lagged at Beechworth no more had revolvers in their hands than you have at present. Fitzpatrick is a liar; you should know that. Every man in the force should know it by now.

"I must say it's a shame to see a fine, strapping man like you in the lazy loafing billet of policeman. Why don't you be a man and get out of it?"

In the moments that followed, while Dan and Joe returned to take up positions in the speargrass and Steve to stand by the tent, McIntyre confessed that he had suffered an illness recently and had been thinking of leaving the force. Finally, he promised to leave the force if Kelly refrained from shooting Kennedy and Scanlon.

"If you get Kennedy and Scanlon to surrender, we'll let you all go in the morning; but you'll have to go on foot. We'll handcuff you tonight, because we want some sleep."

"Will you promise faithfully not to shoot them if I get them to surrender, and will you get your friends to promise?"

Kelly had heard some strange sound in the bush, and was looking down the creek. "I won't shoot them," he replied, "but the others can please themselves. All we want is their guns and horses."

It occurred to McIntyre that, with one spring, he could get hold of one of the guns. He took a short step.

"Look out, Ned, or that bastard will be on top of you," called Steve from the tent.

Kelly coolly turned his head and measured McIntyre. "You had better not, mate," he observed, "because, if you do, you will soon find your match. I know there are not three men in the force a match for me." He added, "Are there any other parties of police out?"

"Yes, there's one at Greta."

"Who are they?"

"They're under Strahan, that's all I know."

At this moment, Kennedy and Scanlon turned out of the twilight of the bush into the brighter light at the end of the clearing.

"Hist, lads, here they are!" cried Kelly. "Go and stand at that log, McIntyre, and you'll get no harm; but mind, I've got a gun for you if you give any alarm."

Slowly the horsemen walked their mounts towards the fire—Kennedy in front and Scanlon a length or so behind. They were about fifty metres away when McIntyre stepped forward on Kelly's instruction. The distance had closed to twenty metres when McIntyre cried out, "Sergeant, I think you'd better dismount and surrender, as you are surrounded."

Kennedy, seeing McIntyre advancing and the fire burning as he expected, could not conceive he was riding into an ambush.

He smiled.

"Bail up! Hold up your hands!" cried Kelly, rising to his feet.

Scanlon slewed his horse about as if to gallop off, but unslung his repeater, wheeled and fired. He was about to fire again when a bullet from Ned's rifle pierced his chest and he fell.

Kennedy, meanwhile, had seized his revolver and thrown himself from the offside of his mount. He began to fire over its rump at Dan, who was advancing from the creek, but the horse wheeled and he ran for the cover of a tree. He fired again—this time at Ned, who felt the bullet part his beard. Standing in the middle of the battle, McIntyre seized his opportunity, flung himself at the saddle and clung on as the animal squealed and sprang up the track down which it had come.

All this had taken place rapidly within a radius of ten or fifteen metres; but now, as Kennedy crashed into the tangled wattle and sassafras scrub, a drawn-out duel began.

Scanlon was dying. Ned picked up his repeater, but not knowing the mechanism, dropped it, seized his shotgun and followed. As the trooper retreated from tree to tree, pausing now and then to take aim and fire, Ned followed, counting the shots and knowing Kennedy would have to reload.

The sound of Kennedy's horse with McIntyre on its back died away. The two men pressed deeper into the scrub, watching each other narrowly. Every now and then, Kennedy broke from cover and retreated while Ned pressed on behind, biding his time.

Kennedy fired his fourth shot as he ran. He fired his fifth from behind a tree, and was withdrawing his weapon when Ned hit him in the armpit with a charge of swandrops. The trooper made a last attempt to run, but thought better of it, turned and raised his arms in surrender, but too late — Ned, mistaking blood covering the policeman's hand for a revolver, had fired again, and Kennedy fell with a bullet to the right of his heart.

Tangled enough are accounts of events up to this; but now, in the interval before Kennedy's spirit was finally snuffed, came an interchange concerning which the wildest tales have been written and told.

Some say that when Ned came up to the dying man, he said, "Well, Kennedy, I'm sorry that I shot you, for you're a brave man. Here, take my gun and shoot me." And Kennedy, acting his part of the melodrama, replied, "No. I forgive you from my heart, and I pray that God may forgive you, too."

Kelly — the only man to know what happened — said that although Kennedy begged his life so that he might see his wife and children again, he knew the trooper was mortally wounded and could not live. As McIntyre had escaped to give the alarm, he and his mates could not wait for the trooper to die, and to abandon him would mean a slow, tortured death at the mercy of ants, flies and dingoes, so he put his gun to Kennedy's heart and pulled the trigger. Had Kennedy been his own brother he could not have been more sorry, he said. He went back to Bullock Creek for a cloak and left him as honourably as he could with the cloak over him.

Some people chose to believe that Kelly demanded Kennedy's watch and finished him off when the trooper objected, "Don't take it, Ned; my family values it!"

The tale that Kelly's mates came up, and that the four of them swore to share the blood guilt and die as one if need be, possibly grew from a misconception caused by the multiple wound from the swandrops blast. The public were told how the outlaws handcuffed Kennedy to a tree and cut his ear off; but there are many ways Kennedy could have lost an ear in the five days before the body was found. The coroner mentioned that a wombat could have chewed it off. Kelly simply said: "As for handcuffing Kennedy to a tree, or cutting his ear off, or brutally treating any of them, it is a cruel falsehood. If Kennedy's ear was cut off, it has been done since."

Some say Kelly lied when he claimed he could have shot McIntyre but let him go rather than break his word. He certainly had good cause to shoot McIntyre as an alarm would bring police parties down on them immediately; moreover McIntyre was the sole witness of the Lonigan shooting and his death would have removed any positive evidence of it. If Kelly lied, why did he say of Lonigan, "I did not begrudge him what bit of lead he got, as he was the flashest, meanest man that I ever had any account against."

As the sun sank on Stringybark Creek, so sank the hopes of these four young men of rejoining their people and living on the open sunlit plains. They were committed to the barren ridges, the sky and storms. The lengthening shadows of twilight were to become the night in which they were to move in stealth for long months ahead. Yet, the brand which they took from the fire and threw into the police tent was to ignite the spirits of thousands of downtrodden selectors and shed a glimmering light into new centuries.

As they returned to Bullock Creek, Byrne was cut up by what had occurred and Dan annoyed with Ned for not handcuffing McIntyre, while Steve was more phlegmatic and interested in getting some grub — yet not unaware that here was a gigantic event eclipsing all he had known or imagined, and that war to the death would be waged against them by the entire force of a colony now committed to avenge blood with blood.

12. War Declared

WHENEVER NED HIT OUT, he did so with supreme decision, force, and rapidity. No wonder terror struck the already shaken McIntyre when he saw another of his mates fall. He clung frantically to his mount as it galloped back over the rise into the bush, then managed to pull himself properly into the saddle. According to his account a slug whistled by his ears and another struck the rump of his horse. He imagined the Kellys were following.

Curious how a man, knowing what lies in front of him, calculates his chances, works out a plan of action and executes it with never a flicker of fear—and yet how the same man, caught unprepared and unarmed, will flee blindly into greater dangers than those behind him, jump at the bark of a dog, or shudder at the crack of a twig.

McIntyre, crazed with fear, galloped violently for three kilometres between trunks, slapped by hanging branches, up and down gullies, until his horse stumbled and he was thrown. He remounted and rode on till the beast fell exhausted. He hid saddle and bridle, so the mount could not be used so readily in his pursuit, and ran on torn and bruised towards the setting sun. He found a wombat hole, and fearing his pursuers might soon catch up with him, crawled in to wait for darkness.

Here, understanding what he was doing about as well as a drunk who writes his name on a urinal, he scribbled this memo in his notebook: "Ned Kelly and others stuck us up today when we were disarmed. Lonigan and Scanlon shot. I am hiding in wombat hole till dark. The Lord have mercy upon me. Scanlon tried to get his gun out."

As darkness fell and no sound came from the bush, he crawled out of his dank retreat and set off, keeping a bright star on his left hand. Twigs crackled under his tread. The sound frightened him, so he took off his boots. He shuddered at the whine and rustle of the wind and started at sounds in the undergrowth. Losing sight of the star behind a ridge, he crouched behind a log with his jacket around his head, and with the aid of three wax matches checked his direction with a small pocket compass. Still confused, he put his boots back on the wrong feet, changed them again, and set off once more through bush and scrub. He descended bracken slopes to cross small creeks and climbed again past fallen trees and moss-encrusted stony outcrops. Sometimes he was forced to scramble on hands and knees through tangled undergrowth.

So dawn came. He pressed on and began to recognise the country. Coming to Blue Range Creek, which runs past Mansfield to join Broken River, he rested and wrote in his book: "I have been travelling all night and am very weary. 9 a.m., Sunday. I am now lying on the edge of a creek named Bridges."

Walking steadily on through uninhabited country, which, however, began to show signs of stock, he came in sight of a station about 3 p.m. To his horror, several horses were standing near the homestead, one of which seemed to be the animal he had abandoned the previous evening. Had the bushrangers outstripped him and cut him off?. He pressed closer, and seeing the mounts belonged to the place stumbled forward to be met by a settler named McColl to whom he told scraps of his story.

An hour later, McColl and McIntyre burst into the sleepy quiet of Mansfield's Sunday afternoon, and drove up the broad street to the police station. Green and lovely—embosomed in its blue mountains—Mansfield did not suspect that the disconnected sentences which Inspector Pewtress, shivering with influenza, drew from the weary McIntyre would soon be flashed across the globe.

When the news of the tragedy became public, a gasp of horror passed through the township. Half the population of 500 gathered at the police station. Volunteers stepped forward. Shortly after, Inspector Pewtress, Dr Reynolds, Constable Allwood, five civilians and McIntyre set off with an array of borrowed firearms and a couple of packhorses to bring in the bodies. They covered the twenty kilometres to Monk's sawmill easily enough. When they arrived at the mill, the night was pitch black and rain was falling in torrents. Monk consented to act as guide; and half an hour later the party continued on its way, riding in melancholy single file through the forest, which answered the clop of horses' hooves with the pattering of rain on leaves, the occasional mournful cry of the mopoke and crash of a wallaby through undergrowth. The creek was reached soon after midnight. Lonigan and Scanlon were found where they had fallen; and, striking matches, members of the party examined the bodies. The tent had been burned down and everything removable taken away. Kennedy could not be found, so the search was dropped.

With daylight came fears that the Kellys might return and annihilate the whole party. Under the grey sky, the forlorn clearing, with its sombre ashes, dead men, and damp, remote silence, gave the fevered Pewtress more reason to shiver and McIntyre more cause to remember the sudden, terrible wrath which was now to become a legend with which mothers might quiet children and small boys frighten policemen. Wet and miserable, the party carried out a desultory search around the borders of the scrub and along the creek, and became more and more convinced of the correctness and convenience of McIntyre's view that Kennedy had surrendered and been led away as prisoner. So at last the bodies of Scanlon and Lonigan were tied together, lifted on to the packhorse, and the party returned to the mill and thence to Mansfield.

McIntyre and the rest of the party were no different from other men whose station in life put them into opposition to the Kellys. They had no special sense of the justice of their cause and merely wanted to perform their daily jobs and enjoy the warmth of their families. If a regiment of Cossacks had landed in the North-East, the police would have been less alarmed than by the simple defiance of this one man and his mates.

Before Pewtress had left for Stringybark, telegraphic communication with Benalla had been interrupted, so he had written a brief report of his interview with McIntyre, and ordered Constable Meehan to take it to Benalla. Meehan left Mansfield at six the following morning in uniform, but after some distance saw two bushmen on the road. He said to himself, "These men have euchred everything. They have shot the police. I have no firearms. I cannot get past them. What am I to do?" So he turned in his tracks and rode back to a nearby farm to get firearms, but without success. Again he said to himself, "I must do something. As I have no firearms, I must use my head." So he removed the bridle from his mare, abandoned the animal, took off his boots which were pinching him, and walked across country all night to Broken River. Here he was picked up by a police trooper, to whom he told how he had come across the camp of the bushrangers and to avoid them abandoned horse.

Meanwhile a cocky found the animal without bridle and with both stirrups over the left side as though the rider had been thrown and led it in to Pewtress, at Mansfield. Pewtress later said to Meehan, "I will never forgive you for making such a fool of yourself." There were more to be made laughing-stock in the months ahead; and mightier men than Meehan!

By Tuesday, news of the double tragedy had been flashed across the colony, and police had begun to trickle into the district from other parts. A second search party arrived at Stringybark on Tuesday, and a third on Wednesday. On Thursday morning, a farmer came across the body of Kennedy in the thick scrub where Kelly had left him. Kennedy had a bullet wound in his right breast, swandrop wounds under his right armpit, and the clothing around the third and fatal wound in the left breast was blackened with powder.

Earlier bushrangers had scarcely been known outside the colonies in which they operated. But new and extraordinary discoveries were tumbling into the world. The sensational electric light invention had caused a panic in gas shares and now the electric telegraph dribbled the news of the tragedy in a curious mixture of dots and dashes to every part of the colony and of the world's greatest power — Great Britain herself.

In a breath, the newspapers denounced the Kellys as inhuman murderers, and the police authorities for sending out men inadequately armed. Lurid stories of torture and sadism were mingled with more objective accounts. One of the State's leading newspapers, the *Williamstown Advertiser*, described the Kelly home at Greta as a "groggery and shanty hell", and stated that the murder of three showed Ned Kelly to be an experienced hand, who had probably murdered twenty in his time. "He spends his money", it said, "among harlots in whose sweet society he is now basking." Bishop Moorhouse, of Melbourne, addressing a meeting at Mansfield, said in a spirit of loving kindness, "We should pity the poor wretches who have caused us to mourn over the recent disasters."

No sooner had the news reached Melbourne than Mr Gaunson, M.L.A., moved the adjournment of the House to discuss measures to mitigate the calamity fallen on the relatives of the murdered men. He suggested the Victorian standing army of 150 men be sworn in and sent to relieve volunteers assisting in the search. The Chief Secretary, in a rapid reversal of form, ordered police to stint no expense. A few Spencer repeaters were issued from barracks store, and a number of double-barrelled breach-loaders were bought for £8 each and sent up with reinforcements of hand-picked men.

At Mansfield, large crowds attended the last rites, in which clergy of all denominations including Fathers Scanlon and Kennedy, cousins of the deceased, participated. Subscription lists were circulated by banks, business houses, government bodies and squatting interests for a memorial in Mansfield to serve as a perch for sparrows for the next thousand years.

In Melbourne, at the Princess Theatre, a highly sensational melodrama entitled *Fleeced or The Vultures of the Wombat Ranges* was produced. The *Age* critic wrote:

> Of literary merit, *Fleeced* possesses but little, the language being senseless and coarse. In point of fact, the dialogue appears to have been regarded as a matter of most trivial importance, reliance for effect being placed on a series of desperate encounters between a band of bushrangers and the police, the latter almost invariably coming off second best. At the conclusion, the gang are exterminated after baffling their pursuers in a most successful manner through the piece, but the leader of the band, even in his dying moments, is made to appear quite a hero, and was evidently regarded in that light by the audience, by whom he was called before the curtain with shouts of "Kelly" and uproarious applause. The drama appeared to be immensely popular with those present, and doubtless the house will be crowded night after night by the very class upon which its moral effect is likely to be most

pernicious. It is a moot question whether some steps should be taken to suppress the present performance.

But the chief reaction was the rapid passing by the Berry Government of the Felons Apprehension Bill, which gave civilians the right to shoot the gang on sight and police power to arrest anyone harbouring or assisting them. Almost immediately, the Chief Justice granted an order against each of the gang to surrender at Mansfield on or before Tuesday, 12 November, to stand trial for murder. Lengthy advertisements appeared in the press naming and describing Ned and Dan and two others believed to be Charles Brown and William King. On their non-appearance, all four were to be outlawed, and notices offering £500 dead or alive were to be posted on boards and tacked on trees from one end of the colony to the other.

The country was seething with interest. The upper classes and their newspapers continued to express horror and indignation, and to demand the rooting out of these blood-stained thieves and murderers. But the poorer people of both city and country could not help feeling that here a blow had been struck against the arrogant authorities who shoved them around.

A band of horsemen galloped through Mansfield one evening yelling with all their might. A few evenings later, as people were going to church, Wild Wright passed a party of police who had just dismounted after returning from a search. "Dogs, curs, cowards," he shouted. "Follow me if you want to catch the Kellys; I'm going to join the gang. Come out a little way and I'll shoot the lot of you." Annoyed, the police remounted, and spurred their mokes after him, but Wright kept just out of reach. "All the police of Mansfield can't catch me," he shouted. Sub-Inspector Pewtress ordered two troopers to arrest him; but Wright steadily drew away and gave them the slip on the Benalla road. However, he was later caught unawares and fined £1 for using threatening language.

The name of Kelly became a stick with which to beat enemies. After the return of the search parties to the sawmill, Monk boasted to a large number of people that he had tracked the Kellys and could track them again. A few days later he received the following letter:

> To E. Monk. You think you have done a grate thing by serching for the traps, but you made a grate mistake for your friend Kennedy is gone although we made him confess many things you told him in confidence and we heard you say you could track us and our horses, but we will track you to hell but what we will have you. We will make your place a Government

camp when we come, and give them some more bodeys to pack. What a fine thing it is to cut their ears off, but we will poke your eyes out.

Yours until we meet,
E. and D. Kelly.

A certain Walter Lynch was arrested, and after being held four months without trial, was sentenced to two years hard labour for writing a threatening letter. Sole evidence was similarity of handwriting.

Ned Kelly had already become the hero of all the pushes and street-corner loungers who, sick of having their pipes pulled out of their mouths and being pushed around by the traps, now commenced to taunt them with the Kellys. Under the flickering fishtail burners in the dimly lit streets of the cities, they started to sing the first of the Kelly songs. A voice struck up:

> *A sergeant and three constables*
> *Set out from Mansfield town*
> *Near the end of last October*
> *For to hunt the Kellys down;*
> *So they travelled to the Wombat,*
> *And they thought it quite a lark,*
> *And they camped upon the borders of*
> *A creek called Stringybark.*

Then came the clatter of boots, the jeers of the lads, the threats of police, and the echo of feet up alleys. From behind a fence came voices singing the next verse:

> *They had grub and ammunition there*
> *To last them many a week.*
> *Next morning, two of them rode out*
> *All to explore the creek . . .*

Then, perhaps, a shower of stones and again the voices:

> *Leaving McIntyre behind them at*
> *The camp to cook the grub,*
> *And Lonigan to sweep the floor*
> *And boss the washing tub.*

Police magistrates announced their determination to deal severely with offenders, whom they fined £2 to £5 or in default one or two months gaol. War had been declared. For his part, Ned Kelly announced:

I have no intention of asking mercy for myself of any mortal man, or apologising, but I wish to give timely warning that if my people do not get justice, and those innocents released from prison, and the police wear their uniform, I shall be forced to seek revenge of everything of the human race for the future. I will not take innocent life if justice is given, but, as the police are afraid or ashamed to wear their uniforms, therefore every man's life is in danger, as I was outlawed without cause, and cannot be no worse, and have but once to die; and if the public do not see justice done, I will seek revenge for the name and character which has been given to me and my relations while God gives me strength to pull a trigger.

13. On Double Pay

WHILE TOM LLOYD mounted sentry after the Stringybark battle, the Kellys and their mates snatched a few hours sleep. Then they sorted out their gear, loaded two packhorses, fired hut and contents and set out in rain and fog for Greta.

It was evident that Steve and Joe could put themselves in the clear if they wished, but neither was willing to do so. Still suffering from the shock of events, all four needed time to work things out and the best place to do it was across the Murray, so after a brief meeting with relatives in Greta, they doubled back on their tracks and headed for the Woolshed. When they emerged onto the Murray plain on Tuesday, all the ditches were brimming.

Pushing ahead, they found their fears realised—the Murray was in flood, stretching out into a tangle of creeks and billabongs, so they turned towards the Bungowannah punt. Here, unfortunately, they were spotted by a neighbour of the Baumgartens whose wife pointed out their tracks to a police patrol out after gold smugglers. They were barely able to escape by tethering their mounts in the scrub and hiding up to their necks in a lagoon. Exhausted and finding the punt sunk at the wharf and the waters still rising, they turned their mounts again and headed back for the nearest haven they knew—Joe Byrne's stamping ground, the Woolshed.

Friday night and Saturday were spent over the range at Sebastopol where Byrne's mate, Aaron Sherritt, lived with his parents. On Saturday night, they set off across the flooded Oxley Plains leading two packhorses and driving four spares, passed rapidly through Everton and made for Wangaratta which they reached at 4 a.m. There, Steve led them along a ledge under the bridge crossing One Mile Creek; then they clattered through the town, waking the townsfolk and struck up into the thickly wooded Warby Ranges which run south to Morgans Lookout at Glenrowan.

They were now in familiar country of hills, swamps and farms. It was early summer and the crops were turning. They handed their tired mounts to friends, lazed in the ripening wheat along the railway by day, and watched police parties following alarms up and down. At night, they were received into the homes of relatives and supporters, united as never before by pride of achievement and hatred of the police. The lads had covered a total distance, as the crow flies, of 210 kilometres which meant they had ridden 320 kilometres in eight days.

During two weeks in which the police were always several moves behind, the pattern of the next twelve months warfare became evident, with the gang, showing remarkable endurance and celerity, whipping across the plains by night and moving freely by night or day along the ranges, and the police, days or weeks behind, running up and down the railway line and striking in from Benalla, Beechworth and the other towns in a vast, slow, spongy encircling movement which never engaged, if only because they preferred riding the country on double pay to risking the fate of Lonigan, Scanlon and Kennedy.

As Superintendent Nicolson had anticipated, Stringybark prompted a dramatic reversal in the Berry Government's attitude to the force and Chief Commissioner Standish was told to spare no expense in running the criminals to earth. Nicolson himself was placed in charge of the case and had barely arrived in Benalla when he received a report that the gang had been seen near the Murray. Sending a party of troopers on ahead, he took a train to Wodonga, and with the aid of a black tracker from the Darling, followed some tracks but lost them at Barnawartha.

Meanwhile, Inspector Brooke Smith had been informed that four young men whose horses seemed exhausted had been seen passing through Wangaratta towards the Warby Ranges. For two days he did nothing; then he ordered twenty-two troopers out. The party came upon a packhorse bearing the police brand, B87, and was preparing to press on in pursuit when the erratic inspector, who had orders from Nicolson not to expose his men unduly, rode up and said, "Halt, form up! Any applications or complaints?"

"No sir, but we found one of the horses taken from the police at Stringybark."

Brooke Smith's reaction was to order his men back to Wangaratta.

Melbourne, meanwhile, was in the temporary grip of race fever. Having delayed his visit to the battlefield long enough to attend the Cup, Chief Commissioner Standish arrived in Benalla on Wednesday, 6 November, to be met at the station by Nicolson. The two gentlemen were at supper in their hotel when a message arrived from Sadleir to the effect that the Kellys had been reported at Sebastopol. Unfortunately for the police officers, Kelly sympathisers had concluded from the Commissioner's arrival that big moves were afoot, so that when they tried to telegraph Beechworth, they found the lines thrown out of circuit.

Not to be discouraged, Nicolson ordered all police to report to the station by midnight. Horses were trucked. Nine troopers and a tracker, looking like bushrangers themselves in civilian clothes, climbed into a van and the officers entered their carriage. Just before the train moved off at 1.30 a.m., three suspicious looking characters were detained and questioned.

On arrival in Beechworth, Superintendent Sadleir led the party to the police station where they were alarmed to see a large body of armed civilians standing about in the moonlight. It was explained these were squatters and professional men organised by one of the constables.

Soon after, a party of nearly fifty horsemen clattered up Ford Street where old Power had once passed in triumph and thudded out along the southern road, the rumble of hooves carrying clearly in the still night. After travelling in a wide detour through wet country broken by granite outcrops, the party came at dawn in sight of a large slab hut in a valley where the Kellys had rested up six days before. This was the Sherritts' hut, said Sadleir, and the gang was believed to be sleeping there.

Parties were ordered out on each flank to place a cordon around the hut, while Captain Standish remained on the brow of the hill ready to throw in his reserve of twelve at the decisive moment. Nicolson and a party of six spurred their mounts and plunged full tilt down the slope.

> Into the valley of Death
> Rode the six hundred.

Logs and rotten ground they would have looked at twice any other time were cleared in a flash. At terrific pace, the party took a sharp turn into the home paddock, splashed through a rivulet, and rode recklessly up a narrow passage between split-rail fences, where Nicolson flung himself to the ground and burst in at the door, bumping one of his constables whose gun went off. At the report, the other parties drove their spurs home, and rifle in one hand and bridle in the other, thundered in from all directions. On reaching the hut, they too rushed in to join the fray.

The building was without windows and so dark no one could see properly. Someone tried to strike matches but more bodies kept crowding in the door. The constable whose gun had gone off rushed from room to room pulling the bedclothes off the lower tier of bunks, while Sadleir, who couldn't see into the top tier, followed, carrying his hat on the muzzle of his rifle. After bumping into a table, some stools and each other and shouting a good deal, the police and their gentleman friends became aware that the hut was deserted.

No time was lost in speculating on possibilities and the party pushed on over the range that forms the northern flank of the Woolshed, and descending a precipitous gorge through giant outcrops and native pines, turned into the Byrnes' clearing and rushed up to the house. Joe's sister was known to be engaged to Aaron Sherritt, and by now, Joe was suspected to be one of the gang. Mrs Byrne appeared rather frightened when such a large party arrived to search her hut, but, finding she was not to be arrested, began to stand her ground and slate them.

It was now 7.30 a.m., and after searching one or two other huts, the police settled down to refreshments brought from over the flat. As diggers, their wives and large numbers of children began to gather around, some of the police set out to fish for information and asked Mrs Byrne to help them save her son. He had placed his neck in a noose, they said, but they would get it out if she could persuade him to hand over his mates. She is supposed to have replied, "He has made his own bed; let him lie on it."

Aaron Sherritt's father, John Sherritt, came up and indignantly demanded why the police should raid his property. Hadn't he been in the Irish Constabulary! Why should he be suspected of harbouring such persons?

Finally came Aaron himself — tall, fair and sauntering along with an axe over his shoulder — quite a dandy even at this hour of the morning in his white shirt and high boots. He was spotted by Senior Constable Strahan, who went over, spoke to him, and then took him across to meet Superintendent Sadleir.

"Here is a man who knows the Kellys well and will be of use to you. He knows all that is going on," said Strahan.

Ignorant bushman or not, Sherritt seemed quite able to hold his own with the respectable, nonconformist Mr Sadleir. Sadleir asked him a question or two and offered him a large part of the government reward if he assisted in capturing the gang. Sherritt was ready to co-operate if paid for his work, but rather nonplussed Sadleir by doubting his power to make such an offer. Sadleir had neither the wit nor alternative but to introduce Sherritt to silent, canny Superintendent Nicolson, whose authority was likewise doubted coolly, but without impudence. So Sherritt was referred to Captain Standish himself. The latter was easy-going, rather bored with the conversation, wishing he were back in Melbourne rather than chasing rumours around the country.

Aaron was promised anything reasonable. He was advised to remain on good terms with Joe and await a favourable opportunity. The officers found him quietly spoken, genial and tactful in his replies. Perhaps he was not as flash as he looked. As the sun rose over Beechworth, the master tacticians, within hearing of a motley crowd of troopers, engaged Aaron Sherritt as a spy. A little time passed; the men remounted and rode off in small parties into the morning.

So concluded the Charge of Sebastopol, otherwise known as the Fiasco of Rat's Castle, which name had been given the place because Morgan and Power had sought refuge there.

Infuriated by the failure to follow up the packhorse lead, Nicolson ordered Brooke Smith out again and set off in pursuit himself, assisted by two old black trackers; but the police were now four days behind the outlaws and the search was abandoned near Glenrowan. Undismayed, the police continued to charge around the country, exhausting themselves and their mounts. Parties were placed at road and river crossings. Shots rang out in the night when timorous travellers bolted on being challenged. The press expected the outlaws to be caught any day, but occasionally a doubt began to creep into reports.

14.   Faithfulls Creek

A PRICE ON THEIR HEADS and fair game for anyone who liked to shoot them, the outlaws — as they now were — stood no chance without an organisation and war exchequer to support it. They therefore decided to rob a bank, set the date for the full moon early in December, and chose Euroa because it was handy to the Strathbogies and one of the two remaining towns in the North-East without additional police protection.

All that Ned knew about warfare had been learned in the cattle duffing business — that Australia-wide trade in which sleight of hand had been developed to the level of art. He knew that boldness depended mainly on intelligence, and with the bad season and impoverished conditions on so many farms, found no shortage of volunteers. Upwards of a dozen men including Sherritt were recruited and instructed to hump their blueys to one point or another along the line of advance and await developments. As Steve was not yet suspected of being a member of the gang, he was sent to Euroa on Saturday 7 December, to make a further check on the position.

Euroa boasted an old town and a new town comprising bank, hotel and store opposite the railway station and school, with most of the business done in the centre near the public hall. Steve reported amongst other matters that many of the townsfolk, including the only constable, would attend licensing court in the public hall the following Tuesday and that the stationmaster daily deposited takings at the National Bank after the 3.30 goods departed, the street door being left ajar until 4 p.m.

The Strathbogies then would serve as the line of approach and retreat, but they needed a staging point to secure their entrance to the town. Younghusbands' station backing onto the Strathbogies and seven kilometres from Euroa on Faithfulls Creek would be suitable.

Situated amid lofty gums and backed by the usual rough outbuildings and stockyards, the Younghusbands' homestead was a solid, twin-gable structure with central passage leading to a spacious kitchen and veranda at the rear. On the Monday, the sun shone down from the meridian and the stationhands were preparing to knock off for dinner when a young man — apparently an ordinary bushman — knocked at the kitchen door and asked in a matter-of-fact tone if Mr Macauley was around.

Fitzgerald, a stationhand whose wife was housekeeper, replied, "The manager's not here; can I help you?"

The stranger replied it was of no consequence and sauntered off. Fitzgerald went on with his dinner, and on looking up a few minutes later, saw there were now three rough-looking bushmen instead of one, leading four magnificent horses, but thought no more of it, finished eating and went off to the stables. Two bushmen now approached the kitchen, and Mrs Fitzgerald was rather surprised when they entered uninvited. One took a piece of bread and jam; the other said he was Ned Kelly and that he needed refreshment for himself and his mates and feed for the horses. There was no occasion to fear, he said, for they would do no harm. Mrs Fitzgerald called her husband, who returned to find that the bushman he had spoken to a few moments before now held a revolver. "This is Mr Kelly," said Mrs Fitzgerald.

The men talked until Stephens, the groom, entered and greeted the strangers, whom he took to be travellers or visiting the station on business.

"I suppose you don't know who I am?" said Ned.

"Perhaps you are Ned Kelly," replied the newcomer with a grin.

Kelly laughed. "You're a damn good guesser." He produced his revolver from behind his back. "And this is my brother Dan."

"I beg your pardon," said Stephens, taking a step backwards. "I thought you were joking."

"All right, I'm glad you take it in good part."

Ned and Dan joined Joe outside; then took their mounts to the stables to be fed.

When the fourth outlaw appeared and announced that the men were coming up for lunch, Ned and Joe crossed with him to a large storeroom facing the kitchen. Placing Joe to guard the door, Ned and Steve met the stationhands as they arrived and marched them inside one by one in cheery fashion. The prisoners were assured they would receive no injury unless they interfered or attempted to escape, and everyone seemed amused by the novelty of the adventure. The door was locked and Steve and Dan mounted guard while Ned and Joe went off to eat.

Mr Macauley was greatly puzzled as he approached the homestead on his return; no one was working, and yet it was the busiest time of the year. As he came up to the house, he called, "Where is everybody?" Fitzgerald, from the storeroom, shouted, "The Kellys are here!" At the same instant, Ned walked out of the kitchen and told him to bail up, adding they were not going to take anything but had merely called at the station to feed and spell their mounts and get some sleep. Submitting to the inevitable, Macauley said they might as well make themselves as comfortable as possible; and tea having been made, they went inside and sat down together.

Before eating, Ned asked his hosts to taste the food.

"Why in the name of heaven?" inquired Mrs Fitzgerald.

"There's too much strychnine and arsenic around," Ned replied. "Do you know Morgan wouldn't eat anything but boiled eggs and he wouldn't eat those if they were cracked?"

When Ned and Joe finished, they mounted guard while Steve and Dan ate and Mrs Fitzgerald fed the prisoners.

During the afternoon, Ned requisitioned a hut and spent some time there in the company of Byrne. The prisoners were allowed out in the fresh air a few at a time and gossiped with their guards. Macauley was given considerable freedom. Mrs Fitzgerald and the maid went wherever they wished without interference; but the outlaws, while not appearing to do so, watched them closely.

A selector seeking men to help him bind his crop was taken prisoner. He explained to Ned that his boy was waiting for him, so Ned and Steve walked over with him and laughed heartily when the boy eyed them and remarked, "They don't look much good for binders."

Shortly before nightfall, a hawker named Gloster drove up to the homestead in a covered wagon. After he had unharnessed his horses and fixed his camp amongst the gums, he walked up to the kitchen to get some hot water for his tea, and when told the Kellys were in charge, laughed and walked off. Ned came out of the building and cried, "Come here!" Gloster took no notice and kept on walking, and when Dan called out, "Bail up, or I'll shoot you on the spot!" ran for his van. He was climbing in when Ned and Dan ran up and caught him by the legs.

Gloster's assistant, Beecroft, was finding it hard to keep a straight face, for the visit was prearranged. Rather than leave the people at the bank to give the alarm, the gang intended bringing them to the Younghusbands', and the wagon was needed to transport them.

"Come out of that or I'll blow your brains out," cried Ned.

"Who and what are you?" demanded Gloster.

"I'm Ned Kelly, son of Red Kelly, and a better man never stood in two shoes. I've a good mind to put a bullet through you because you didn't obey. It's a very easy matter for me to pull a trigger."

"Well, if that's the case, there's no use resisting you."

"You'll get no harm if you keep a civil tongue in your head. Have you got any firearms?"

"I don't keep firearms for sale."

"I know you have a revolver; give it to me or I'll burn your wagon."

Under the guns of the brothers, the hawker climbed back into the wagon and brought out a revolver. For the benefit of the onlookers Ned then clapped handcuffs on him and took him and Beecroft to the lock-up.

The brothers ransacked the wagon and found a rifle and ammunition, then discarded their old clothes and put on new outfits, making regular bush dandies of themselves. Finally, they sprinkled scent liberally on their cravats and handkerchiefs, and went up to relieve Joe and Steve, who likewise climbed into new outfits.

75

That night, the outlaws stood guard on the storeroom by pairs. The evening was warm, and as he squatted by the door, Kelly conversed with the prisoners, many of whom were playing cards. Some asked him about Stringybark, and he replied, "If there was any shooting, I did it." They asked about Kennedy. "He was a good shot as well as a brave man, for one of his shots came through my whiskers," he said. They asked was it true he had killed Kennedy in cold blood. "I had a long conversation with him, and seeing he could not live from his wounds, to end his misery, I shot him," he replied. "It is not murder to kill one's enemies; the police are my natural enemies." Was it true he had taken Kennedy's watch? "Yes, I intend to return it to Mrs Kennedy in course of time." He told them of his life, his family. They thought he showed no desire to conceal anything or to lie.

Next morning, the outlaws were astir early, released the twenty-odd prisoners, and kept guard while all had breakfast. Then they locked them up again, telling them they would be kept close prisoners for the rest of the day. Little occurred during the morning, except that Ned and Gloster had a conversation in which the outlaw told Gloster he had stolen, altogether, 280 horses. Gloster said later Ned declared that if the police had taken him for anything of that nature, he wouldn't have cared; but if a man ever did anything wrong the police wouldn't leave him alone. He declared his mother had been convicted on the perjured testimony of Fitzpatrick. "My mother has seen better days," Kelly had told him. "She struggled up with a large family, and I feel keenly about her being convicted on the statements of Fitzpatrick."

For this reason he had prepared a statement setting out some of the facts of his case and addressed it to the local Member, Mr Cameron, who had shown the good sense to speak up against the Felons Apprehension Act in the House.

Shortly after lunch, a shooting party in a springcart driven by a farmer named Casement approached the homestead and were opening the gate when Ned rode up followed by Byrne on foot.

"Bail up!"

The members of the party were astonished when Ned pointed to their shotguns and said to Byrne, "My God, if it's not Ned Kelly and his mates." When he added, "Where did you shake that horse and cart?" Casement was outraged and demanded on what authority they were accused. Argument waxed hot as Kelly produced handcuffs. An elderly member of the party, a Scot named Dudley, was sparkling with rage. "I am not a thief and I never was a thief in all my life," he cried. "I will report you to your superior officer."

As the outlaws marched the shooters towards the lock-up, the Scot did not let up for an instant, and by the time they had reached the yard, Kelly was fed up and grabbed him by the collar. "If you don't hold your tongue, I'll blow your bloody brains out," he threatened.

"Don't shoot the old man," said another of the party, by now somewhat alarmed.

"I won't shoot him if he holds his tongue," grumbled Kelly. On reaching the lock-up, he said to Stephens, the groom, "Introduce me to these gentlemen; they don't appear to know who I am."

Stephens lifted his hat. "Gentlemen," he said, "allow me to introduce you to Mr Edward Kelly, the bushranger, and his party."

"Now," said Kelly, taking the Scot by the arm and shoving him in the door, "is it not bad enough to be a proscribed outlaw without taking such cheek from an old man like you?"

Events now began to move more rapidly. Dan made a remark about having a lark with the women, but Ned discouraged him. While Byrne, shotgun in hand, revolvers in belt and two rifles in reach, remained at the lock-up, the others took axes and proceeded to cut down telegraph poles along the railway. Four fettlers who came up to ask what they were doing were taken into custody and handed over to Byrne. When sufficient line was down, Ned returned to the homestead and asked Macauley if he had an account at the Euroa bank.

"Yes," said the manager.

"Then write me a cheque."

"I will not."

"All right."

Kelly crossed to Macauley's desk and picked up a cheque on the Oriental Bank, Melbourne, which he shoved in his pocket, and Macauley then sat down and did as requested.

Ned helped Dan to empty Gloster's wagon; then, leaving Joe to guard the homestead, set off for Euroa in Casement's springcart, while Dan followed in the wagon with Beecroft. Steve had cantered off along the dusty road some time before.

In the warm, silent afternoon, the womenfolk continued to move around the homestead doing their chores while the prisoners in the storeroom kept up an interminable whispered discussion as to whether or not they should break out. Against the wall was a pile of tools which the outlaws had not bothered to shift. Enthusiasts pointed out how simple it would be to hit Byrne with a pick-handle as he walked past the gap that served for a window, but gradually succumbed to the inertia of the majority who had come to have some liking for Kelly in the past few hours and respect for the silent threat of two or three unknown swagmen amongst them. They realised that these men might prove a powerful adjunct to Byrne's armoury.

There was one bit of entertainment. The outlaws had scarcely gone when a train stopped opposite the homestead and a telegraph linesman alighted and came up to get assistance for repairing the line, but found himself locked up with the prisoners. The train rattled away into the distance, and soon snores replaced the conversation. Outside, Byrne watched and listened, and occcasionally sauntered over to say a word to the women.

15.   At Euroa

NED AND DAN jolted along the summer road into Euroa to find the main street quiet; Steve's horse was flicking the flies away outside the hotel. Pulling up, they entered the street door of the bank and knocked at the banking chamber to be answered by Booth, the junior clerk, who stuck his head around the door and told them the office was closed for the day.

"I have a cheque from Mr Macauley who told me you would be sure to let me have the money," said Ned. When the clerk hesitated, he wedged his foot in the door and forced his way in, took a bank revolver off the counter and added, "I'm Kelly; if you two buggers don't watch your step, I'll drill daylight through you!" He then locked the street door securely and crossed the chamber to the manager's office.

The manager himself, Mr Scott, was busy writing. Expecting one of the clerks, he did not bother to look up until he saw his revolver lifted from the desk, whereupon Ned introduced himself and demanded the keys. Scott, however, answered coolly that he would give what was entrusted to his care to no one, so Ned walked into the strongroom and proceeded to rifle the drawers, becoming increasingly disappointed and annoyed at the haul. One drawer he could not open, but when he demanded the keys, Scott replied that he did not have them, which prompted Ned to return to the chamber and search the clerks, all to no purpose.

A new thought struck Kelly. He told Scott he intended entering the house, but the manager objected that he had no right in his private apartments.

"It's no use objecting, for I'm going; but I promise you I won't do any harm," Ned replied, opening the door and entering the hall, followed closely by Scott.

In the meantime, Dan and Beecroft had taken the wagon and springcart into the yard to find Steve on the veranda. The maid, who was ironing, looked up and said, "Hello, Steve Hart, what are you doing here?" Her name was Fanny Shaw and they had been to school together in Wangaratta.

"Oh, nothing much, Miss Shaw; I had a little business to do with the boss." Then, after a moment or so, he added, "I think your missus wants you inside."

"Oh, no, she does not; I have just come out of the dining room," said Fanny.

"I'm sure she does; you just go in and see."

So Fanny disappeared to find on her return that Steve had shut the door and was standing against it.

The Scott family was going to a funeral, the children were at various stages of preparation, and when Ned and Scott entered the parlor, Mrs Scott's old nurse, who had been having nightmares about the Kellys for weeks, was seated on the couch putting the baby's bootees on. "My God, it's the Kellys," she cried. Next moment, Mrs Scott, a lively woman of forty dressed in a mourning gown, found herself standing in front of the outlaw and looking up into his face.

"Are you Kelly?" she said.

"Yes."

"Are you Ned Kelly?"

"Yes."

She gazed at him — his powerful frame, new tweed suit, felt hat, polished boots and cravat — and sighed.

"You are not quite what I expected," she said.

In the next room was Mrs Scott's mother, Mrs Calvert, who on leaving her home on the Loddon to visit Euroa, had jokingly said to a friend, "The next thing you'll hear is I'm in the hands of the Kellys!"

Ned could see she was nervous as he entered to check the windows and said, "Don't be frightened! Nothing will happen to you; I have a mother of my own."

Once he had inspected all the rooms, he returned to the Scotts and again demanded the keys. Getting no change from the bank manager, he turned to Mrs Scott and said, "Those keys must be found; have you got them?"

Mrs Scott could see Ned was becoming impatient. "No, I know nothing of them but will try and find them. Do you know where they are, Bob?"

When her husband answered that Bradley must have them, she went up the hall into the bank and searched the senior clerk who was in a state of near collapse, but having no better luck than Kelly, entered the private office and found them in the drawer of her husband's desk. At that moment Ned and Dan arrived, and Ned smiled when the recalcitrant drawer in the strongroom opened and he pulled out £2000.

With the sun blazing squarely on the bank front, the building was very hot. By now the old nurse was hysterical, and when Scott tried to comfort her with a nip of whisky, she began to cough and set the baby crying.

The outlaws, meanwhile, had raked together a total of £2060 plus thirty ounces of gold, eighty rounds of ammunition and a number of deeds and mortgages, which they placed in a bag. When they returned to the parlour and asked for a drink, Scott offered them whisky, which they drank after he had sampled it. Likewise, when Mrs Scott filled a jug from the waterbag on the veranda, none of them would touch it until she had drunk a glass herself.

Ned went outside briefly. When he returned, he said to Mrs Scott, "You drive, I believe?"

"Yes."

"Well, I'm going to take you away with me."

"What, take me away? Where to?"

"I can't tell you where, but you have to come; you will likely be away all night."

Scott looked on glumly while his wife said, "If you insist on us going, of course we must obey; but won't you leave my mother, the old nurse and the young children behind?"

"I am very sorry, Mrs Scott, but you must all come for my safety. You can drive your own buggy and take your mother, nurse and the young children; I'll manage the rest."

When Ned went outside again to harness the horse into the buggy, Mrs Scott realised that Harry, her thirteen-year-old who had been ready for some time, was in tears and asked what was the matter.

"Oh, mother, are we all to be shot?" he said.

"Don't be silly, George, we are all right."

But then a thought flashed through her mind and she looked wildly at her husband who put his hand on her arm and said, "Don't get nervous now, Susy; it will be all right in the end."

Dan was standing by the dining room door. He pointed across the room and said, "That blind wants to be drawn."

"Yes, it does; suppose you do it," said Mrs Scott. Entering her bedroom, she told Steve she must close the door, but Steve would not agree, because, he said, she might open the shutters and try to give the alarm.

"Well, how am I to change; I can't leave the house like this," she replied.

Finally, after Steve had inspected the room, she agreed to leave the door ajar and went to the wardrobe; then stopped.

There would never be another Saturday like this! It was now or never; she would wear the French muslin with its lace and ribbons just arrived from Robertson and Moffats! Yes, the muslin, her shearer's hat covered with tulle and flowers, and her long white driving gloves!

Beautiful horses, yes; but beautiful women, no! The outlaws merely looked surprised when Mrs Scott finally stepped into the hall, whereas a Frenchman or Italian would have paid a compliment.

"Well, are we all ready now?" said Ned, moving outside. Apart from the bank clerks there were twelve in the party — the Scotts, Mrs Calvert, the old nurse, seven children and Fanny Shaw on whose information the police were soon to identify Steve as the fourth member of the gang.

Ned helped the women and small children into the buggy, finally handing up Mrs Scott. As he gave her the reins, he said, "I know you drive, but remember, none of your larks!"

Then he put Fanny, the larger children and the clerks into the wagon, and, spotting a cake wrapped in a shawl someone had forgotten, handed it to Mrs Calvert.

Mrs Scott understood the outlaws were concerned lest she signal someone along the way and noticed as she flipped the reins to follow the wagon out the gate that they had cut a hole in the canvas; in fact, Dan was watching her through it, revolver in hand.

The townsfolk were either at the licensing court or the funeral and the street was almost deserted, but instead of moving through the town, the cavalcade — with Casement's springcart making up the rear and Steve riding alongside — headed smartly past the Common School, through the creek and towards the Sydney road and the Strathbogies.

Approaching the cemetery, all Mrs Scott could think of was how horrified the dead boy's mother would be to see her drive past at such a bat, but a wave of Dan's revolver prompted her to whip up the horse.

Following behind with the treasure at his feet, Ned smiled and turned off into the timber. "What road do you intend taking?" asked Scott.

Ned laughed. "Oh, the country belongs to us; we can go any road we like."

Approaching Faithfulls Creek, Mrs Scott found herself ordered direct to the homestead while the rest lingered until a green flag made its appearance on the fence.

And so peaceful Euroa sank into forgetfulness. With the exception of the inhabitants now making an excursion into the country, the life of the town flowed on as gently as ever before or since. Trains pulled in and out of the station, dropping and lifting passengers, including the same Mr Wyatt, Police Magistrate, who, following the Fitzpatrick episode, had suggested that the authorities negotiate with the Kellys.

Mr Wyatt had stopped off in the town to preside at the licensing court. Yet he had had a curious experience and suspected something unusual was afoot. Perhaps also some of the town's citizens thought it amiss that the bank manager should go picnicking, but Euroa, and even Mr Wyatt, were to remain in ignorance for several hours yet.

When the Scott party arrived at the homestead, Mrs Fitzgerald was preparing tea. There was a great deal of bustle and excitement. Everyone seemed delighted with the novelty of the occasion, while the station people expressed amazed admiration that the outlaws had not only robbed the bank, but had brought away such a large party without an alarm being given or a shot fired. The outlaws were preparing to sit down and eat when a train appeared and Byrne called out, "Here come the traps!"

Shouting, "Come on lads, we'll give it to the cocktails," Ned seized a couple of rifles and set off towards the track. The train, bound for Benalla, slowed to a walking pace and a couple of men jumped off. The outlaws no sooner appeared, however, than the men climbed aboard again and the train steamed away.

This further increased excitement in the crowded homestead. The outlaws were in gay mood, yet no less vigilant than previously. Ned was asked how he came to be outlawed. He took some trouble to reply, and the more he spoke, the more attentive and sympathetic became his audience. He outlined the Fitzpatrick affair and the steps that had led to the imprisonment of his mother. As he had been wronged, he had a right to defend himself; and he had killed the policeman in a fair fight, and was sorry to do so, because he had never met a braver man than

Kennedy. Scott asked him if it were true he had stolen Kennedy's watch and then shot him dead. Kelly replied that he had taken the watch because he had needed it, but had not finally shot Kennedy in anger. He then gave an outline of the crimes committed against selectors which had led to the police persecuting him. "I have never molested workmen or farmers, except when they come between me and the police. I have never taken from a poor man when I could help it in my life, but I'll rob the banks, and if I get my hands on any mortgages, I'll burn them, the same as those I got this afternoon."

This gave Scott the cue to ask for the return of some property deeds which he declared were of no use to Kelly and a severe loss to the bank; but Ned walked out, and when Macauley suggested Scott send his wife to Kelly's hut to ask for them, Scott looked at the manager as if he had gone mad.

Mrs Scott, her mother, the children and the maids, meanwhile, were on the front veranda around a tray of bread and butter and tea which Steve had brought them from the kitchen. As the afternoon grew cooler, Kelly emerged from the hut and entertained all hands with a display of trick riding, then secured his swag on the pommel and hung the bridle of his horse near the front veranda. It was a beautiful grey mare.

"Let's move a little nearer and take the brand; it might prove useful," Mrs Scott said to Booth, the junior clerk. Scarcely a minute had passed when Byrne bellowed from the kitchen, "Shift from that horse, Mrs Scott; it might kick you!"

Evening was falling and Mrs Scott was sitting on the veranda trying to find some cool air when her thirteen-year-old, who earlier in the day had shown dire expectations of the Kellys, approached her and offered to run in to Euroa and give the alarm. Mrs Scott told him to wait and at suitable opportunity consulted her husband. Scott glared at her through his spectacles, which he took off. "Woman, are you mad?" he hissed. "For all you know if Harry brought the police, the Kellys would shelter behind us and we would all be shot down. The police are so reckless. Besides, the boy would soon be missed and someone would have to suffer, and you know who that would be!"

By now, the stationhands had been locked up. Mr Booth had left her. Suddenly, Mrs Scott was aghast to find no one in sight; all she could think of was that Kelly was nearby in the hut. She gathered her skirts and ran to the veranda; then hurried the children into the sitting room and placed the fire-irons in a handy position, prepared to defend herself. Ned, however, had other thoughts; he and Joe were adding the finishing touches to the letter addressed to Mr Cameron M.L.A. Soon after, they entrusted it to Mrs Fitzgerald who promised to post it.

As night approached, the gang made final preparations to leave. A couple of prisoners under Ned's supervision burned the outlaws' old clothing and Ned tossed more bank papers into the flames. A charred portion of a bonnet found later gave rise to the theory that a woman, who was rumoured to ride with the Kellys, was actually Steve in disguise.

The horses were brought to the kitchen. Three were bays—one of them a Younghusbands' horse which Steve had taken in place of his own—and the fourth, Ned's grey mare, Mirth, which he had recently acquired. Byrne asked Scott to hand over his watch. When Scott replied, "No, I won't; but you can take it if you like," Byrne smiled, stretched out his hand, and unhooked the timepiece from the bank manager's waistcoat.

Now that everything was ready, Ned said a few words to the prisoners, mounted his mare, and, placing the spoil on the pommel, commanded Macauley on pain of his life to see that no one left the homestead for two hours. With this, the outlaws wheeled and leapt the fences to show off their mounts, before riding off rapidly into the fading light.

Still excited by the extraordinary events of these past thirty-four hours, yet relieved that their imprisonment would soon come to an end, the prisoners were settling to wait when Macauley unlocked the storeroom and everyone sat down to supper amid general rejoicing. However, neither the intractable Mr Scott, the hard-headed Gloster nor the choleric Dudley saw fit to break the injunction Kelly had placed on them—least of all Mr Macauley. The Scotts left about 11 o'clock. Perhaps the unidentified swagmen acted as a deterrent, but in addition, was a certain admiration for the consideration and humanity with which Kelly pursued his purpose.

Many years later, Mrs Scott wrote: "There was a great deal of personality about Ned Kelly and he knew how to control men and circumstances. His management of the Euroa affair was good; he seemed to consider everything and knew exactly what to do for the best. He would have made a magnificent general . . ."

16. The Telegraph

DURING THE SIX WEEKS between Stringybark and Euroa, there came a sharp drop in the length and optimism of newspaper reports. At first, the police spoke frankly and boldly; they were close behind the outlaws and would pounce on them at any moment. The weeklies carried black and white sketches drawn in Melbourne offices showing the dramatic precipices, ravines and jagged rocks of the sombre fastnesses around Mansfield. The outlaws were terrible and romantic. Resembling illustrations to Dante's *Inferno,* the sketches created the cataclysmic background to a mid-Victorian hell, whose fires had somehow been lifted from earth's centre and placed against heaven itself at 1000 metres amid the Mansfield hills.

But now, a day or so went by with nothing to report. Was it that fifty police and a hundred horses were knocked up? No, it was rather that police were so hot on the trail, that reports might imperil the next delicate move. Reticence replaced confidence as the police virtue. Sir Bryan O'Loghlen said outright that sections of the press were doing a disservice to the community by informing the outlaws of police activity.

Yet, strangely, Standish remarked that there wasn't a police party to move from barracks any time of day or night but someone would be galloping off to report to the outlaws. As for the settlers in the Kelly country and the mass of Victorians — not being as wise as either Sir Bryan or the press — they had already begun to laugh.

Nicolson, having exerted himself sufficiently, now commenced to treat reports of the outlaws' appearances with greater suspicion. He found plenty of co-operation from the Kellys, who, through their hundreds of supporters, now commenced to disseminate information as well as collect it.

A fortnight before Euroa, he had advised Chief Commissioner Standish that a bank would be stuck up in the near future; nevertheless, no attempt had been made to fill the gaps at Euroa and Violet Town. Instead, bridges and crossing places on the Murray had been given special attention as it was thought the outlaws might try to escape to remote parts of New South Wales or Queensland.

On the Monday, while the Kellys were having tea at Younghusbands', Nicolson returned to Benalla tired and dispirited from another wild goose chase. On entering the barracks, he met Sadleir, who informed him that Pat

Quinn — Ned's uncle by marriage, whom events would show to be an outcast amongst his own people — claimed that the gang was at the head of the King. "How can I travel seventy miles with horses in this condition? He's never been engaged as an agent; I don't trust him," said Nicolson.

Nicolson had scarcely had time to study the reports when a telegram from Constable Flood, of Edi, reinforced his opinion that the gang was not in the Kelly country. Flood, who had found a means to intercept and open mail, stated that he had seen a letter dated six days earlier concerning arrangements for the gang to cross the Murray and receive fresh horses; it contained references to passwords, a place where tired mounts could be left, a boat for crossing the river, scouts who were to watch the banks up and down stream and two men who wished to join the gang. It sounded genuine enough, for the Kellys had tried to cross the Murray after Stringybark and no doubt would try again. Nor would worn-out Benalla police mounts be needed for the search.

So Sadleir made arrangements to visit Albury, and next evening, when Nicolson returned from a further search, the two gentlemen drove down to the railway station. They had scarcely gained the platform when they were embarrassed to find themselves bundled into the ladies' waiting room by an excited Mr Wyatt, who, of all things, had a coil of wire sticking from his pocket. Four hours before, Wyatt had caught the down train at Violet Town and chatted with a telegraph linesman who was looking out of the window for a break in the line. Approaching Faithfulls Creek, the train slowed to a walking pace and the linesman jumped to the footplate, took a look at some fallen poles, picked up a length of wire and swung back on board.

"Look here, Mr Wyatt," he said. "I can't repair this line. I wish you would send a message to Melbourne through the stationmaster at Euroa."

"Will I get down and help you, Mr Watt?"

"No, I'll try and get help over there." The linesman pointed to a station homestead about 300 metres distant.

"Very well, then; I'll tell them at Euroa."

"I want six telegraph poles, thirty-six insulators and a corresponding amount of wire. The peculiar thing is the government line has been placed over the railway telegraph."

"Very well."

As the train picked up speed, the linesman walked towards Younghusbands' homestead and Joe Byrne.

On arrival in Euroa, Wyatt heard talk of a whirlwind, so told the stationmaster the line had been broken by a whirlwind and to telegraph Melbourne for a repair gang. He then walked rapidly across to the public hall, granted various applications and set off back, still thinking about the wire the linesman, Mr Watt, had held in his hand. Instead of entering the station, he turned towards the Sydney road and De Boos' Hotel where he hired a springcart and set off for Faithfulls Creek to investigate.

But the horse wouldn't trot and he got tangled up in the roads. Finally, remembering he had a train to catch, he looked at his watch and went to turn about, whereupon he all but ran into a stationhand riding a remarkably fine horse from the direction he had just come. "Is this the way to Faithfulls Creek?" the man asked.

Wyatt hesitated and said, "I can't tell you."

"Surly old bastard!"

Wyatt did not stop to reflect whether or not the abuse was merited. What was it? — the tone of the man's voice, his appearance, or perhaps the contrast between his appearance and the thoroughbred he was riding. He had not gone half a mile before he said aloud, "It's the Kellys!"

He dropped the vehicle at the pub and hurried to the station.

"Has Watt turned up?" he asked the stationmaster.

"No."

"That's funny; he had only three miles to go. Mr Gorman, there is something up. You must give me permission to stop the train."

So, again, the train slowed down opposite Younghusbands'. Wyatt and the fireman jumped down and inspected the damage. Perhaps fortunately, they did not waste time, and jumped aboard again. "It's clear the line is cut," said Wyatt. "I believe the Kellys are about. Don't tell the passengers. Tell them it's a whirlwind."

As soon as the train pulled in at Benalla, Wyatt jumped off. Eventually, he found Nicolson and Sadleir standing by a carriage door. "Come with me!" he said. He bustled them into the waiting room and closed the door in the face of one or two ladies. "Look," he said, pulling the wires from his pocket. "The line between Violet Town and Euroa is cut, all six wires. They're cut, not broken. The Kellys are about. Now, you know as much as I do."

The conversation had scarcely begun when Nicolson and Sadleir drifted back on to the platform, Sadleir to question the train crew. He returned saying something about a whirlwind being responsible. The whistle blew, and as they walked to the carriage door, Nicolson remarked, "We know what it means Mr Wyatt; it will not influence our plans."

It was unlikely that the wires could have been cut all afternoon and the police not hear of it, he said as the train steamed into the dusk. Sadleir agreed; seven telegrams had been despatched to Melbourne, he said. Nicolson, who was tired, lay back in the corner and was soon asleep, but Sadleir was thoughtful as he gazed out over the dark country. As the train passed through Glenrowan, he noticed a man looking out from the shadows of the station building and recognised McDonnell, a local hotelkeeper and friend of the Kellys. He felt uneasy and wondered if he should wake Nicolson. Well, perhaps not — Nicolson took little notice of him at the best of times.

At midnight the train reached Albury, where a New South Wales police officer took a restrained pleasure in giving certain information to these two representatives of an upstart colony, which was waging a tariff war along the Murray and trying to swing Australia by its tail. "Gentlemen," he said, "I regret to have to inform you that the National Bank at Euroa was robbed by the Kelly gang eight hours ago. I have here a telegram."

Not in the happiest frame of mind, Nicolson and Sadleir crossed to Wodonga, to return south by special train at 2.30 a.m. Sadleir got off at Wangaratta, and started down the Warby Ranges on horseback to intercept the Kellys as they returned to their usual haunts. Nicolson, however had received instructions from Standish to go direct to Euroa.

When Nicolson eventually reached Faithfulls Creek, he was already exhausted. It was a blistering day. Since daybreak, the police had been riding around the homestead trying to pick up tracks. In every direction, the earth bore evidence of horses cutting, turning and criss-crossing in every direction. The small cockies and lads of the Greta Mob who looked to the Kellys as their champions had converged on the area and wiped out all chance of following the outlaws. Such, probably, was the horseman, who — coming on the respectable Mr Wyatt and getting a short reply in an English accent — grumbled, "Surly old bastard!"

Nicolson tried to make some sense of the tracks; then an old woman told him the gang had gone towards Violet Town, and Stephens, the Younghusbands' groom, volunteered to act as guide.

Nicolson's party crossed and recrossed the line, turned towards the Strathbogies and finally lost the tracks in the centre of a paddock in sight of Euroa. By noon, the superintendent was fed up and ordered the troopers back to town where they left their mounts at the barracks and piled into the hotel near the bank. While dinner was being prepared, Nicolson went in next door and talked with Mr Scott.

Many of the troopers had been up all night. Most had been on the search with Nicolson a day or so before, and were almost as exhausted as he. The day was one of stifling heat, which shimmered in the air against a cloudless sky. Overpowered with fatigue, men fell asleep over their food. Johnston, one of the toughest horsemen in the force, went to sleep on the sofa, while a decrepit rouseabout, who did odd jobs round the pub, treated him for sunstroke by pouring water over him. But the trooper merely stirred.

Nicolson, almost blind with fatigue, sat on one chair with his feet on another. A tough and patient man, he felt heartbroken. He decided to change his tactics and await his chance. Better still — he would seek relief from a hopeless task.

17.   In Parliament

CAPTAIN FREDERICK CHARLES STANDISH, short service in the Royal Artillery, was a younger son of an English county family, who, somehow — there being no move in England to open up the estates to the land-hungry — had gravitated to Melbourne. Of liberal upbringing although born a Catholic, with wider views and greater sensibility than most, he was a pleasant companion and a man of fashion and educated taste who found other things in life than hard work. As a leading Mason and a member of the Melbourne Club, where in fact he lived, he was on cordial terms with leading society figures who had set Superintendent Freeman aside to make room for an officer and gentleman.

Standish had been in the saddle for twenty years, when, shortly after 11 p.m. on 10 December 1878, he returned from a dinner in the Town Hall to receive advice of the Euroa robbery. He jumped into his gig and hurried to the post office. As the line was down on the direct route, he wired Nicolson instructions via Deniliquin; but next morning he received word from Berry, who felt the Kellys were a reflection on his administration and suggested that, if he were Chief Commissioner, he would go to the North-East and refuse to leave it until the outlaws were taken, dead or alive.

So Captain Standish sighed for the fleshpots of Melbourne, and caught a train for Euroa, perhaps reading the daily paper in which he may have found the words: "That four young fellows should set at defiance every effort of that mighty Engine of Civilisation — the police force — is one of the most extraordinary things of the age — as ridiculous as it is reproachful."

On arrival in Euroa, Standish found Nicolson red-eyed and knocked up. Nicolson asked to be relieved, so Standish consigned him to take charge of his own office and sent Superintendent Hare instructions to come up and take over the pursuit. Standish had no liking for the dour, yet efficient, Scot, and his mood did not improve when Wyatt told him of the conversation of two nights before in the ladies' waiting room at Benalla.

But he had a genuine liking for Hare, who had never been able to agree with Nicolson as to which one of them had played the major part in the capture of poor old Harry Power. Tall, convivial, with a peculiar voice, Hare was full of enterprise and dash. He had so much self-confidence, that when he made a fool of himself, he was unaware of it, so he remained unworried and his extrovert mind found new clues and his confidence new directions. Confidence was what Standish needed—Hare's laugh and pioneering confidence. He, at least, would make life bearable in this desert of ignorant bushmen and beer-swilling crop-growers.

The news of the Euroa bank robbery spread throughout the country like a bushfire in the hottest summer. Muddled, contradictory, and referring to the outlaws as blackguards, murderers, mean-spirited and miserable cowards, the newspaper reports could not conceal that the coup had been a complete success—and that four ignorant Australians, scarcely out of their teens, had played a colossal joke on authority.

The upper classes were infuriated and spoke of the outlaws with contempt one minute and awe the next. The shooting at Stringybark had been bad enough; it simply proved that four bush roughnecks in their own element were superior to four troopers. Eight months of leading the authorities a dance over 5000 square kilometres of country had been a good deal worse. It not only demoralised the police, but incited the contempt of the "lower orders" and "dangerous classes", both for the police and for all who proclaimed by their palatial homes and fashionable dress that they were superior to ordinary mortals.

But the latest insult was many times worse than the deaths of Lonigan, Scanlon and Kennedy, for, without spilling one drop of blood, the outlaws had affected some odd sort of bush gallantry and even tried to convert people to their cause. They had sent the police rushing in the opposite direction while they themselves, with perfect timing and good-humoured élan, had executed a tactical plan which bore comparison with the exploits of Hereward the Wake or the Three Musketeers. Where would their ambition end? If the farmers in the North-East were assisting Kelly and the lower classes of the cities were cheering him today, what could happen tomorrow in a colony where none of the political factions could agree? They wondered as they heard stones thrown by street larrikins descending on the slates.

On the other hand, most people had little to gain or lose; Mr Kelly and his friends were enterprising rascals, and their deeds made exciting reading. The following advertisement appeared in the *Ovens and Murray Advertiser*

HOW TO CATCH THE KELLYS
Pay a visit to J.T. Mitchell, coachbuilder, wheelwright, and general blacksmith, High Street, Beechworth. His wheels run so fast, that anyone patronising him who is anxious to go Kelly-hunting must succeed in getting the £4000 reward.

Newspapermen, themselves by no means specially sympathetic to either side, but intent rather on filing stories that suited their own advancement, found they had a goldmine in the Euroa story.

As for the poor—it is seldom recorded how they feel about things. Half could scarcely read, let alone write. But the poor, from the Bluff to Cape York, talked constantly of Kelly. The barefoot kids ran down to the corner or out to the butter box beside the road to get the paper. And by word of mouth, from pub to pub, along a thousand roads and rough bush tracks, yellow at noon and purple in the twilight, spread and grew the legend of four bush lads who could imagine nothing better than to live and love lightheartedly and die in nonentity along the green plains between their stony hills.

The official reactions to Euroa were many and rapid. The banks instituted their own escort system and wrote to the Chief Secretary, enclosing a list of towns having bank establishments and asking for special measures to protect them. Bank officers were armed and feverishly commenced revolver practice, frightening neighbours and children. The Government meanwhile sent police to guard all banks in Melbourne and the country not already protected. Fifty noncommissioned officers and men of the Garrison Artillery rattled up to the North-East and parties of seven men were assigned to banks at Seymour, Avenel, Euroa, Violet Town, Wangaratta, Chiltern and Wodonga.

Mr David Gaunson, M.L.A., wrote to the *Argus,* which sought to oust Berry in favour of the conservatives:

The sticking-up of the Euroa bank is a striking instance of Ministerial incompetence. We now discover the whole time of the Ministry is devoted to H.M.S. Nelson festivities and

91

embassies to England, continuous breaks, etc. Truly, they travel in old historic company. Even Nero fiddled when Rome was burning. Why should not Mr Berry eclipse Nero?

Again, the Kellys were reported from many parts of the colony.

An engine fitter, visiting his girl out of Benalla, put his hand on the door knob and shouted, "Bail up!" It may have been a great moment for her, for Ned was already the object of feminine hero worship, but unfortunately, her brother ran to the police who galloped out and took the surprised joker into custody. A bank manager at another centre hammered and shouted outside his premises to test police a hundred metres away, and on checking their quarters, found them fast asleep. At Euroa, Mrs Scott was so offended by remarks of passengers on the night train that she refused to visit the station again for months. When a police party met Mrs Skillion returning to Greta from a shopping expedition, she asked them if they would not like to know whether she had received any of the stolen sovereigns.

The *Sketcher* came on to the streets with a full-page engraving of the bushrangers seated around a fire amid the forest fastnesses dividing the loot, while, actually, they were moving between the homes of their relatives and the ranges behind, using the £2500 to pay the costs of those who had helped to make the Euroa campaign a success. Ned and Joe had not lost hope of reconciliation with authority, but had decided it must be on terms which included Mrs Kelly's release and a fair trial for the gang.

Mr Cameron, M.L.A., in the full hearing of the House, had asked the Chief Secretary whether he would cause a searching inquiry to be made into the origin of the outbreak and police steps for their arrest, and although Mr Berry's reply had been inconclusive, it was not entirely negative. After all, what was Berry's history? In England, he had been considered a dangerous revolutionary because of his connection with the Chartists. He had followed his political interests in a new land, and had ridden to power with a huge majority on the votes of all except the squatting and banking interests. Had he not immediately proposed a progressive land tax on all big estates, and drastic reform of the Legislative Council? Did he not point out that only the rich could afford to stand for the Assembly, and that thereby the poor were unable to get competent representation? And what had he done when they blocked his bill for payment of Members? On Black Wednesday, he had dismissed County Court judges, Police Magistrates, Coroners, goldfields wardens and heads of important departments — with the result that the Imperial

Government had sacked the Governor for his weakness and replaced him with the Marquis of Normanby.

Kelly had seen the effects in his own area where the discontent among the selectors had never been more vocal and where police stations had been broken up and new men placed in charge. The shadow of Black Wednesday was still over the service. Discontent and favouritism were rife. In the country, there had never been such inefficiency and high-handedness, while in Melbourne, Collins Street residents could not sleep at night for the chaffering and bargaining of men and women on the street. Constables were rarely seen on the beat, but at any hour of the night half a dozen could be found at Martin's Brewery or at the brothels at the top of Bourke Street, in one of which, they said, the parliamentary mace had been found. Anybody could tell the state of affairs by the way the Collingwood cabbies raced each other down the long slope of Bourke Street, shouting wildly and sending pedestrians scuttling. Berry knew how things stood and made no secret that the force could be run without officers.

So Ned had composed the letter addressed to Cameron, M.L.A., and with help from Joe, finally penned the twenty-two pages of it at Younghusbands' in red ink. It was a document showing terrific vitality and resentment, giving evidence of a man who had mastered fear, and who, if he did not get what he considered justice, was willing to be obliterated rather than yield.

Kelly admitted stealing from those he claimed were crushing the selectors and manipulating the law. He accused police of brutality, provocation, false witness, and taking bribes from squatters. He named witnesses. He accused Fitzpatrick of perjury and blackmail of a witness and Brooke Smith of persecuting his brothers and sisters. He described what took place at Stringybark and bitterly rejected accusations of brutality. Finally, he suggested the police had no real desire to apprehend him; they were on double pay and had country girls to play around with. He concluded the epistle with a hint that, if he didn't get justice, he would derail those harbingers of a hostile world motivated by percentages — in his own stylish words:

. . . I have no more paper unless I rob for it. If I get justice, I will cry a go. For I need no lead or powder to revenge my cause. And if words be louder, I will oppose your laws. With no offence (remember your railroads) and a sweet goodbye from

Edward Kelly, a forced outlaw

Mr Cameron received this little token of the outlaw's esteem a few days later and was rather embarrassed. It was all very well asking questions in the House, but to be regarded by the notorious bushranger as a possible champion of his cause put the Honourable Member in an awkward position. The banks, the manufacturers, the joint stock and land companies, the squatters, everyone in authority was liable to become warm on the question. If he offended them, they could easily discredit him with his electorate. His interest in searching inquiries rapidly faded. He declined to make the contents public, despite the curiosity of reporters, and consulted Mr Berry.

The *Age* reporter could only record:

> . . . .but as the writer's only object is to have it made common property, it is doubtful if Mr Berry will consent to allow it to be published. The letter is full of diatribes and threats against the police; and the writer intimates his intention of forwarding a further communication as soon as he can obtain paper on which to write.

Two days later, the Government released a summary in which all charges against the police had been eliminated.

So it seemed that Kelly could place little hope in the Berry administration. In order to break the political power of the squatters, Berry and the selectors' movement had been used by the *Age* and the interests which backed its policy of protection for local industry, and the rich had been forced to sacrifice some of their number to the landless diggers in order to become even more wealthy and more firmly seated in the saddle. Like many other leaders who commence fired with the honesty and conviction they get from the common people, Berry had ceased to champion lost and dubious causes. He passed by in silence, and next time the Kellys did not bother to address themselves to Parliament.

18.   More Arrests

HARE spent his first month at Benalla going through documents, interviewing spies, making friends with leading citizens of the district, and catching up with the case. Meanwhile, his men continued to rush around the country following clues and bogus reports and even tracking each other's parties. Luckily for them, the weather was warm and they could make themselves comfortable at night even in the ranges. Nevertheless, the sooner they knocked up their steeds, the better they liked it. Their camps were well known to the gang. Ned later told a member of one of these parties how each morning two young constables caught the horses, while the others boiled the billy and packed the quantities of gear they carted around.

Hare's idea was to keep the Kellys on the move and force them into the ranges where it would be more difficult to obtain supplies. However, having little success, he and Standish decided to put out of action the chief members of the extensive organisation which kept the gang in supplies and information. Standish obtained Government approval for this plan, and early in January, 1879, called a conference of detectives and officers in Benalla.

The scene must have been such as has been repeated many times before and since — a dozen or so men collected in a large, rather bare room at the police station, while the Captain explained that the Government had decided to apply Section 5 of the Outlawry Act and arrest leading Kelly sympathisers. The matter was one demanding the utmost secrecy and rapid execution, as otherwise it might result in driving more larrikins to join the outlaws. The object of the meeting was to draw up a blacklist of offenders. Mr Hare wrote down many names, and finally, on the advice of Detective Ward and others, twenty-three names were selected.

New Year's day was something of a celebration for the Kelly supporters. Up at dawn, hundreds of farmers packed their families into wagons and jaunting carts, and set off along the dusty roads for the Benalla races. News spread amid the concourse that Tom Lloyd was on the field riding Ned Kelly's grey mare. Moving in pairs around the edges of the crowds, the police heard remarks made for their benefit: "Yes, Ned's here; I saw him a couple of minutes ago on the fence over the other side of the course," or "Why, that mare's worth a thousand pounds to the police if they're game to take her."

Who knows — some of the gang might have really been there, for, like the young people in any age, they loved the flamboyant gesture.

Next day, the police sprang a New Year surprise and arrested six people from Mansfield district, five from Benalla-Greta, four from Wangaratta, two from Chiltern and three from the King, adding several more in the next day or so. The bag included Ned's cousin Jack Lloyd, his uncles Jimmy Quinn, John Quinn and Tom Lloyd, and Steve Hart's brother Jack; as well as Wild Wright and various others reputed to be friendly either with the Kellys or with Steve Hart.

A quiet old man, Robert Miller by name, so the newspapers reported, was taken from his fields while getting in his small crop. When offered a cup of tea en route to Benalla in the Crawford coach, he burst into tears and said he wanted nothing while in handcuffs. The widower of one of Kelly's aunts, he had been arrested because his daughter was said to be friendly with Ned.

At Lake Rowan Hotel, police arrested Ned's cousin, John Ryan, instead of his brother Joseph, the one who had bought a horse from Kelly on the night of the Fitzpatrick affair. Noticing the prisoner had a wooden leg and realising their mistake, they sent a trooper to the farm to tell Joseph his brother had been thrown and was in a dangerous condition. So Joseph Ryan rode in to find a reception committee with handcuffs. As he was hustled into the coach, one of the onlookers shouted, "Good luck to you, Joe!"

The constable responsible for the arrest replied, "Shut your mouth or I'll put my boot through you!"

"You would have more than that coming to you if I had my hands free," the prisoner told him.

The police said Ryan had been arrested for "annoying the police in every way and watching every move they made".

When Tom Lloyd senior was taken in Benalla, he explained to the constable that an urgent job had to be done on the farm and asked permission to send a telegram. The telegram to Greta read, "Let the four bullocks out of the paddock," and was interpreted as a call to Ned and the boys to strike another blow.

Who would be next? When would the police suddenly descend on others? After the names became known, it was realised that some of those arrested were perfectly innocent. As crops went unharvested and wives went without husbands, relatives and neighbours became increasingly critical of police and government. As early as 7 January, the Beechworth paper incurred official displeasure when it accused the police of going too far. Then farmers began to get up petitions.

At the end of a fortnight six of the prisoners were discharged; but seventeen others were dragged into court week after week. Remand after remand was granted on grounds that to call private evidence would endanger the lives of witnesses or that to call the police away from active duty was impossible. Counsel for prisoners protested bitterly against the travesty of British justice. The magistrates, under official pressure, declared exceptional cases demanded exceptional measures. The public was incensed, the prisoners defiant, and even the police disgusted at their false position.

Wild Wright derived great satisfaction from looking around the court and making sarcastic remarks. On his first appearance he declared, "You might as well remand for life as like this. The police keep on the main road and will never catch the Kellys." On his next appearance, he came before Mr Wyatt, P.M. Between softly-spoken Wright and Wyatt, of the scientific bent, existed a regard based on mutual sincerity. Wyatt felt somewhat awkward when confronting the prisoner. It was as though their positions had been reversed. "Wright," he said, "you and I have met before."

"Yes, your worship."

"You know I would give you fair play if I could. I told Patrick Quinn I remanded him to save him from the Kellys, and I think it better for you and the public if you are left in custody."

"There is no fear of the Kellys killing me, your worship. The police won't find the Kellys until Parliament meets and lets Mrs Kelly out and lags Fitzpatrick. If Parliament doesn't do that, then the Kellys will attack the police and lag Fitzpatrick themselves."

On his next remand, Wright said: "Your worship, you said you would give me fair play, but this doesn't look like it." He turned to Superintendent Hare, to whom the remand had just been granted, and remarked: "No wonder you blush; you ought to be ashamed of yourself."

Joseph Ryan observed laconically: "It's getting rather stale now, your worship. Don't you think there should be a change?"

Counsel for the defence, Mr Zincke, asked: "Are men to be kept from their wives and families and their crops rotting in the ground without any evidence given against them? The prisoner for whom I have just appeared has a wife nearing confinement; I intend to contest the legality of these proceedings before the Supreme Court."

Wyatt became increasingly concerned and told the Acting Chief Secretary, Sir Bryan O'Loghlen, that the situation was indefensible in a British community. Unless evidence could be produced, the prisoners should be discharged. So, on his next appearance on the bench, he was able to assure prisoners that he had taken certain steps and that the time was approaching when the police must produce evidence.

Wright said: "I hope this will be the last. You can't get any Kelly evidence against me unless you buy it."

Meanwhile, the Chief Secretary had received a note from Kelly:

Sir,
   I take the liberty of addressing you with respect to the matter

of myself, my brother and my two friends, Hart and Byrne. And I take this opportunity to declare most positively that we did not kill the policemen in cold blood as has been stated by that rascal McIntyre. We only fired on them to save ourselves, and we are not the cold-blooded murderers which people presume us to be. Circumstances have forced us to become what we are — outcasts and outlaws, and, bad as we are, we are not so bad as we are supposed to be.

But my chief reason for writing this is to tell you that you are committing a manifest injustice in imprisoning so many innocent people just because they are supposed to be friendly to us. There is not the least foundation for the charge of aiding and abetting us against any of them, and you may know this is correct, or we would not be obtaining our food as usual since they have been arrested.

Your policemen are cowards — every one of them. I have been with one party two hours while riding in the ranges, and they did not know me.

I will show you that we are determined men; and I warn you that within a week we will leave your colony, but we will not leave it until we have made the country ring with the name of Kelly and taken terrible revenge for the injustice and oppression we have been subjected to. Beware, for we are now desperate men. — Edward Kelly.

Soon another of Joe Byrne's ballads was to echo in bush pubs and ring out under the roofs of selectors' cottages:

> It's when they robbed Euroa bank
> You said they'd be run down,
> But now they've robbed another one
> That's in Jerilderie town,
> That's in Jerilderie town, my boys,
> We're here to take their part,
> And shout again, "Long may they reign,
> The Kellys, Byrne and Hart."

19. Another Bank?

THREE MONTHS HAD PASSED since the gunshots rang out at Stringybark and the more public interest turned on these four men, the further they withdrew into the shadows of selectors' huts and the rustle of the timbered ranges. Little is known of them in the days between their occasional brief and startling appearances. We can only deduce that following Euroa, when the forces aligned against them had never been stronger, they were in a measure amazed at their own young strength and fame, and more than ever determined to enforce their will and their justice.

Among the Kelly supporters, enthusiasm had never been greater; bitter defiance of the authorities had been followed by contempt.

Neither before nor after was the gang so bold as now. Magically, one sundown, Joe appeared in the back bar of the Commercial Hotel in Beechworth. There was a momentary lull, the square gin bottle hung poised in air and the curtains were pulled back on one or two cubicles; then by common unspoken agreement the talk and laughter rejoined the splash of the fountain in the front bar and rattle of wheels from the street. Joe said good day to half a dozen acquaintances. He appeared to be unarmed. He ordered a three-star brandy and yarned briefly to a farmer about the yearling sales. Then he went as he came, while one or two men drifted out into the street and another followed him through the rear towards the stables. A group of commercial travellers in the bar seemed astonished. Yet the rank-and-file drinkers remained unmoved though possibly more thoughtful than usual, and the cubicle curtains were drawn shut.

At this time too, Ned's name was associated with that of his cousin, Mary Miller, who had been the cause of her father's arrest. Some say Mary's interest in Ned was merely that she was a loyal relative. Others swear she loved Ned, that she was the girl from Greta to whom he later threw kisses from the dock in Beechworth and who prayed for him on the steps of the old Melbourne Gaol when the bell tolled at the hour of his hanging. In the twilight of these summer nights, she was seen riding into the ranges, a bundle behind her on the saddle, and someone told the police. On several occasions the troopers lay in wait as she came leisurely across the rising ground south of Greta, but when they spurred their mounts she tricked them on the creeks.

On 3 February, a professional gentleman was walking through Wangaratta near midnight, looking for refreshment, when he came to the rear of a small hotel. Entering, he found himself in the midst of a noisy crowd of thirsty cockies who clapped him on the back and cried, "Have a drink on Ned Kelly! He's not here, but his money's as good as the bank's."

Amid laughter, this gentleman, still a little dazed, lifted his glass to the Kellys and soon came to the conclusion there were as many Kelly sympathisers in the North-East as law-abiding citizens. From the conversation of the barmaid and the licensee's wife, he concluded that there might be quite a few women around who were dazzled by the exploits of the four. They asked him what good the police thought they were doing by arresting twenty innocent people when there were hundreds around who would see Kelly got grub any time he wanted it and he found himself giving answers that would have alarmed his professional friends in Melbourne. His new acquaintances informed him the Kellys would do something of note any day now and it wouldn't be in Victoria.

Next afternoon, Joe and Dan rode up to where Aaron Sherritt was working on a new selection opposite the Sugarloaf in the centre of the Woolshed. Both outlaws were armed and kept on the watch, particularly Dan, who remained on horseback and regarded Sherritt in characteristic fashion with suspicion. Joe squatted beside his old mate and explained they were going across the Murray to Goulburn, where Ned had a cousin, and they wanted Aaron to act as scout. They were going to stick up a bank on the New South Wales side. As they talked at length, Dan became more and more impatient; Sherritt hadn't a cent to his name yet he spoke and looked like a squatter. Finally, Aaron excused himself from going and Joe remarked, "Well, you are perfectly right; why should you mix yourself up in this trouble with us," whereupon the boyhood mates parted and Joe and Dan rode off.

That, at any rate, was what Superintendent Hare was later to conclude. When Aaron turned up next day at the Benalla barracks, he did not give Hare quite the same story.

It must have been a curious affair, this first meeting between these two men who were to have such a close relationship in the year ahead. Sherritt, save for a few talks with Detective Ward, had had no further dealings with the police since the morning the party had charged down on his father's place on Sebastopol Creek. Now he came to speak to Captain Standish. Hare replied that Standish would not be back that night, explained who he was and asked Aaron his business. "I have some important information and wish to speak to him privately," was the reply.

The two men talked for an hour and a curious bond grew between them. Both were tall, genial, and liked a yarn. Each had the spontaneous charm of men brought up to no strict code, so while each had his own selfish interest, he was quite prepared to view the other tolerantly. For Hare, Aaron even exerted a physical charm. He later recorded: "He was a splendid man, tall and strong. He made a wonderful impression on me. He was a

100

remarkable looking man. If he walked down Collins Street everybody would have stared at him — his walk, his appearance and everything else was remarkable."

As they talked, Hare came to believe he had a remarkable influence on Aaron, and Aaron warmed up sufficiently to explain that he was the chief centre of the bush telegraph for the Beechworth area and knew as much as anybody of the gang's movements. He had been at school with Joe and they had been together in crime all their lives. Finally, feeling himself at home, he said, "Well, Mr Hare, I think I can trust you with my information." He explained what had occurred the previous afternoon, but refrained from saying the outlaws intended to rob a bank, so that Hare concluded they were about to leave the colony. Aaron described the brands of a grey mare Joe was riding and of Dan's bay, and Hare gave him £2 and told him to avoid being seen in Benalla any more than was absolutely necessary.

That night, Hare, after receiving a report that Dan and Joe were riding towards the Murray, telegraphed the New South Wales police and instructed his own men at Chiltern to watch the river upstream.

20. Across the Murray

THE OUTLAWS certainly knew something of Sherritt's dealings with the police, in particular his meetings with Detective Ward who was well known in a district where his affairs with servant girls were common gossip and whose waxed moustache gave the lie to his many disguises.

They had gone close to disaster in their previous approach to the Murray and possibly needed someone to scout out a crossing for them; but, in any case, they gave nothing away in saying they were headed for Goulburn 'since the real direction of their strike was well to the west — towards the Riverina where menfolk from Greta district went each year for the shearing and where they had many friends and associates. When they set out for New South Wales a day or so later, they approached the Murray along the Warby Ranges by the route Morgan had used some twelve years before.

It was the height of summer and the river, unimpeded by weirs, sluggishly uncoiled its sleepy reaches between bright clay banks. They secured a flattie downstream from Yarrawonga and pulled across the stream, swimming their horses behind, to discover dry scrub plain ahead, broken here and there by a line of green following a damp creek-bed. In Victoria, a traveller on the plains anywhere but in the unsettled Mallee would meet scores of folk in a day's march, but here the land was still unbroken squatters' country, and the homesteads with their precious wells were well apart. Taking it easy in the heat of the day, they travelled rapidly between times past clumps of scraggy gums and occasional lagoons which still managed to give their wild inhabitants a living.

Late on the fourth day after the meeting with Aaron, the gang pulled up at Pine Rise, close to the coach road which ran 65 kilometres east to Urana, and rested their mounts. Nearby lay Billabong Creek, fifteen minutes ride down which, in the opposite direction, lay Jerilderie, a sociable little place whose population of two or three hundred was hardened by the frosts of winter mornings and bright sun of cloudless skies. No one knew better the distances of this flat land, and to travel across it in summer only made the beer cooler at journey's end, so these folk, more than most people in this hearty, garrulous Australia, loved to talk.

It being February, with the harvest done and the shearing past its peak, the small town lazed in the heat; business drifting between its five hotels, as many stores, a single bank, a post office and a blacksmith shop. Jerilderie had not even a railway to bring a modest hurly-burly twice or thrice a day; coaches, suspended on tough leather thongs, lurched in from Urana, Narrandera, Deniliquin and Corowa, the last of which linked the township directly with Beechworth, hub of the great Crawford daily system. The coaches pulled up at the pubs. There was a pub for every fifty men, women and children; and the townsfolk gathered there to collect the mail and papers and see who was coming and going.

The Kellys were not an infrequent topic of discussion. Several of the nobs had swelled with pride, as under the veranda of the Royal Mail, they declared to the molten air how they would annihilate the murderous band should it dare to make its appearance in New South Wales. Thank God Richards and Sergeant Devine were not like the Victorians! Devine had kept the local horse thieves riding, and at Tocumwal shortly before, Richards had fired at some men believed to be the Kellys. Moreover, the town had an apostle in its newspaper proprietor, Mr Gill, whose criticism of police methods was excelled only by his demands for increased protection.

As the sun sank and the first stars began to glimmer, the gang prepared for action and turned east. Ten minutes ride brought them to the Woolpack Inn where Dan and Joe went inside, contacted the bush telegraphs and sent them out to Ned and Steve on the banks of Billabong Creek. Dan was quiet as usual. Joe, rather more genial, became friendly with the barmaid, Mary Jordan. Being Jerilderie's first and last pub, the Woolpack was where folk gathered to let off steam, so Mary was well informed on the habits of Devine and his assistant. When Dan and Joe went in to dinner, Ned and Steve entered the bar and all four left about 10.30 p.m. The moon was up and the scene almost as light as day when they approached the police barracks on the outskirts of town.

A few minutes before, Mrs Devine had woken and told her husband of a nightmare. The Kellys had been crawling along outside the fence, on the inside of which her husband and Richards were standing. The outlaws were lifting their rifles to shoot, and she, paralysed with fear and unable to warn them, had suddenly woken and found she was safe in bed. Devine had comforted her and they had gone back to sleep.

Now Ned withdrew some distance, wheeled his mare and came at the station full tilt, shouting, "Devine, Devine, get up; there's murder at Davidson's!"

Devine and his assistant jumped out of bed; nothing that happened at the Woolpack surprised them. Devine appeared at the front door, while Richards hurried around the side to join him on the veranda. Meanwhile Ned kept talking wildly, at the same time backing his mare. The troopers had advanced no more than two or three steps when three armed men appeared at their rear, and at the same moment, Kelly presented a revolver and called on them to surrender. Finding no alternative, they were handcuffed, pushed inside and forced to join a drunk in the lock-up.

By now, Mrs Devine was out of bed and looking on in her nightdress. Her husband, a determined man, was extremely truculent. Kelly said, "I know all about you, Devine; you're the one who reckoned we were too scared to cross the Murray."

The talk further upset Mrs Devine. The outlaws told her to prepare a meal, stabled the horses, searched the station and found some arms and ammunition, then allowed her to join her children. Ned took first watch while the others slept.

Next morning, the blinds were kept drawn to discourage visitors; but otherwise, the outlaws made everything to appear as usual, and when Mrs Devine said she had to prepare the courthouse for the weekly celebration of Mass, Dan accompanied her across the road and gave her a hand.

After lunch, Ned and Joe donned uniforms, gave Richards an empty revolver and accompanied him on foot around the town where the few casual strollers took them for visiting police. After specially noting the Bank of New South Wales, a low, single-storeyed building under the same roof as the Royal Mail and one of the stores, the trio returned to find things much as they had left them except for an additional prisoner.

Towards nightfall, Byrne changed out of uniform and disappeared to the Woolpack, where he spent several hours in the bar and was pleased to find the Kellys were popular. He left somewhat the worse for wear, and one of the regulars who assisted him into the saddle, spotting his revolvers, concluded he was a new policeman. On his return, Ned angrily demanded why he had been so long.

In the interim he had had a long talk with Devine and Richards about Stringybark and other matters. Kennedy and Scanlon would have shot him on sight, he said. By shooting on sight, a policeman abrogated the rights of judge and jury. The man who had first suggested the idea was a Goulburn squatter, Rossi by name, who claimed to be a count, and Ben Hall had threatened to horsewhip him for it. He explained that one object of the raid was to show how he was independent of the so-called Kelly sympathisers. The Victorian police could arrest as many again and it would make little difference to him; in fact, it would make things more difficult for the police as it might well encourage others to join him. Devine was gloomy; what had happened would ruin his career in the force, he said, and Kelly urged him to get out and start life afresh.

After a good night's sleep, the gang was up early next morning, and Joe and Dan took their mounts into the township to be shod. When Rea, the blacksmith, commented on the fine thoroughbreds and inquired where they were headed, Byrne replied, "Do you mind going on with your work; we are in a hurry."

Then they told Rea to charge to the police account, bought him a drink over the road at the Royal Mail, and rode around to the post office to inspect the telegraph wires. They were too high to reach. On return to the barracks they found Ned and Dan in uniform ready and waiting with Richards to whom all the outlaws had taken a liking. Byrne had set out the plan of action on paper earlier in the day. He made a few minor adjustments, the outlaws held a general discussion, and then, when every man was clear about his role, they were ready to go. As they left the station, Richards said to Ned, "Who is your best man, your brother?"

Indicating Byrne, Ned replied, "No, that man; he is as true and straight as steel."

The party entered the township with Byrne and Steve riding in front and rear and the three uniformed men on foot, Richards in the middle. At noon, Ned, Dan and Richards walked under the veranda and in at the front entrance of the Royal Mail, while Joe and Steve rode into the yard, and, entering the back door, rounded up the kitchen staff and ordered them to the front. Meanwhile, Kelly had called for Mr Cox, the landlord, and Richards was proceeding to introduce him when he interrupted, saying, "I'm Ned Kelly the outlaw; what I want I must have. I won't do you any harm. I want a room in which to place my prisoners as I intend to stick up the bank."

Cox had rapidly concluded that the new police trooper was not quite what he appeared. "Certainly, Mr Kelly, you can have any room in the house," he replied.

The prisoners were herded into the bar parlour, where Steve took over, while Dan stood guard at the street entrance and gave anyone entering the bar a count of three to vault the counter and join them.

21. Town at Gunpoint

WHILE THESE EVENTS were taking place, life continued much as usual in the bank next door, except that the clerk was out and the manager, Mr Tarleton, had shortly returned from a long and dusty journey. The accountant, Mr Living, was at his desk in the banking chamber when he heard footsteps in the bank dining room. About this time of day, the waitress came up the passage from the hotel with dinner. On turning his head, he was surprised to see a drunken bushman. He told him these were private apartments and ordered him back, and was even more surprised when the intruder staggered forward, then coolly presented a revolver and announced, "Hands up; I am Kelly!" At the same moment, a police trooper entered by the front and seized the bank revolver from the ledge.

Living was soon to find that the trooper and not the bushman was Ned Kelly; but now they wanted to know where Tarleton was.

"I suppose he's in his room changing his clothes."

The clerk entered, gaped even wider than Living and rapidly raised his hands.

"Who are you?"

"I'm J.T. Mackie."

While Kelly sent Living to find Tarleton, Joe delivered Mackie to the tender mercies of Steve Hart and returned.

Living rushed from one room to another. He was somewhat jumpy. Perhaps the manager had cleared out to give the alarm. Eventually he opened the bathroom door to find Tarleton in the bath.

"Oh, excuse me, sir, but we are stuck up," he said. "The Kellys are here."

"Don't talk rubbish!"

"They've stuck up the police too."

Tarleton glanced past the excited accountant and saw strangers at the door, one a constable, the other a stationhand. Both had guns.

"Good God!"

"You'd better come out of there," said Kelly.

The outlaws held a rapid consultation; then Byrne walked through to the hotel and returned, placing Hart in charge.

"Don't take all day," he told Tarleton and disappeared up the passage with Ned.

Tarleton set out to milk the young outlaw, who suffered two or three questions, then levelled his guns and said, "No more of these questions; I'll not have any more."

"All right, you don't have to answer if you don't want to."

When Tarleton had donned his trousers, silk coat and smoking cap, Steve conducted him into the pub and resumed position at the entrance to the bar parlour, permitting Dan to return to the bar. A dozen or so prisoners stood uneasily around the wall, and a drunk, for whom liquor and shock had proved too much, lay on the table. A revolver in each hand and another in his belt, Steve demanded quiet. Twenty times he exclaimed, "There must be less noise."

Excited by events, yet cooped up, the prisoners attempted to whisper to each other when Hart looked away, and if he caught them, he threatened to shoot them. Several near the window tried to look into the street, but he grabbed them by the shoulder and pulled them back. "You'll get a bullet through you if you're not careful," he warned angrily.

Any such diversion gave the remainder opportunity to gossip. Tarleton, standing near the door, asked Richards, who was leaning against the wall next to him, to back him up if he knocked Hart down when he returned to the doorway; but the trooper had been treated kindly by the gang and pointed out that Dan had them covered as well, and even if he missed his aim, would be sure to hit someone.

Meanwhile, in the bank, Ned ordered Living to hand over all

moneys. Living replied, "We have only got a little; we've sent it all away. We've got six or seven hundred pounds."

"Oh, you've got nine or ten thousand pounds here," said the outlaw.

"We've got nothing like that," the accountant replied. "All we've got is teller's cash."

Kelly went behind the counter and found a quantity of coin, mainly silver, with some gold and coppers; but not having anything sufficiently large to hold it, he left and came back a minute later with a sugar-bag, into which he threw coin amounting to £691.

"Now, where's the rest?"

Getting no satisfaction, he entered the manager's office and proceeded to search the safe. Unable to open the treasure drawer, he asked its contents, and Living replied, "There's nothing in there but a lot of old papers and things; they are no good to you."

"Open it!"

"I can't open it; there is nothing of any good."

Kelly turned sternly to the accountant and repeated his command.

"I can open only half of it; it's a check-lock."

"Then open half."

The key turned in the lock, but Kelly still could not get the drawer open. "I'll get a sledgehammer from over the road," said Byrne.

"Wait; who's got the other key?" said Ned. "Tarleton?"

Living replied in the affirmative, so Ned went to bring the manager. He had no sooner left than the local schoolmaster entered, to be told to throw up his hands. The newcomer made no attempt to obey and looked inquiringly at Living.

"It's no use, old fellow; these are the Kellys."

Footsteps approached along the street and Ned returned with Tarleton and directed him to open the drawer. "Who are you?" he asked the teacher.

"He's the schoolmaster," said Living.

"What's your name?"

"Elliott."

Tarleton had opened the treasure drawer containing £1450 in sovereigns and sterling.

"So this is your six or seven hundred pounds," Ned said to Living.

"Jump over here Elliott!"

"I can't jump over that."

"You bloody well have to; come on!"

The teacher scrambled over and held the bag while Ned threw in the treasure.

"Now, you can write out a notice giving the children a holiday in honour of my visit." He turned to Tarleton, "Is that all the money?"

"That's all there is."

"No more bloody lies or I'll shoot you."

Ned ransacked the drawers and cupboards. "Where are the bills and securities?"

"That's all there is; there's nothing more," Tarleton repeated.

Ned took down a steel box, placed it on the floor and opened it. "What's in here?'

"Stock mortgages and deeds."

"Good; I'll burn them."

"My life policy's in there," cried Living.

Both Living and Tarleton pleaded that head office in Sydney held duplicates and their destruction could benefit no one. Kelly, who found it difficult to distinguish between one document and another, was becoming annoyed. He seized a handful of deeds. "Which are the bloody stock mortgages; they belong to poor men?"

"My life policy's there. For God's sake, don't burn my life policy," cried Living.

The outlaw allowed the accountant to retrieve his policy.

"Look, Kelly, there's no sense in destroying those," said Tarleton. "You'll only get me into trouble, and they really are of no use to you. I give you my word of honour you have all the money and there is nothing else of any value to you."

"I am an outlaw and must have all I ask for. Are there any deeds of town allotments?"

"Perhaps there may be one or two, but it would take some hours to pick them out."

"Where are the bills and promissory notes?"

Unwilling to answer the question, Tarleton touched a deed Kelly was shoving into the sack. "This is no good to you."

Kelly attempted to read some of the legal jargon. What in the devil was it about? He wanted to wipe out evidence of indebtedness, yet not to wantonly destroy assets of bank clients.

"Where's your revolver?" he asked Tarleton.

"In my office on the table."

Kelly went inside, and not finding it said angrily, "It's not there; I must have it!"

"I must have left it in my room when I came back."

Ordering Living to fetch the revolver, Kelly returned disgustedly to the papers and remarked, "I have no time now, but I will be back directly to look them over. What's more, I'll burn every ledger in the place."

On Living's return, the outlaws conducted their prisoners into the hotel. For the tenth time, Living explained to Byrne that he would have shot him had he not thought Byrne was someone from the hotel. The schoolmaster carried a notice for Ned to sign, but Ned disappeared to the hotel yard with three or four ledgers and books under his arm.

By now, quite a few Jerilderie folk were aware that some new policemen were in town, not least the local newspaper proprietor, Samuel Gill, who had seen the party in the main street earlier and remarked that they looked exactly the smart sort of coves to go after the Kellys. Gill took a walk to the barracks, where a mysterious reply from Mrs Devine sent him back to see the town's leading citizen, Mr J.D. Rankin, whose store was situated a stone's throw from the bank; and the pair picked up another storekeeper called Harkin and entered the bank to find papers strewn in confusion.

Rankin knocked on the counter, a voice from the manager's office replied, "There in a moment!" and within the twinkling, in jumped Kelly, bringing the butts of his revolvers down with a thump on the counter and calling on them to stand. Both storekeepers ran. At the same moment, Kelly leapt the counter and caught Rankin who fell in the doorway and Harkin who gained the veranda, while Gill jumped over Rankin and doubled back into the store next door.

Kelly hustled the storekeepers into the hotel and returned but could not find Gill anywhere, so went back to the hotel. He had had enough annoyance in the past few minutes, and his voice rang through the bar. "He's got away; this will do our plans no good. What's his name? Look out, Hart, the shooting will begin now. Where's that big bugger I last brought in?"

Steve shoved Rankin forward.

"Put the bugger on his knees and I'll shoot him!"

He dragged the now thoroughly frightened shopkeeper into the passage, pushed him against the wall, levelled his revolver at him and cried, "What in the hell do you mean by running when I told you to bail up?"

Someone now thought it suitable to mention that the escaped man was Gill, the local newspaper proprietor, and the general silence gave way to pandemonium.

Amid cries of protest a man called Brett stepped forward, "You've had it all your own way, Kelly, and no one has interfered, but shoot Rankin and you'll have to shoot the lot of us."

Ned looked at Brett steadily for a moment, then said, "All right!" He handed Rankin to Steve and added, "Take him back inside, Revenge, and shoot him at the first sign of resistance."

It was apparent Kelly's anger stemmed from fear Gill might give the alarm; but Gill was frightened the Kellys held a grudge against him for the articles he had published and was still running along the bed of Billabong Creek.

The gang had not intended to cut the telegraph line until time to depart. With the bush telegraphs watching the post office and police barracks, they had little fear that anyone could get a message away; but Gill might, and Ned wanted to see Gill on another matter. Directing Joe to the telegraph office, he set off across the street accompanied by Living and Richards. It was apparent rumours were flying and that the few people about did not know what to think.

The printery abutted Gill's home. When Mrs Gill came to the door, Richards introduced the outlaw and explained that her husband had given him the slip. Kelly added, "Don't be afraid. I won't hurt you or your husband, but he shouldn't have run away."

Kelly was rather surprised when the woman replied, "I'm not afraid, but he's not at home. He hasn't come back. If you shoot me dead I don't know where he is. I expect you gave him such a fright he is lying dead somewhere."

Inclined to believe her, Ned was nevertheless disappointed.

Living said, "You can see, Kelly, the woman is telling the truth."

Ned pulled a bulky document from his pocket, the product of many hours of discussion and exasperating work between him and Joe. Why he had chosen to have it printed in Jerilderie when Beechworth and Wangaratta had half a dozen or more printing works remains to be seen.

"All I want your husband for is to have him print some copies of a statement I have here concerning certain acts of my life. I'll pay for them and I'll come back to collect them later. I wanted to see your husband and explain."

"Well, he's not at home," said Mrs Gill, who for one, did not find Mr Kelly attractive; and she refused point blank to accept the document.

Ned could be as naive as the next man, for when Living offered to hand the statement to Gill, he gave it to him. The trio then set off for the telegraph office.

110

His main objectives achieved, Ned had already regained his good humour. As they were passing the yard of McDougall's Hotel, he glanced in, then entered and took a fine black mare from the stables.

Richards and Living were getting used to surprises.

"Richards, can this mare jump?"

"I know she can gallop. She is one of the millionaire stock, but I've never seen her jump."

Kelly had a bridle on the animal. He put a hand on her rump, vaulted onto her back and did a couple of turns of the yard.

Richards was amazed to see him ease the mare around and suddenly gallop at the dividing fence. As he said later, "At that time Kelly had a price of eight thousand pounds on his head, and at the risk of being thrown and injured—which would have hampered his getaway—he raced that mare at an eight foot fence . . . He was a bushranger, but Ned Kelly was the gamest man I ever saw."

As it happened the mare baulked. Tying her up, Ned shepherded his charges into the bar, and while a few stray drinkers goggled at his uniform, clapped a revolver on the counter and announced that if anyone tried to shoot him, Jerilderie would swim in its own blood. Calling for drinks all round, he told the landlord he would return the mare in three weeks, and soon after left to join Joe.

In the interim, Joe had stuck up Jefferson, the postmaster, checked all telegrams sent that morning and smashed the switchboard. What happened was described thus by Jefferson's assistant, Jim Rankin, whose father had received such a fright at the Royal Mail shortly before:

> On Monday afternoon at about two thirty, Jefferson came up from dinner and said the waitress had told him the Kellys had stuck up the bank which we wouldn't believe. We were standing in front of the office when a man came charging across the street and pulled his horse up at the fence. I said, "There's Hart!" and walked inside; I had no idea who he was. He passed Mr Jefferson and stopped at the telegraph forms, put his hand in his pocket, pulled out his revolver, and told us to bail up and come inside which we immediately did. He then commenced jawing to Jefferson about stopping the line from working and cut the wires in two places inside the office. Had a drink, first asking if it was good. We then went outside and met Ned Kelly who immediately started to cut down poles, but finding it hard work, gave the contract to Charley Naw. We

111

then proceeded to the Royal where we saw a whole crowd of people vainly trying to look as if they relished the joke.

Eight telegraph poles lay felled across the gutter when Ned marched his growing family back to the Royal Mail.

22.   Goodbye Jerilderie

As soon as Byrne was safely off along the road to the Murray with the treasure on the packhorse, Ned shouted drinks all round and re-entered the bank. He cleared up a few odds and ends in the banking chamber, collared a pair of riding breeches and a gold watch and chain belonging to Tarleton, and finally secured Living's saddle which he carried out and threw across McDougall's mare. On his return to the hotel, the prisoners were drinking freely, but Dan and Steve were still on lemonade and ginger beer.

Ned called for silence, mounted a chair and bowed satirically. Steve had abandoned all attempt to keep order and another crowd was jammed into the street entrance.

"Well, I suppose you all want to know how it is I'm an outlaw and what I'm doing here today," said Ned. "I want to say a few words and give you one or two warnings."

He told them he was 400 miles away at the time Fitzpatrick claimed he had been shot. He described the argument in his mother's hut and declared that Fitzpatrick had hurt his wrist in a scuffle. Dan had been innocent when the trooper came to arrest him.

"Supposing you came home and heard that two or three detectives had been to the house and presented revolvers at the heads of your mother and sisters, saying, 'Where is Ned Kelly? If you don't tell us where he is we'll shoot you.' How would you like it? Why, no man could stand such a fright, let alone a woman. Wasn't that enough to make me turn outlaw and shoot those police? When I came back and found there was a reward of a hundred pounds on my head, I set out with a bloody old crooked musket in which you could see the curves when you put it up to your shoulder. I shot Lonigan with it. It could shoot round a corner. Here's Lonigan's revolver if you want to have a look at it."

The bar was silent as Ned spoke. The only noise came from the drunk, who was snoring on the parlour table, and from people in the street. He rapidly sketched the events of these last months. He accused the Whitty and Byrne families of stealing poor men's stock

112

and bribing police to lag innocent men. He had stolen 200 horses, many of which had been purchased by Baumgarten, who was on trial at Beechworth. Horse-stealing had been his only crime. The outlaw's love of talk now got the better of him.

"I have come here today," he said, "not so much to stick up the bank, but to shoot these two policemen. They are worse than any black trackers, especially that man Richards there. Richards, I've particularly got a down on, and I'm going to shoot him directly."

This was greeted by protests and laughter. Several attempted to intercede for Richards, who leant against the bar not in the least upset.

"No, he must die," said Kelly.

At this moment the drunk fell off the table and staggered in demanding to know what was going on. There were roars of laughter. Someone gave him the skin of the dog and Kelly continued.

"I also came here to get Gill to print the story of my life so you can all read about it. I might say that I am immensely obliged to the Victorian police for the manner in which they are acting. If they continue in a similar manner, we won't have any reason to complain. It must be very pleasant for them to roam the country on double pay, and it does not worry us."

This was received with laughter and cheers. Then Kelly became somewhat graver. He warned the postmaster that if he attempted to mend the wires before next day, he would shoot him. To ensure that he wouldn't, he intended to take him a few miles into the bush and let him walk home. Finally, he told the company he was going to rob the Urana coach that night and if anyone attempted to give the alarm they also would be shot. Ned had no sooner concluded and entered the street than he was accosted by the Reverend Gribble, who asked him to return J.B. McDougall's black mare as Miss McDougall had a great affection for it. Then Living rushed up to ask the outlaw not to take his saddle, as he could not afford another. Kelly eventually agreed to both requests, and disappeared to return the mare.

He had no sooner returned, than Gribble, a lean and hungry Methodist, complained indignantly that one of his lieutenants had taken his timepiece, an object of sentimental value which he could ill afford to lose.

"Show me the man," said Ned.

The parson pointed to Hart.

"Steve, did you take this man's watch?"

"Yes, I took the bloody thing."

"Then give it back."

Hart looked sulky and handed over the timepiece; but, after inspecting it, Ned returned it, saying, "It's not worth a bloody chew of tobacco; you took it, you give it back."

After playing the heavy all afternoon, Steve was made to look like a naughty schoolboy. The crowd was milling around. Dan put the postmaster and his assistant in a hawker's wagon and did another retreat from Euroa. As the remaining outlaws, with Richards, set off after him for the barracks, Steve called Ned a fool for returning the mare because a girl wanted it, and Ned eventually became annoyed and started to take off his coat, saying he had taught him a lesson before and he'd have to do it again. But Steve wasn't having any; and when he continued his grumbling, Kelly said, "Shut your mouth; you're nothing but a bloody thing!" On reaching the barracks, he told him to catch Devine's grey.

As Steve walked down the paddock with Richards, he continued to complain. "I'd sooner be shot than called a thing," he said. "Kelly's a fine man and I like him, but he shouldn't have called me a thing."

Meanwhile, the brothers had shed their uniforms and donned bushman's garb. When the outlaws had burned a few odds and ends and locked Richards up with Devine and the post office men, they jumped on their mounts and rode back to the Royal Mail; no sooner done than Steve relieved Cox of a gold watch and chain worth £100 and threatened to ill use him if he said anything to the others. The publican immediately rushed out the back to drop his wife's rings and valuables into a tub of water, then returned to the bar and complained, and again Steve was brought to heel before the crowd.

Tarleton had taken the opportunity of the gang's visit to the barracks to dispatch a rider with a warning for the bank manager at Urana of the intended attack on the coach, while Living had set off for Deniliquin. Noting their absence, Ned uttered dire threats, warned what he would do if he ever came across them again, and ordered that the police must not be liberated until 7 p.m. He then left, and the prisoners surged out onto the street where Dan and Steve were amusing themselves, galloping up and down, brandishing their guns and shouting, "Hurrah for the good old times of Morgan and Ben Hall!"

Ned mounted his grey mare, and amid cheers from a section of the spectators, the outlaws rode out of Jerilderie into the mid-afternoon, each in a different direction.

Ned set out up the Urana road, along which, somewhere ahead, galloped the man Tarleton had dispatched, but soon turned Mirth's head south, and making use of cover, outflanked the township and headed for Wunnamurra station, on the direct route to the Murray and home, where he guessed Living might have called to get a mount.

The three mates checked on the Wunnamurra boundary, and while Dan and Steve pushed on, Ned went into the homestead only to find the horses had not even been mustered; the accountant had apparently gone elsewhere.

"I'll shoot Living when I see him," he told the surprised kitchen staff. "I gave the bastard everything he asked for that belonged to himself. He almost begged and prayed in the bank for me not to destroy his life policy, and when I was taking his saddle he again begged me to give it back. Seeing he was a poor man, I gave it back; and now, as soon as he gets a chance, the bastard rushes off to betray me." He asked for a drink of water and rode off.

After the gang's departure, the excitement in Jerilderie scarcely lessened; in fact, it increased as the rest of the townsfolk discovered what had been going on under their noses. Workers set about repairing the telegraph and by 9 p.m. police at centres throughout the Riverina and as distant as Wagga were preparing to repel boarders. At Urana in particular, the authorities were in a panic of preparation. Gill had meanwhile reached Carrah Farm, ten kilometres down Billabong Creek, and told the astonished Wilson family that the Kellys were killing people right and left. Out on a lone shooting expedition a day or so later, Gill demonstrated the sensitivity of the press again by dropping his gun and diving into the creek when Tarleton, Elliott and the two junior bank clerks rode into sight.

Prior to the visit of the Kelly gang, Jerilderie could boast six teetotallers, but for several days it was difficult to find one. The Royal Mail, The Woolshed and McDougall's did a roaring trade. It was not until a week later that Mr Cox recollected that he had dropped his wife's rings in a tub in the yard.

Jerilderie became a mecca. Hundreds visited the town. As the tobacco smoke rose in clouds inside the bars by day and night, the word became liquored and magnificent and quite vanquished the heat of noon. Jerilderie, a dot on the face of the great Riverina plain, became a mountain on which learned men received the tables of the law from on high, discussed modern history, and told how once, after Euroa, they had warned that the Kellys would come to their town.

Nor was that strange, for the story created its own little sensation in mighty London; and in the American West there were plenty who were reminded that Jesse James was still at large.

23. The Cave Party

WHILE THE GANG was busy at Jerilderie, Benalla police
headquarters received a report from the upper Murray, and
Superintendent Sadleir was sent to direct a search at Tallangatta.
Then, with the sensational news that the Bank of New South
Wales had been robbed, parties were immediately dispatched to
the crossings downstream.

No previous coup by bushrangers had been so spectacular. The
outlaws had entered another colony, taken the police at their
barracks, locked them in their cells, masqueraded in their
uniforms, and—after hoodwinking a whole township—left
holding ten years wages or more without a shot being fired. The
affair had shown unsurpassed psychological and tactical insight.

Across the continent any four men seen riding together were
immediately suspect. At Urana, three sightings of the gang were
reported in four days. At Gundagai, a telegraph linesman who
entered the Salutation Inn wearing a tomahawk in his belt found
himself addressed as Mr Kelly and was amazed to hear that he
had just ransacked the Commercial Bank and locked the manager
in his safe. A "gentleman from the forest", whose name the Colac
newspaper was not at liberty to publish for fear of reprisal,
reported that the gang was on its way to the Western District. And
in South Australia, Superintendent Peterswald marched into
Millicent with a strong force of police to prevent the gang escaping
by sea.

By the time Superintendent Hare had opened the telegram and
told Standish of this latest stroke of "colonial law", the outlaws
were approaching the Murray. Once across, each man followed
his own route through a series of common meeting places to home
pastures; then the Man from Snowy River and his mates took
over, horses were commandeered out of paddocks and the tracks
wiped out between sundown and dawn. Hare's men hit out
blindly, harassed by false alarms, sometimes chasing each other
and sometimes close behind the gang without knowing it. So the
fiction grew that the gang shod their horses backwards.

The outlaws had the golden touch. They had no newspapers or
pulpits to press their point of view; but their deeds spoke with
magic. They became the heroes of the children from one end of
the land to the other. Police and the Kellys became the game of the
day, and the Kellys emerged alive and victorious from a thousand
breathless encounters. Their deeds became bush ballads, sung
and recited wherever poor men met . . . the one which tells of

Ned's melancholy and resolution when forced to leave his people, which begins;

> Farewell to my home in Greta,
>   My loved ones, fare thee well,
> It grieves my heart to leave you,
>   But here I cannot dwell.

. . . the humorous and tragic Stringybark ballad, which ends:

> But brave Kelly muttered sadly as he loaded up his gun,
> Oh, what a bloody pity the bastard tried to run.

. . . the rollicking parody of the Bould Sojer Boy:

> Oh, there's not a dodge worth knowing,
> Or showing, that's going,
> But you'll hear (this isn't blowing),
> From the bold Kelly Gang.

. . . and the heroic one:

> High above the mountains,
>   So beautiful and grand,
> Four young Australian heroes
>   In bold defiance stand.
> In bold defiance stand, my boys,
>   The heroes of today,
> So let us join together, boys,
>   And shout again Hooray!

Hare found disillusion on every side, starting with Standish. Of course, everything would turn out all right eventually and the wretches would be caught, but there were many difficulties. The selectors had never been more obliging, yet given him so little information. He said to one of them, "Look, it's your duty to assist us to run down these scoundrels. Not even his own folk and the lower classes, but even people like you are holding a candle to the devil."

But what had the man replied?

"Do you realise if the Kellys hear I have been aiding the police they'll burn down my stacks, break my fences and steal my stock?"

"Yes, that's just it," said Hare. "You withhold information, so how can you expect us to rid the country of them?"

The man had taken on a wooden expression and replied finally, "I want nothing to do with any part of the Kelly affair; I've got my farm and family to think of."

And then there was the flagrant case of one of his spies, who, it had been reported, was spending notes from the Euroa haul. Hare questioned him and the man had replied with a grin, "Why, between ourselves, they accuse me of getting them from you."

But in one direction, Hare's confidence had been increased — Sherritt's claim to have been approached by Dan and Joe had been justified by the Jerilderie events and spy reports from the Woolshed. Hare remembered his marvellous influence on Sherritt and one of his first moves was to visit Beechworth and summon him and Detective Ward. Nor was he disappointed. Sherritt told him Dan had breakfasted with Mrs Byrne two days before. Although he had been warned against Sherritt, he felt his confidence vindicated, for Dan had been reported riding for the stiff country of the Buckland Gap on the very afternoon of the day Aaron mentioned. When Aaron added that he expected the rest of the gang to turn up at Mrs Byrne's next night and suggested they take a party there, Hare was only too glad to concur and passed him a couple of pounds to go on with. When Aaron had left, he said, "Ward, you think Sherritt will sell me to the Kellys; well, if I don't know a man when I see one I deserve to be sold."

Ward and Hare could not afford to be seen together any more than either could afford to be seen with Sherritt, so next day Ward hid in the boot when Hare drove his buggy to Eldorado to muster men for the night's mission. However, when the trio met that evening in the hills behind Byrne's there was no sign of the Eldorado party. Eventually Sherritt said, "Mr Hare, if we don't go at once, we'll lose all chance of getting the gang."

Hare was upset. Three of them or perhaps only two, against three or four of the Kellys! Yet the path of duty lay ahead, and ahead they must go. So he turned to Ward, "Will you stick with me if we go by ourselves?"

"I will," replied Ward.

The two policemen and their guide mounted and set off in the thick darkness. Aaron cantered and galloped in front as if it were his own garden; but it was with something approaching panic that the two officers allowed themselves to be carried through the moonless night of giant looming rock shapes and dwarf pines, whose arms grabbed and slapped invisibly. At last Aaron reined in and waited until they caught up. "This is bushranger country; nobody ever comes here but them. Go carefully now," he said.

As they walked their mounts, Hare and Ward were keyed up at the thought of meeting the gang. Again Aaron reined in and waited for them to draw level. "They are back from Jerilderie, all right! Do you see that fire?" He pointed ahead. "I've never seen a fire here before; but for some reason they've lit one. They must have some drink in them or they'd never do a thing like that."

The two officers dismounted and tied their mounts to a sapling. Hare felt the big moment had come and regretted having no armed support.

"What do you wish me to do?" asked Aaron.

"Are you sure it's them?"

"They're the only men who come into this country."

"Well, you had better find out just what they're doing — whether they're sitting by the fire or sleeping. Take off your boots and crawl up as close as you can."

Sherritt melted into the darkness leaving the two policemen with their thoughts.

"Well, it looks like do or die tonight," whispered Hare at last.

"Yes; I don't know why those Eldorado men were late. Still, of course, it might not be the outlaws."

Ten minutes passed during which they checked their arms and discussed how to launch the attack; then they heard rapid footsteps approaching.

"Who's this? He's sold us," Ward whispered.

"Keep quiet!"

Both cocked their revolvers and stood stock still.

"How far off do you think that fire is, Mr Hare?"

"Oh, it's you, Aaron? Oh, about a hundred and fifty yards I thought."

"It's nothing of the kind; it's some miles away on the opposite range."

"What? You're not selling us, are you, Aaron? You haven't warned them to be off?"

"No, Mr Hare; get on your horses and come with me."

The trio mounted, cantered through the darkness, slid down through a formation of rocks and came onto the brow of a natural fortress overlooking Byrne's.

"Where's your fire now?"

"You are right," said Hare. He looked across the shadowy diggings, now silent beside the rippling stream. There were lights and here and there the glow of a kitchen fire from the diggers' huts, and on the far side of the valley was the fire they had mistaken for that of the outlaws.

It is doubtful at this point if either Mr Hare or Detective Ward discussed with themselves whether they were glad or sorry.

"What is to be done?" said Hare.

"Hurry as quick as you can and come along down to Byrne's house." Aaron had dismounted and was securing his horse.

Eventually, after slithering over rocks and tripping over boughs the small party reached the bed of the valley. It must have been past midnight, but there was still a light inside. The policemen waited under a gum while Aaron edged up to the house. There was a sudden stir and a cackling amongst the geese. He came back as silently as he went and whispered, "They expect them tonight. They've left the candle burning and there's supper on the table." He pointed to a clump of trees some distance from the house. "That is where they tie their horses when they come here. Sometimes they lie down there after meals."

Hare's confidence in Sherritt had met with setbacks that night, but here was further proof of the man's sincerity. Detective Ward had told him of this same clump.

"We'll look at it," he said.

They moved cautiously across the clearing, and entered the clump. Yes, it was just the same — the droppings of horses and the bark eaten off the tree trunks. It was close to the stockyard. This was the way the outlaws would approach the house. This was the place to watch. Aaron explained it all and they decided to wait until daylight. Hare found it pleasant talking to Sherritt as they lay under the dark trees. He was amazed by his shrewdness and bush skill. The sky paled, and at last, as there was no sign of the outlaws, they withdrew to escape observation.

"They've disappointed me tonight, but they'll turn up within a day or so," said Aaron. "If you want to catch the outlaws, Mr Hare, you'll have to watch that place." He could have added that the outlaws also used Wall's Gully nearby to tether their horses when visiting Mrs Byrne.

Next day, Sherritt was sent into Beechworth for supplies with a plain-clothes constable from Melbourne. Knowing they would be taken for Kelly sympathisers, the pair put on an act in Ford Street; and then Aaron felt moved to confide in his new-found friend that he expected the gang back from Jerilderie any night.

"Joe will be leading the packhorse with the gold and notes," he said. "Directly Mr Hare opens fire, the packhorse in all probability will break away. Now, what you and I do is follow it, take off the pack and hide it in the bush, and later divide the treasure."

The trooper reported the conversation to Hare, who, however, did not bother to remonstrate with Aaron, let alone sack him.

So the cave party began, and so was sealed the association of Hare and Aaron Sherritt, scarcely then or later characterised by that peculiar power which the former believed he exerted over the latter, but by the reverse. Soldiers of fortune both, they continued on the best of terms. After years of loafing around the Woolshed, Sherritt had found a congenial occupation which tickled his mental palate and his new-found pride soon sprouted feathers in a new set of clothes.

On his return to Benalla, Hare had a lengthy talk with Standish and they decided to watch the Byrne home, Mrs Skillion's and the Harts'. When Hare declared his intention of keeping with the Woolshed party, Standish was not at all happy at the prospect of being left with Sadleir, but in view of growing criticism of the force, finally agreed.

Still smarting from Victorian gibes about Ben Hall and how the Victorians had put an end to Morgan inside a week, the New South Wales authorities had been watching the predicament of their Victorian brethren with ill-concealed glee, but were now forced to eat humble pie and add £4000 to the reward money. Notices announcing a total reward of £8000 were circulated, and in many cases no sooner posted than torn down.

24. Black Trackers

POLICE ACTIVITY had reached its peak between Euroa and Jerilderie, and although the police continued all the motions of war, activity waned gradually to create a spurious armed peace under the surface of which mounted ever blacker tides seeking decisive conflict. By now, people were becoming used to the Kellys and to the idea that the police couldn't catch them. The squatters, whose impounding of stock and bribery of police had contributed to the crisis, began to see that too much pin-pricking of cocky farmers might lead to sudden vengeance from the outlaws—or from the farmers themselves, emboldened by the gang's example. Witness a member of the Stock Protection Society who had set his dogs on a mob of sheep which had strayed on to his property. He awoke one morning to find a hole in his dam and the sliprails removed from his gates, and when he voiced his suspicions, the reply came quick as a flash, "Put the traps on to me, and I'll get Ned Kelly to put a bullet through you!"

Recognising at last that the bushrangers were effective with or without the support of the so-called sympathisers, the *Ovens and Murray Advertiser* called for the injection of a bit of fair play into the court proceedings.

Late in February, another five were discharged on application of the police. The defence counsel, Mr Zincke, pointed out that no evidence had been brought against the others, and as they had been remanded eight times, they had cause for damages. Unless they were given an opportunity to clear themselves, their lives and reputations must be blasted forever. Remanded again, Wild Wright attempted to make a speech, and when removed from court on the order of Mr Foster, P.M., turned with a savage look and cried: "You bloody old bastard; I'll do for you."

For some reason, Wright was not punished for contempt.

So, with the police keeping the people in order and the Kellys keeping the squatters quiet, the North-East had seldom known such peace. With the Kelly campaign paying its bills in New South Wales banknotes and the police spending thousands each month, there was plenty of lip service to catching the Kellys, but who wanted to end such a profitable state of affairs? Stealing? Did not the banks, year after year, grow fat on the sweat of farmers and townsfolk alike by stealing?

Police pressure for remands lost all claim to respectability in March when a defence lawyer said, "There, you have seven days in which to manufacture evidence," and the prosecutor replied, "That is sufficient."

Yet finally, when the last of the sympathisers was discharged four months after the initial arrests, Mr Foster, P.M., was able to utter this benediction: "I have felt it my duty to act independently and to do what which my conscience seems just and legal; and I do not feel justified in granting a further remand."

It went hard with Captain Standish, but the Chief Commissioner had found cause recently to agree to a number of proposals which normally he would have given short shrift. For instance, the Queensland Government had offered a detachment of black trackers for use in the search. These men could track at the gallop. The *Age* recorded:

> Their bravery is undoubted, for it was proved by conflicts with Chinese rioters in the north of Queensland, and with mobs of predatory and murderous Aboriginals, when these were attacked within their strongholds. It might seem an easy thing for troopers armed with rifles to attack and defeat a mob of Aboriginals, but the spears of the blacks of tropical Queensland, with the aid of woomeras, are most terrible weapons, and carry almost certain death with them at a hundred yards. It requires no small amount of courage to face a shower of them or to chase through long grass or thick scrub those who were capable of hurling them with almost scientific precision.

Despite such praise, Commissioner Standish was not impressed by the Queensland offer, for he could not concede it possible or desirable for blacks to succeed where white men could not. He was intent on a refusal until Hare pointed out that the new Governor, Lord Normanby, lately in Queensland, had been impressed by the trackers and it might be advisable to accept before the blacks were forced on them.

Then some fool had written to the press suggesting the capture of the gang be let to tender as the police were not bushmen enough for the job, and another had proposed that Standish's salary be withheld in line with the Chinese custom of stopping payment of physicians until the patient recovered.

Then again a few extracts of the fifty-seven page statement Ned had left for the printer at Jerilderie had eventually found their way into the press. Not that Gill had printed it — Living had taken it to Melbourne — but a correspondent of the *Age* had got hold of a precis which contained some pointed quotations.

The Queen should be proud of her force, wrote the outlaw. He had seen eight or ten mudcrushers in court in Melbourne, big and ugly enough to lift Mt Macedon out a crabhole, who could not arrest one poor, half-starved larrikin without the aid of a civilian. He himself — here he referred to his Jerilderie plan — would astonish them all, including the British Army itself, by showing what a little stratagem could do. Finally, he advised those who belonged to the Stock Protection Society to withdraw their reward money at once and give it to the poor of Greta where he had spent so many happy days and would again, fearless, free and bold.

Such material, Captain Standish must have concluded, was neither pleasant nor edifying reading, and it was scarcely patriotic of Mr Syme to publish it. Mr Syme may or may not have agreed. At any rate, it certainly did embarrass the very Government he had so recently put into power. People were beginning to repeat a new rhyme:

> *Berry, Berry, you are making a mulberry;*
> *Your father, the elderberry,*
> *Would not have been such a gooseberry.*

But it made bright reading!

So the police established themselves amid the small pines, the mongrel gum and the dramatic rocks of the hillside behind Mrs Byrne's. There were two positions — one in a natural fortress towards the brow of the hill where there was a small cave formed by cubes of rock thrown into primitive architecture in geological time. From the brows of the rocks they could look over the valley of the Woolshed with its meandering stream, its white and yellow road down the centre, its huts and Chinese shanties. This, Aaron asserted, was one of the strongholds to which the outlaws might resort and Hare agreed that with good riflemen defending it, it would be well-nigh impregnable.

Hare took another party a mile down the sharp hillside and formed a second camp from where they could more easily descend to the clump of trees near the stockyard. To this they were to retire each dawn after sitting on guard all night.

It proved a monotonous life. Day after day they waited expectantly. It was irksome hiding in the shade and loafing on the backs of the sun-drenched titans, and equally tiresome descending by night to lie in the cold near the stockyard to watch for something that might happen too fast or never happen at all. Hare, speaking of it at a later time, said he never left camp at night without thinking the outlaws might be waiting down the hill ready to fire. He felt terribly the responsibility; but added that the prospect of engaging the outlaws cheered everybody up.

The stores for the cave party were delivered to the Sherritt farm on Sebastopol Creek by the Beechworth storekeeper, and were carried to the cave by the police, one or other of Aaron's younger brothers, or by Aaron himself, who also brought water up from the creek in bags. At the same time, the party's antics were well known to Aaron's three young sisters, one of whom, on occasions, spent the night with the Byrne children over the hill.

The police often watched Mrs Byrne searching for tracks. She was a neat, active woman, considerably younger than her late husband, Paddy, who had come out in the potato famine, and stuck at the job whenever she had time from her chores in the hut or the kitchen garden. The valley was so steep it seemed that a stone flung from their watching places would strike her.

While the police lay asleep after their night vigils, Sherritt continued to roam about between the Woolshed and Beechworth, much as he had for years. The diggings, now twenty years past their prime, still supported hundreds of miners, and at the western end opposite Byrne's remained the huts of many Chinese. Each evening he called at Mrs Byrne's to court Kate Byrne. Then he would return to Superintendent Hare, who seems to have spent these nights in a state of semiconsciousness. Each night Hare set off from camp with some hopeful tale Sherritt had collected in the valley during the day, and each morning returned disillusioned. Yet his faith never wavered. Tall, ungainly Hare of the high peculiar voice felt secure in a certain power over Aaron Sherritt, who on his part evinced an almost superstitious respect for Ned

Kelly. "I look upon Ned Kelly as an extraordinary man," he declared. "There is no man in the world like him — he is superhuman. I look on him as invulnerable; and you, Mr Hare, can do nothing with him."

Hare would have nothing to say to this as they lay near the stockyard, guns at the ready. Hare was amazed that Aaron could go with so little sleep. At any time of day or night Aaron could curl up, head between his knees like a dog, and drop off for half an hour or so. He could sleep anywhere — on a rock, under a tree — like an animal. And what was even more remarkable, he wore nothing but a flannel shirt and trousers. The nights were chilly now and Hare would say, "You're mad Aaron, lying there like that." Sherritt replied, "I don't care about coats."

Once Hare asked him if the outlaws could endure as he endured. "Endure? Why, Ned Kelly could beat me into fits. I'm a better man than the others. I could lick Dan and Steve into fits. I always beat Joe. But none of them travelling in the very depths of winter in the mountains sleeps in anything more than an overcoat."

Hare was amazed too at Aaron's knowledge of police activity. One night Aaron appeared anxious and asked, "Is there any news of the Kellys?" "No," replied Hare. "Then what is the meaning of all this activity that has taken place among the police today in different parts of the district?"

"What do you mean?"

"Why, this morning at four o'clock two men left Beechworth in the direction of the Woolshed, three others started from Eldorado and three or four others started in the direction of Wangaratta."

Hare's eyes opened wider.

"Tommy," he said, calling Sherritt by one of his aliases. "Tell me how you get all this information."

"I can give you any information about the movements of your men in any part of the district."

"I don't believe you."

"You can question me if you like and see if I don't."

"Well, tell me what occurred the day before yesterday."

"Yes," replied Sherritt. "Detective Ward and another man rode out from Beechworth, a party of police came into Eldorado, and some men through near Everton, but I don't know the particulars beyond that there are some policemen there!"

"Now, Aaron, tell me how you got to know."

"I will not."

"Why — are you not in my confidence?"

"No, there are certain things I will not tell. I will tell nothing against myself to convict me, although I have been in all the crimes with the Kellys for years past. You would be perfectly astounded if you realised how much we knew."

"Tell me, do the other agents in this district know as much as you, Aaron?"

"Oh, yes, but I am head over all of them."

And so it continued. Every night Hare was encouraged with some tale or other of the approach of the outlaws or discouraged with accounts of their prowess.

"No party of men on horseback will ever catch them," declared Sherritt. "They haven't got the horses or the riders. There are a few men in the force like Johnston or Lawless who might ride them on level ground, but they can't gallop down the ranges like the Kellys. If a strong party is sent they'll keep out of the way — if a small one, they'll surprise them and shoot them down."

Then Hare was liable to get a lecture on the various stupidities of police behaviour. One night, as they waited under the trees, he broke off a twig and commenced to pull off the leaves.

"Hey, you better stop that," said Sherritt. "You'd never do for a bushranger. If Ned Kelly saw any of his men do that he'd have an awful row with them."

Hare even wondered if he could save Aaron and make a solid citizen out of him. One night when Aaron brought promising information, he said, "Well Aaron, what will you do with the eight thousand pounds if we secure the Kellys?"

"I don't know; I should like to have a few mares and a stallion and get a nice farm."

"The best thing for you to do would be to get out of here, leave all your old associates, get a respectable girl, marry her, and start life afresh among new people."

"Oh, yes," yawned Aaron, for whom Kate Byrne and her watchful mother were quite respectable enough. "That would be the best thing, of course."

Suddenly he turned with a little laugh. "Mr Hare, if you got me the best mares you could buy and the best stallion you could buy, do you think I could withstand the temptation of stealing my neighbour's horses and selling them?" He gestured as if to brush such an idea aside as ridiculous. "No more than fly!"

Hare came increasingly at a loss to understand how the outlaws eluded him. When he returned to camp in the mornings, the men begged him to allow them to light a fire to boil a billy of tea, so after a while he gave in and they got into the habit of making a small fire of dry sticks between the rocks and dousing it as soon as the brew was made. The days were hot and water had to be carried. The nights were sharp, yet they dared not light a fire. The diet of stale bread, preserved beef and sardines became monotonous. And all the time was fear of the outlaws lurking behind the rocks in wait.

The twentieth day of the watch was hot. The sun burnt the rocks and a north wind struck down over the Woolshed. One of the troopers from the cave party sneaked down to a watercourse in the valley and Mrs Byrne sent for Aaron. When Aaron turned up at the house in the evening she said, "There is a party of police up there. You better go and have a look for them tomorrow."

"I haven't seen any sign of them, but I'll have a look."

"A man like a constable was seen walking with a bucket towards the creek," she said. "I myself went to the creek and found where there was some soap. The fellow had washed his hands there and had been whittling this." She produced a piece of stick.

The next night when Aaron said he had looked everywhere but couldn't find them Mrs Byrne regarded him sardonically.

25. Aaron Plays Up

On the morning after Mrs Byrne discovered evidence of the police party, there occurred what Superintendent Hare described as an extraordinary accident. The troopers had barely returned from the stockyard when the sentry rushed down from the lookout and said, "Mr Hare, the old woman is in the camp!"

Hare sat up, his back to a rock, and saw Mrs Byrne crawling into the camp. She stood up, glanced at a few articles lying on the ground, advanced a few steps further and looked towards one of the sleeping men; then halted and retreated. Hare waited as she crept down the hill, then went down to find out whom she had seen. To his horror, he found it was Aaron, lying on his side, hat over his face, no blanket and wearing his usual distinctive dress—white flannel shirt and dark trousers tucked into high Wellingtons. Hare was dismayed. He woke him, and when he described what had happened, Aaron turned deathly white and beads of perspiration broke out on his face. "Now I am a dead man," he whispered.

"Come on!" Hare exclaimed. "The best thing for you to do is to be off as fast as you can and show yourself to your friends somewhere else so you can prove an alibi." Clapping his helmet and greatcoat on Sherritt so the old lady would not recognise him if she looked that way again, he sent him off over the back of the range.

The police watched Mrs Byrne cross to the opposite hill, pick up something off a rock and mount a new spur leading to the rear of their camp. Evidently under the impression she had not been seen, she was intent on finding just how many men were present. She crawled like a rabbit, showing only her head, and when it became apparent she was making for a certain rock above the camp, Hare instructed one of his men to give her a fright. The old lady was about to look down on the camp when a trooper sprang at her with a terrible shout.

She tottered and almost fell; then trembled from head to foot for several moments. "What? What? I am only looking for cattle," she stuttered.

But gradually she grew calm, and when she had recovered her courage, her anger grew and blazed. "I'll get my son and the Kellys to shoot the whole bloody lot of you just like they did Kennedy," she screamed.

Sherritt returned at dusk, nonchalant as usual, and when Hare asked what he had done with himself during the day, replied he had visited some friends and drawn attention to the early hour; nevertheless, he was in a mortal funk because the old woman had seen him.

"Are you going to see your young woman tonight?"

"Oh yes; I must see if the old woman recognised me this morning."

"Don't you funk it."

"I must find out if she knows it was me. I have bought a penny whistle," he said artfully. "I will commence playing it within a hundred yards of the house, and perhaps Kate may come out to meet me and I can find out whether the old woman has said anything."

So, as Hare went to the watching place that evening, Aaron visited the Byrnes'. He returned silently about midnight and sat down beside the superintendent. He had played his whistle to the door and walked inside still playing. The old woman had said nothing, and watching her face, he was sure she had not recognised him. Then they had gone outside and she had said, "A nice trick you have been playing on me."

"What do you mean?" he had replied.

"Who could have put the police into that camp in the mountains but you?"

"I don't know what you mean."

"A pretty fellow you are, going to search," she had retorted. "I found the police in the mountains today. There must be a great number there because of the way the ground is beaten about, but I only saw one lying there."

Aaron must have held his breath, but the old lady continued, "If I could only find out how many are in the camp I would get Joe to shoot any number under fifteen or twenty for what they did to me." And she told him how she saw a sardine tin shining across the valley and went to see what it was and had been frightened out of her wits.

"How could I find them when you couldn't?" she had finally demanded. "I'm certain you knew all about it."

"I don't know," Sherritt had replied. Her parting words had been, "Well, you go there tomorrow and see for yourself."

As he spoke under the trees, Sherritt seemed a good deal easier. "She didn't recognise me, but she had lost faith in me," he told Hare. "I'm all right; I'm still on terms of intimacy with the others in the house." And this was true. Now that he had a regular income he had presented Kate with a horse and there was some talk of them getting married.

Now that the lower camp was known, Hare concluded he was wasting his time in the Woolshed, but at Sherritt's earnest request remained a few days longer. Aaron explained that Mrs Byrne had no means of communicating her discovery to the outlaws; only he could do that. "And when they come, I'll get the news," he said.

His fascination had its limits, for Hare replied, "I don't believe it."

"Believe it or not; don't go because the old woman has discovered you," came the reply.

A day or so later when he found that Mrs Byrne and some other woman had been examining the police watching place near the stockyard, Hare packed up and returned to Benalla, leaving Sherritt and party to fare as best they could.

As the weeks wore on, Aaron got deeper and deeper into mischief. Finding Kate becoming cool towards him, he would have taken his horse back; however, she had swapped it for a bay mare. Then Kate learned from one of Joe's old schoolmates that Aaron was friendly with Detective Ward and broke off the engagement.

Aaron was so piqued he stole the mare and sold it to Mrs Skillion, with the result that Mrs Byrne got a warrant for his arrest and the police had to rig the case to save him from a gaol term.

Hare was amazed—Aaron was worse than a vaudeville show. "Why did you do a damn silly thing like that, Aaron?" he asked. "I could not help it," replied Aaron. "I did not want the horse, but the way old Mrs Byrne has been behaving to me lately, I had to do something to her."

But Aaron had no sooner been dropped by one Kate than he set out, on Hare's advice, to win Kate Kelly and ran up against Mrs Skillion, who, after the gaoling of her husband and her mother, was now the real power of the Kelly family next to Ned himself. Mrs Skillion wouldn't have Aaron on the place, and when he managed to entice Kate out for a walk one day, rode into Oxley and lodged a complaint.

The constable was naturally excited at the opportunity to arrest one of the Kelly gang's agents and went to the homestead; but Aaron saw him coming and bolted out the back door with the policeman's bullets skipping around him. Again Hare stepped in, and so Mrs Skillion's case was quashed as well.

About this time, Aaron got his second and final offer from the gang, made at the Sherritt farm by Ned himself, possible because he knew of Aaron's link with the police and wanted to offer him a way out. What Ned thought as he looked at the pictures of hollyhocks, Queen Victoria and British warships on the wall remains to be seen. Two girls were at home with the five-month-old baby. He asked for Aaron, took the baby and nursed it for a while, and then said he was hungry. There was dough on the table and bread baking in the oven, so he broke off some dough and placed it on the coals, which he pulled out with his boot, meanwhile asking the girls to put the kettle on as he wanted some tea for his men on the hill. When he had eaten and drunk, he put the child back in its crib, drew a flask from his pocket, poured some brandy into a tumbler and placed it on the cupboard.

"Give that to Aaron," he said. "Tell him a gentleman called who wanted him to assist him with some cattle, and that I'll be back in two or three weeks. Tell him I believe there is a warrant out for his arrest, and the best thing he can do is come along with us."

But Aaron was not interested. Although the police froze in the winter dawns and winced from rain and wind, he seemed to thrive. Once dressed in a modest attempt at flashness and well known as a pal of Joe's, he now rode into town as flash as Lucifer. A strapping fellow with a full-featured and mobile face, he wore buff corduroys, white-and-tan calfskin vest and a brown tweed jacket which Hare had given him, set off by Wellington boots and wide-brimmed hat at gay and evil angle. Anyone would think: Who the hell's this — an advance agent of the circus? But no, it's King of the Woolshed Sherritt, riding a police-bought thoroughbred up Ford Street. They say he's with the outlaws.

Before the Kellys came to fame he rarely had a penny; now he always has a quid or thirty bob — that's it, thirty pieces of silver from Caiaphas Hare with which to buy a round of drinks.

Hare returned to Benalla thinner and graver, to find Standish overjoyed to receive him. The situation had been steadily deteriorating. Following Stringybark, the police machine had gone into action to the echo of loud newspaper cheers and police numbers in the North-Eastern district had doubled in a month. After Euroa, the throttle was pushed forward full bore, and almost 300 officers and men, including an artillery corps, guarded a district where, a few months before, a mere 80 had been employed. Now, following Jerilderie, the numbers began to dwindle and the offensive declined. The press at last admitted the police were incompetent to grapple with the situation and clamoured for results. Under the title of Outlaw Hunting in Victoria, the following satire appeared in the *Ovens and Murray Advertiser.*

By sticking to his plan, Captain Standish is confident of capturing the outlaws before they die of old age. When he had surveyed the situation with his eagle eye from the window of a railway carriage and his gigantic intellect had grasped the whole particulars, he determined to draw a cordon around the stronghold in which the outlaws were supposed to be concealed. This cordon was constructed in a triangular shape, its base forming a straight line extending from Mansfield to Wahgunyah. The apex of the triangle is situated in the South Pacific Ocean. Its exact locality has hitherto been kept a profound mystery, as upon it Captain Standish rests the success of the whole campaign. The secret is kept carefully guarded night and day by six picked troopers and Detective Inspector Secretan.

Having fixed this triangle with mathematical accuracy, Captain Standish, aided by Professor Ellery (of the Melbourne Observatory), took a number of lunar observations with a view to obtaining the exact position of the outlaws. It was found that Ned and Dan Kelly were concealed exactly in the centre of the lines of circumvallation, while Hart was standing on a rock three points to the northward, and Byrne was smoking a cigar eight points to the south-west of that spot.

To further isolate the outlaws and deprive them of such necessities of life as whisky and tobacco, the police were withdrawn from the townships and concentrated all in a heap. It is a well-known rule in modern warfare that garrisoning a town invites attack. Therefore, taking the police out of the north-eastern townships was the most effective way of protecting them against assault. But the Kellys, being deplorably ignorant of the canons of war, did not comprehend this move, hence the Euroa affair.

There are 840 000 people in Victoria. Of these, 839 996 — barring children in arms and ministers of religion — are deeply interested in the doings of the remaining four. The troopers who form this impenetrable cordon are all picked men, specially selected on account of their thorough knowledge of the wilds and intricacies of Little Lonsdale Street, Romeo Lane, and similar classic localities.

Another rule of modern war is to protect the men under your command. Therefore, the troopers are kept in the towns and only allowed to travel on the main roads or by railway trains. Large bodies are kept together in order to inspire mutual confidence.

The headquarters of the force is at Benalla. The first consideration is to preserve Captain Standish. He is constantly guarded by a detachment of fifty men. Telegraph wires are laid to the chief's bedroom, also to the card room of the hotel in which he is staying, to enable him to obtain, without delay, the latest bushranging and sporting intelligence. His orderly has a telephone permanently attached to his ear.

The arrangements made for the final "bursting up" of the outlaws are very complete. The program is this: When the Kellys are confronted with a reasonable number — say 200 — of troopers, the Chief Commissioner is to be sent for. He is to proceed to the spot by special train and drag, both of which are kept in constant readiness. When he arrives near the scene of operations, he is met by the artillery band, which, playing "See the Conquering Hero Comes", will precede him to where the main body of troopers is stationed. Then, bowing to the outlaw chief in the fascinating manner which has rendered him invincible on the shady side of Collins Street, he is to fire the first shot out of a silver-mounted pistol. Then the fight is to proceed to Wagner's music of the future.

This is given in confidence and I trust none of your readers will convey it to the outlaws. — Q. Vive.

For once, Standish thanked his stars he was in temporary exile from the Melbourne Club!

Reports, meanwhile, came in about Mrs Skillion, whose selection lay among the low hills connecting the uplands of the south with Glenrowan and the Warby Ranges; the hills had been Morgan's line of retreat to the Murray. The spies reported that Mrs Skillion fed the gang by concealing supplies in a hollow log and signalled them in the ranges by pinning out sheets on the clothesline. The police had missed their chance to arrest her with the sympathisers, and in the ensuing uproar, found it advisable to leave her at liberty on grounds she might serve as bait to trap the gang. Her every move was watched. The spies reported that she and Kate Kelly frequently rode into Benalla and ordered large quantities of canned fish, sardines and hams. After Jerilderie, it was noted that they paid in New South Wales banknotes. Large bakings were reported at the Greta home, along with nocturnal expeditions, following which Mrs Skillion's mare, Whitefoot, was invariably knocked up. On several occasions police parties followed her; yet, despite superior numbers, which should have enabled them to outflank her, she managed to elude them.

One morning, shortly before dawn, from their lookout above the rough home, they saw a woman come out, catch a horse, secure a large bundle to the saddle, and set off towards the Warby Ranges. Without doubt it was Mrs Skillion on one of her expeditions. They lay low as she passed, then silently rose and toiled up a steep gap on foot, keyed up at the prospect of coming on the camp of the outlaws. They rounded a bend and stopped aghast. It was Mrs Skillion right enough — coolly seated on a log with thumb to nose and fingers spread out in derisive gesture. The chagrined troopers stumbled forward and seized the bundle. When they opened it and found nothing but a harmless old tablecloth, she laughed scornfully and they shook their fists in her face.

Aged only twenty-one, with her mother and husband in gaol, her brothers outlawed and a family and her mother's farm to care for, Maggie Skillion had aged five years in a few months; yet she represented the heart and soul of the Kelly family and carried herself with a pride that was a challenge, and the troopers quailed at the prospect of the sudden and terrible reply her arrest might elicit. Police watched closely each time the sisters took a load of supplies to Eleven Mile Creek. Very soon the sisters learnt to make the circuit of the house with their dogs before going to bed each night. There would be a burst of yapping and the police would be forced to retire hurriedly. Hare himself was caught, so the next time he appointed a man to drop strychnine baits. From then on the dogs wore muzzles day and night and Mrs Skillion and Kate walked brazenly through Benalla, muzzled dogs on leash.

So the battle went on—move and counter move, with sometimes half a dozen or more parties roaming the hills and following all sorts of tracks they happened across in their travels. A party which lay watching Tom Lloyd's in the Bald Hills was discovered one dawn by two boys with dogs. The boys immediately called Lloyd, who fired three shots and hit a hollow log three blows with an axe so that the echoes rang out sharply along the hills. The sound would have carried for five miles, said Hare. "The outlaws could not have been seen if they were twenty yards away, nor could I have put a cordon round the place if I had five hundred men."

26. Whorouly Races

AT LAST the press announced that twenty native police were en route from Queensland. Acting Chief Secretary, Sir Bryan O'Loghlen, declared angrily that publication of this fact was a deliberate attempt to foil his efforts to capture the bushrangers. The press replied: "If police organisation is complete, knowledge by the murderers of their movement would be a matter of perfect indifference. It becomes imperative to inquire into the cause of failure."

The twenty proved to be six and arrived in March after a voyage to Sydney in which all were terribly sick, and one of their number, Corporal Sambo, contracted congestion of the lungs. With Snider revolver on hip, and dusty brown feet projecting from the trousers of their blue and red-piped uniforms, they seemed raw and incongruous when Standish inspected them at Albury; but although several were still in their teens, all had a great deal of experience. Enlisted when boys and trained by their commanding officer, Inspector O'Connor, they had proved their bravery in the anti-Chinese riots and in punitive expeditions against their own race. Standish watched their uncanny skill with some surprise.

The trackers were given quarters at Benalla police barracks while Inspector O'Connor joined his brother officers at the Commercial Hotel, so becoming the fourth member of the Board of Officers which Standish, Hare and Sadleir had formed to conduct the campaign.

Within a few days, the trackers left with some troopers to follow the Broken River into the Wombat Ranges where Hare believed the gang might be hiding. After a week they were suffering from exposure, Sambo was dying and nothing more exciting than the tracks of some stockmen had been discovered. Yet it was already apparent that they were of value. The police were accustomed to establishing camp after dark, and, not daring to strike a light, dossed anywhere — on sticks, stones, sheoak apples and bare earth. Now, with the trackers to reconnoitre, they could choose a site before sundown and collect bracken and tussock for beds. There was no longer need to hobble the mounts; and while breakfast was being prepared, a couple of trackers, bridle on arm, quickly mounted the first horses found and rounded up the remainder, tracking them into the bush if necessary. This meant the animals could graze freely overnight and that both the mounts and the men could continue the search next day without tiring so rapidly.

But although life became more bearable for the troopers, it scarcely improved their determination to catch up with the gang. Some boasted of running the scoundrels down, but the chatter around the campfire at night showed that the trackers suffered from nerves. Perhaps each race had its way of saying the same thing.

On the track, O'Connor never forced his Aboriginals towards cover until they had reconnoitred. They would jog along detecting signs whites could make out only after close examination — sweat marks where a horseman had taken hold of a rail, impression of a spur's understrap where the rider had dismounted for a drink, the remains of a fire covered over, or horse dung — the age of which they could tell with their toes. In rough country, when signs showed fresh, everyone dismounted and crept along on hands and knees dreading what lay ahead, yet with a sense of wonder at seeing the noses of the trackers flatten and distend with excitement as they followed the scent.

In the first month the trackers covered Power's old haunts along the King. There was some brief excitement when they tracked to an old hut in the hills near Greta and found the names of Ned and Steve carved on the door. Meanwhile Hare and party searched the Warby Ranges where they found stones arranged in a curious manner on the peaks, and some tracks — which led to an exciting chase that ended in the discovery of another police party and some honey collectors.

"We never lay down at night, but we knew we might have to fight for our lives before morning. Ned Kelly described my men and everything they did," Hare wrote later.

Hare favoured forays at random, with his men stretched out on a broad front to comb the country. Sadleir thought this was fooling; the only way was to follow up reports of the gang's appearances. O'Connor wished to conduct the search with his trackers and no more than two or three white troopers, while Standish and Hare favoured attaching one or two to parties of white troopers. The blacks, they contended, were suffering from the Victorian cold and carried so much bedding that they reduced the pace of the pursuit.

Relations were cordial at first but began to deteriorate. Captain Standish made several trips to Melbourne to escape the boredom of Benalla, but always returned complaining that Sir Bryan O'Loghlen chased him out of the city. O'Connor remarked to Sadleir that Standish would not talk on the Kelly affair for two minutes and seldom went out with search parties. Just mention the matter and he would shake his head, throw himself on the sofa, and pick up a novel.

The Commissioner became restless and uneasy when Hare was out of his company and sat on the barracks fence waiting anxiously for his return from a ride of no more than a few miles. Such devotion only increased Hare's egotism. Moreover, Standish's antipathy for Nicolson and O'Connor became increasingly evident, leading towards an open breach. Mr O'Connor had scarcely arrived in Benalla when he fell for the charms of a sister-in-law of Superintendent Nicolson. A society wedding was out of the question, so the couple married quietly and planned a public ceremony for Flemington during the racing round. In the meantime, the good Captain took the evidence of their living together, as Mr O'Connor and Miss Smith, as moral laxity, and in May, when O'Connor remonstrated with him for sending Hare out without trackers, replied caustically, "I will endeavour to get the Kellys without your valuable assistance."

Of course, as Standish later confided to Mrs Hare, what was appalling was O'Connor's coarseness, and equally the ignorance, poverty and suspicion so evident among the farming families who came into town on their shopping expeditions each Saturday. Thus came an open breach and the initiation of Queensland moves to withdraw the detachment. From now on, Standish and Hare ran things and O'Connor devoted himself to his romance.

One day Aaron brought Hare a letter couched in peculiar phraseology, the purport of which was that Joe Byrne wanted Aaron to ride his black mare in a hurdle at the Whorouly races and would meet him there. Hare told Aaron to accept the offer, and on the day, directed three of his best horsemen to the course—one to make a book, another to set up a dice table, and the third to play yokel and patronise the other two. Hare himself drove down in a buggy, mixed with the uniformed police and the crowd and waited for Aaron to signal the outlaw's appearance. When some of the local gentry pointed out Aaron as a notorious Kelly sympathiser and urged Hare to arrest him for theft of the fine bay he was riding, the superintendent felt somewhat embarrassed and pleaded ignorance of Sherritt's doings despite the fact he himself had bought the bay a few days previously. In the event, there was no sign of Byrne or his black mare, but laughter spread among the crowd when the disguised policemen were recognised. As the yokel remarked to the bookmaker, "I told you he wouldn't turn up. Byrne's not such a fool as to put a thirteen stone man like Sherritt up!"

But if Hare could afford to laugh, few other police could. He said frankly that the police, in or out of uniform, were all as well known as the town clock and had only to put their noses outside the barracks for some member of the bush telegraph to go galloping off with the news.

It was openly stated that the refusal to allow local police to follow reports promptly without the Board of Officers' approval was motivated by the officers' concern for the £8000 reward. Jealousy spread amongst the ranks because Hare's men from Bourke District were run about by special train on double pay whilst the police elsewhere were hamstrung waiting for instructions. A running fire of contemptuous ridicule and angry reproach was aimed at the force and its heads were unmercifully slated.

Hare tracked the outlaws to a haystack and sent his bravest trooper up the passage leading to it, and all Victoria laughed when the trooper was chased out by an old sow. A correspondent of the *Age* suggested that ". . . we pardon the romantic Mr Kelly and constitute him head of the police force."

The Government had given Hare and Standish carte blanche and they had run up a bill of £11 371 in seven months with nothing to show for it. Hare's health began to fail and he asked to be relieved. Standish, having lost six kilograms in weight, gave out a story of muddle on the part of Nicolson, and so obtained permission from Berry to return to Melbourne.

Safe behind stone walls in the garrison town of Beechworth, Inspector Brooke Smith, to whom Kelly had directed special attention because of his treatment of his sisters, felt the hand of terror fastening on his heart and was rapidly approaching imbecility. As if he had known Brooke Smith was shortly to be removed from his post, Kelly had written:

I would like to know who made that article who reminds me of a poodle dog half-clipped in the lion fashion called Brooke E,

Smith, Superintendent of Police. He knows as much about commanding police as Captain Standish does about mustering mosquitoes and boiling them down for their fat on the back blocks of the Lachlan . . .

Strange things were happening in the colony of Victoria!

On a trip to Melbourne, Tarleton ran into Scott, his opposite from Euroa, and said, "Hello Scott, still in the bank?" adding, "Well, my people got rid of me; you'll go next."

As Mrs Scott said, "With eight children, we were left to sink or swim."

Having fewer troubles than his friend Standish, Chief Justice the Hon. Sir W. Foster Stawell could afford to be amused when he received a telegram from a Euroa resident to the effect that Ned Kelly and his mates were cutting cabbages in his backyard.

Along the bush tracks and in the shanties they were singing a new ballad:

> *The Kellys are having a very fine time*
> *In the ranges not far away.*
> *And we on their tracks think it mighty fine fun*
> *To be doing nothing all day.*

> *For our boss, the sergeant, is a very fine man,*
> *And he lets us out, do you see;*
> *So we settle in a shanty and play forty-fives*
> *And it suits Moriarity.*

27. Heat on Nicolson

Now, as the autumn days fled and the clouds dropped the first snow on the shoulders of Buffalo and Bogong, it might have seemed that the outlaws, like the strange, savage beasts some people pictured them, had curled up in their lair and dissolved in winter sleep. Rumours and the grandchildren of rumours describe their life from the time they returned in triumph from Jerilderie into that new autumn of 1880 when came those warnings of the final storm that would expunge forever their mortal flesh.

Some were of the opinion they had left the colony. Some imagined them fleeing without rest, sleeping on hilltops, eating out of cans, cooking on small fires, then burying both cans and embers before passing on. Tales were spread of their fear of the trackers, of Kelly's threats to obliterate them, of the gang abandoning their horses and travelling by foot to put the trackers off the scent. No doubt such tales had some basis in fact; yet it seems that the outlaws spent some of their time in a broad drive opening off the bottom of some old mine workings within 100 metres of the crossroads linking Beechworth, Chiltern, Kiewa and Yackandandah.

The hideout was strategic in more ways than one. It was dry and spacious—it even contained a broken dray which had been used to cart ore to the shaft. They had the support of the few people who lived around—mostly old prospectors or miners. It was handy to Beechworth where Joe got all the daily papers from a barmaid in a pub on the Chiltern road. And they could even win a bit of gold if they had nothing better to do.

Around this time, Ned received an offer to join forces from the one-time Anglican lay-reader Captain Moonlite, who had recently returned to the bushranging life after doing seven years for bank robbery. Kelly knew his reputation from Pentridge and sent back word that if Moonlite or his gang came to the North-East he would shoot them down. So George Andrew Scott, alias Captain Moonlite, kept his distance to be run to earth in a full-dress battle before 300 spectators out of Wantabadgery station along the Murrumbidgee.

When Standish and Hare left Benalla, thirty-five constables and twenty-three artillerymen were withdrawn. Late in June, Nicolson, who had been given seven months to think things over since his Euroa defeat, was ordered back to Benalla. His plan of action was to protect the banks and to leave the outlaws alone, lull them into a false security, hem them with spies, locate, and finally seize them. Within six weeks he was convinced they were hiding around Greta, so encouraged the fiction that he believed they were in the Strathbogies.

Meanwhile, he altered the nature of police activity. At Benalla he maintained a special force for emergencies. At Wodonga, Wangaratta, Bright and Mansfield, he secretly recruited a few townsmen "of the right sort" to assist local police in event of an attack on the local banks. Search parties were discontinued except in cases of specially good information when he gave his subordinates full authority to call in the trackers and act without reference to him. He was thus able to lift the morale of men who for too long had winced under the general laughter attending random forays.

One of his men shot a comrade while handing down rifles in the barracks yard. He found troopers ignorant of their weapons, so instituted firing practice and taught them how to engage and surround. So that his mounts would not pack up when forced off stable feed on pursuit, he fed them grass and hay and brought them to the same pitch as the outlaws' mounts. In answer to the demands of the Government, which had withdrawn the carte blanche under the jeers of the Opposition, he permanently stationed the remaining special constables at Benalla so that the department would not have to foot travelling expenses. Thus, expenditure was cut to less than one-third of the former rate.

Finally, he cultivated an extensive spy system, building up a personal relationship with his agents and guaranteeing their security, meanwhile watching the movement of sympathisers and reading their mail. At the same time, all police were ordered to cultivate friendly relations and appeal to the public spirit of farmers and townspeople. Yet it was slow work and the quiet months rolled by. The *Ovens and Murray Advertiser* recorded;

> We no longer have the marching and counter marching of armed men which at one time gave the town the appearance of a garrison settlement in war country, the Kelly gang, indeed, being all but forgotten. The murders of the police took place on 26 October last year, so that in close on twelve months the police do not claim to have once seen the gang.

Indeed it might have seemed that the conflict was over. The outlaws, driven by the first fires of indignation, had risen to notoriety and fame, and envisaged winning freedom for themselves and those they championed by the power of their young arms. But all threats and appeals had gone in vain.

The Berry Government, which had swept into power offering hope to all who were disenfranchised, in fact had achieved little for its supporters, and the political situation was rapidly approaching anarchy under the impact of violent bigotry directed against anyone who was Irish or Catholic, while the Victorian Irish themselves raised funds for their republican brothers in the Emerald Isle.

The gang must now have realised the bleak alternatives facing them. For how long could they bear to live in the twilight, never knowing when someone had laid a trap? Who was friend and who was foe? Fields went untilled as their allies devoted long hours to watching the police and fighting the battle of threat and intrigue that raged along the farms. Were they the champions of their people, or could their very existence become a curse? It was necessary to rob more banks; yet the banks were constantly improving their defences, making any attempt a hundred times more dangerous than Euroa or Jerilderie. And would robbery bring any permanent solution nearer?

140

Could there be a solution?

To clear out of the colony to Queensland or New Zealand would mean exile in shadow of the hangman's noose, and the constant thought that for all their deeds and boasts they had finally been unable to do anything more than run away. Could they leave their country in the shadow of the Divide where they had ridden with songs and defiance? Their very peril had tied them closer to its stones and silences. Could they by some unparalleled deed hold a gun at the heads of the elite of the land and enforce their freedom? Could they be stronger than the mightiest? Could they?

As they asked themselves these questions, they received new intimations of support from various people who had had their applications to the Land Boards rejected on police advice. The systematic vetting of applications over a wide area was evidence of the continuing intention of the authorities to rid the North-East of anyone suspected of being a Kelly adherent, much in the same way as they had earlier rid Glenmore of the Quinns.

Although the outlaws showed themselves seldom, spy reports received in Benalla began to increase under Nicolson's expert hand. At first, reports of appearances were invariably a month or more late, for the spies, while relishing the small sums Nicolson handed them, had an active fear of Kelly's vengeance. But gradually, as Nicolson built up confidence, they came in more promptly. In September, members of the gang were seen at Eleven Mile Creek. Early in November, acting on a note from Joe Byrne which suggested a meeting near Lake Rowan, Aaron Sherritt's younger brother, Jack, was returning disappointed to Wangaratta when Byrne appeared out of a gully, blood on his spurs from hard riding, and asked him to find out how much money was in the bank at Eldorado.

On the suggestion of Detective Ward, who was experiencing some embarrassment related to a pupil at a girls' school, all Beechworth banks were connected to the police barracks by telegraph. But nothing happened.

Aaron had found a new sweetheart, Mary Barry by name, aged only fifteen; and as she was a Catholic too, like Kate Byrne and Kate Kelly, he had had a quarrel with his father. This, combined with his dislike for Nicolson, had meant that various police jobs in the locality had fallen to his younger brothers. However, with the rapid progress of the romance, he sank his inhibitions in the need for cash and reported new appearances of the outlaws at Mrs Byrne's.

So Nicolson re-established the cave party early in December and Sherritt and four constables watched from the long grass at night and slept in the cave by day. Once they came across the mark of a very small riding boot—believed to be Byrne's—with high larrikin heel, where a man had been seen among the rocks. Then, in February, something curious occurred—the theft of a number of ploughshares from farmers between Oxley and Greta. Trackers were sent out and, in the soft clay near one of the dismantled ploughs, found the imprint of that same riding boot with the high heel. But why should the outlaws steal mouldboards? Perhaps to line some redoubt?

Each week as fresh reports came in Nicolson became more convinced of the correctness of his strategy and Standish more convinced of Nicolson's "masterly inactivity". Meanwhile, the savage conflict between the Upper and Lower Houses that had erupted with Black Wednesday 1878 had resolved in the temporary defeat of the Berry Ministry, with renewed doubts as to the worth of the police. Standish had long known Detective Ward was getting a sling from the storekeeper who supplied the cave party; now he wrote to Nicolson, "I certainly cannot ask the Chief Secretary to approve the purchase of jams, sardines and suchlike items—including 150 bottles of liquor" and told him to reduce his spy expenditure.

Bit by bit, Nicolson was learning the price of Culloden; in anguish he replied that to cut spy expenditure on top of other cuts would imperil his whole endeavour. Again he wrote, "I have the outlaws surrounded by my spies and have my hands upon them. It is not a chase of weeks and months, but one of days and hours."

Standish had never been happy about the gaoling of Mrs Kelly; he feared and loathed the sheer, ruthless inhumanity of his hypocritical lieutenant whose breath he could feel down his neck whenever he picked up the *Argus,* but he was not happy at the increased pressure from above either. On the one hand he told the Government that the gang was secure in the goodwill of the great majority of the inhabitants of the North-East, "a poor but semi-criminal class" whom they frequently assisted and who supplied them with food and information. On the other, he instructed Nicolson to curtail rifle and revolver practice and announced that he had decided to dispense with the trackers.

Standish had closed the Greta station the year before; and now, on reports of the doings of members of the Greta Mob at McDonnell's Hotel, ordered establishment of a station at Glenrowan.

For all Nicolson's boast that the chase was one of days and hours, the weeks dragged on. Nicolson feared that if he lunged and did not connect, the outlaws would retire to inaccessible country around Tom Groggin, cancelling at one stroke his work of months. Thus on one occasion he decided not to follow a day-old report of an appearance of the outlaws and Tom Lloyd out of Benalla.

Reports were now coming in more promptly, but were still not new enough for Nicolson to act on. As April 1880 came around his spies told him the outlaws were hiding in the Greta ranges. They were supposed to be in great straits. Their horses were either worn out or abandoned for fear of trackers and when they moved, it was at night on foot with several of their closest sympathisers scouting front and behind. They concealed themselves in the ranges by day, and sometimes travelled to Sebastopol, or to the Pilot Range, near Wodonga. Tom Lloyd had told them they must do another bank. Then reports stated they were concealed in a gully between Greta swamp, the Kelly home and Tom Lloyd's and had a small tent for use when it rained. And so Nicolson anticipated one dawn he and his men might surround the tent as they had surrounded Power ten years before.

Standish suddenly ordered the closure of the cave party. "You think it a secret, but not a man in Richmond Barracks does not know," he wrote. Nicolson should immediately discharge Sherritt, who, he said, could not be trusted. The finishing touch was added when the Government decided to withdraw its share of the Kelly reward as from 20 July.

Political pressure brought to bear by the *Argus* and Nicolson's father-in-law, the Hon. John Thomas Smith, had created for him the title of Assistant Chief Commissioner, so Nicolson, already deeply incensed, felt secure enough to ignore orders, with the result that he was given notice that he would be replaced by Superintendent Hare. He replied to Standish requesting an interview with the new Chief Secretary, Mr Ramsay; and early in May paid a visit to Melbourne.

It was not with the greatest cordiality that the two police heads met. Standish said coldly, "Well, if you wish to interview the Chief Secretary, I should wish to be present," to which Nicolson replied somewhat stiffly, "Certainly, I have not the slightest objection to you or anyone else being present." The Chief Commissioner then told the Assistant Chief Commissioner that Mr Ramsay would not be available till 2 o'clock. But, unfortunately for him, the Chief Secretary's Department was in the same building, and as Nicolson left the office, who should he see ascending the stairs but Ramsay himself. According to Captain Standish, Nicolson *rushed* up the stairs, intent on stealing a march on him, and *forced* his way into Mr Ramsay's room. Nicholson claimed he *followed* Mr Ramsay up the stairs, *arranged* an immediate interview, and was proceeding to call Standish, when along came the brave Captain himself at the double looking at him in a most insulting manner.

Next day Nicolson was told he had been given another month and returned to his lonely room at Benalla barracks to pen the following lines to Hare:

I need not tell you what misery it has been for me to reside in this district for so many months continuously. I do not affect to be prompted by higher motives than my neighbours, but to me this Kelly business seems too serious to be trifled with.

If you come up here and supersede me, and yet *do not succeed* — then the *deluge* (not for you) for the department, because the police will be considered played out and the condemnation of the present organisation will follow as a matter of course. What this means in the present state of the country may easily be imagined . . .

During the interview Mr Ramsay was most diplomatic, and assured Nicolson his withdrawal from the North-East cast no reflection on him. It was merely a change of bowlers, as in cricket. Nicolson reminded Mr Ramsay that the Kellys were not playing cricket, and the Chief Secretary, in his best bedside manner, finally promised he would consider his application to remain.

Day after day went by and the spy reports brought in little fresh news. On 14 May Dan was seen at Tom Lloyd's. Tom himself made no secret of his loyalties and came and went like Mrs Skillion, polite enough, but showing complete contempt for the police. Then Nicolson received a sensational report from one of his agents who went under the alias of Kennedy, Williams or the Diseased Stock Inspector — "diseased stock" being the term applied to the outlaws. This man was a local resident whose professional standing brought him the talk and family gossip, but although he moved even among the Kelly relatives without undue suspicion, there was an inner circle he could not reach. He it was who had advised Nicolson that as long as the bank money lasted, no further outbreak need be expected, and who, for some time, had been saying that funds were dwindling and that friends were urging the outlaws to make a fresh haul.

The note which Nicolson received read as follows:

Nothing definite re the diseased stock of this locality. I have made careful inspection, but did not find exact source of disease . . . Missing portions of cultivators are being worked as jackets and fit splendidly. Tested previous to using, and proof at ten yards. I shall be in Wangaratta on Monday before when I may learn how to treat the disease. I am perfectly satisfied it is where last indicated, but in which region I can't discover. A break-out may be anticipated, as feed is getting very scarce. Five are now bad . . . Other animals are, I fear, diseased.

Realising he had a week before he was relieved and that the report might prove a means of securing another extension, Nicolson telegraphed Melbourne that he was coming down again. On presenting himself, Standish said, "Ah, Nicolson, I was dining at the Governor's last night and I saw the Chief Secretary and he does not think there is any occasion to have further interview with you," and thereupon held out his hand. But Nicolson shoved both hands into his hat, and Standish, despite all his efforts could not get another word out of him, so said he would send him on an inspection of the country.

Nicolson left, went straight to the Chief Secretary's office, showed him the agent's letter, told him Standish had no experience of the Kelly affair, couldn't concentrate his attention on it for ten minutes, and that it was a great pity that the decision to replace him had been made without his being consulted. That afternoon, he saw Sir James McCullough, and asked him to use his influence with Ramsay.

Later, as he was boarding the train at Spencer Street, up came Standish in a rage. "I am paying you an amount of courtesy which I suppose you would not show me," he fumed, handing Nicolson a telegram. "I hear you have had an interview with Mr Ramsay and have been abusing me. I consider your conduct very disloyal. I believe you conducted yourself so violently that Mr Ramsay had to check you."

The bell was ringing and the train was about to go.

"Never," cried the Scot fiercely, as he climbed aboard.

28. Carte Blanche

THE CHIEF SECRETARY called Hare in and said, "Mr Hare, Cabinet has decided to put you in charge again at Benalla. We give you carte blanche, and anything you do, the Government will bear you out in."

Superintendent Hare was not merely prepossessing; as brother-in-law of Sir William Clarke, the colony's richest squatter and leader of Melbourne society, he was an instant success. Guests by the score arrived at the private railway station north of Melbourne to spend the weekend at the Sunbury mansion. The Clarkes entertained splendidly.

Hare replied that he was very flattered; nevertheless, he was not specially keen to go. After Nicolson's letter placing the very survival of the force on his shoulders, he had received another from Sadleir begging him to keep out of the affair; and this further added to the reluctance he had felt ever since he had given up the search, tired in body and mind, eleven months before. But the Government's offer was generous, more compliments came, the Governor was in favour of his reappointment, Standish had recommended him for the post of Chief Commissioner on his retirement, and his ambition overcame his doubts and scruples.

He arrived in Benalla on 2 June and entered the barracks while conversation was in progress between Nicolson and the Diseased Stock Inspector. He listened to them talking of the stolen mouldboards which Nicolson still believed would be used to line a stronghold. The agent persisted they were making armour; it was so fitted they could ride in it. When the spy departed, Hare remarked, "Rubbish!" Even more formal than usual, Nicolson handed over the reins and departed, leaving Hare to make his peace with Sadleir. Hare found O'Connor bitter because Standish had written to his Government behind his back, criticising his handling of the trackers; in fact, Standish had reported to Ramsay that as long as O'Connor and his men remained, the outlaws would not show their hand. Meanwhile, in response to O'Connor's protest, the Queensland Government had announced its intention of withdrawing the trackers.

Hare had been in Benalla a few days when the theft of two thoroughbreds was reported by a Mr Ryan, of Cashel, and agents gave the opinion that the gang or their friends were responsible. Then came information from Melbourne that Tom Lloyd, Mrs Skillion and a young woman believed to be Kate Kelly had been visited at the Robert Burns Hotel, Lonsdale Street, by a young man who had been followed to various houses in the city and eventually emerged from Rosier's gunshop in Elizabeth Street carrying a parcel. Inquiry had shown that he had purchased 400 Webley revolver cartridges, told the gunsmith he was leaving the colony and promised to return in three days for further supplies. If the young man had ever intended returning, he would have been deterred by reports of the incident in the press next morning; but a squad of detectives made a pest of themselves playing hide-and-seek at Rosier's for the rest of the week.

In the meantime, Mrs Skillion and party slipped away as

quietly as they had arrived. The police searched the train at Spencer Street, and the party, which had climbed aboard at Essendon, was detained briefly at Benalla while Hare's men repeated the exercise.

Everything suggested that Ned and his mates were preparing for another, grander coup. Nicolson had sent sealed instructions to all police stations that in the event of a new outbreak, troopers were to proceed to strategic points through which the outlaws were expected to pass when returning to their bases. Their passage was not to be disputed, but police were to report by telegraph so the gang could be followed and surrounded by an overwhelming force.

Meanwhile, Hare set out to interview Nicolson's spies and revive the watches on the outlaws' relatives. With the gaoling of her husband, Mrs Skillion had returned to her mother's home, and parties were established at Glenrowan and Wangaratta whence constables tramped out nightly to watch the Kellys and Harts.

Nor did it take Hare long to arrange a meeting with Aaron, who, on receiving Nicolson's assurance of a job with the cave party, had married Mary Barry and set up home in a deserted hut in the middle of the Woolshed. Aaron had flirted with both police and outlaws. He had compromised the police, quarrelled with Mrs Byrne, had Mrs Skillion set the police on him, was on bad terms with his father and had received warnings from Byrne. Perhaps, as his mother said, he was naive.

Mrs Sherritt had heard horsebells in the home paddock one morning, and on investigation, found Byrne lying on the grass with a bridle on his arm. Joe had risen and spoken to her in a friendly way; it was he who had let the horses in. Then he said, "I have come down to take Aaron's life and also Detective Ward's. These two have nearly starved us to death. Ward goes about the hills like a black tracker."

Mrs Sherritt had begged him not to kill Aaron, scarcely knowing what she said, and Joe had replied, "You need not try to impress that on my mind because I tell you there was Ward and him and Mr Hare very nearly twice catching us."

So Aaron had been in a curious state most of Nicolson's time. He did not relish the job, stayed away for days on end, turned up from nowhere without explanation, even neglected to bring food to the cave party and was liable at any hour of night to leave camp and curl up under a bush somewhere.

The meeting between the two old friends — Sherritt the larrikin, and Hare, hail - fellow - well - met among the lions of

Melbourne—took place in the bush near Beechworth. They shook hands, and Hare told Aaron in a fatherly way that he was disappointed he had not worked well under Nicolson. "I could not work for that cranky Scotsman; he distrusted me in everything I did, and I told him I did not care about working for him," Aaron replied. He added that the outlaws were still about and he would turn over a new leaf and do everything he could to help Hare run them down.

So the party, which had been withdrawn when Nicolson left, was re-established with Senior Constable Armstrong in charge on the understanding they would spend the days at Aaron's and keep out of sight. As the building had no veranda or skillion and only one bedroom, conditions were cramped; then the owner appeared and threatened action if Sherritt didn't get out. Not wishing to be ordered out by the Eldorado police and discovered, the four constables clubbed together with Aaron and bought the property.

Yet at heart, all of them believed the gang knew they were there. After all, the hut was in plain view of several houses and a stone's throw from the main road which led to the pub nearby and to Byrne's. Most days supplies were delivered, and Mary Sherritt's young brother often hailed Denny Byrne as he passed to and from the Common School up the valley. One day Denny came into the hut, and soon after that his older brother Paddy began to hang around on his grey mare—or so the police imagined. The days were growing colder in these Beechworth hills and the nights becoming bitter. After the watch, the policemen trooped home from the long grass around Byrne's and warmed themselves at the broad fireplace until Mary Sherritt got up. Breakfast over, they went into the other room to sleep on the floor or in the bed still warm from the body of the young wife. After loafing around in the afternoon they left to take up the vigil again about 8 p.m.—it was no life for a dog, let alone a constable.

During one of Hare's visits, Ward reported Dan seen riding from Myrtleford towards Beechworth. Sherritt started up. "Then he will call at my mother's place tonight. I wish, Mr Hare, you would bring a couple of men as some of the gang are sure to call there if they're passing." Hare agreed and lay for two nights in a barn behind the Sherritt homestead at Sebastopol Creek, lapped in the stench and grunting of pigs and the rustling and chirping of mice in the hay, scratching himself for fleas, and seizing his rifle in alarm each time the dogs barked.

This much may be said for Hare, that none of his constables would have suffered it with more fortitude. But, with little supervision and the bitter cold and futility of these supposedly secret night watches, the troopers began to slack on the job, and one Saturday night Hare surprised two of them in the hut when they should have been watching Byrne's. There was no use telling Hare that they didn't set out for Byrne's until the pub had finished. Ward, who was scared he might lose the sling he got from the Beechworth storekeeper if the cave party was closed down again, hurried around the back to give the others the wink, and then to give them time to get well in front, led Hare through an icy cold stream. Unfortunately for him, Hare had heard whispering outside the hut, and on arrival at Byrne's gave the conspirators a dressing down. He found Sherritt under a tree. It was bitterly cold and ice would form on the pools before morning and here was Aaron lying on the bare ground without a coat. Hare was amazed at the man's hardiness and mentioned the matter as he had more than a year before. "I do not care about coats," came the old reply. The two men walked back to the hut together and when Hare invited Aaron in to have a cup of tea, Aaron declined. "No, Mr Hare, I must get back at once to the men."

Hare reflected, "Here is a man who has been working for the last eighteen months — is this put on or is it reality?" Once Sherritt had disappeared, he went outside and sat by the creek. As he heard the footsteps fading down the road he realised the night had not been wasted. "I felt confident his whole heart and soul was in the work," he said later.

Talking to Armstrong next morning, Sherritt said, "My belief, Harry, is that the gang are in the ranges between Rose River and Gippsland. I've known nothing of them since they passed to Jerilderie." Armstrong said, "Why did you tell Hare a different story?" Came the reply, "Well, I must use a little policy. I am as true as you are; I'm just working for the pay I'm getting for my wife."

So talked trooper and police agent as they sipped tea in front of the log one dawn, crsip and young with promise as so many others. Such talk had long continued to froth on the cauldron of hate which boiled and sputtered among these north-eastern hills. But time was running out.

"My boy and his mates will shortly do something that will not only astonish Australia, but the whole world!" Thus like a fist flung up and shaken against the sky came the reported boast of Mrs Byrne. Perhaps it brought a leap to the heart, or a small bristling of fear as it travelled beside the chattering creek along the yellow road through the valley of the Woolshed. Perhaps the confident Hare of the peculiar voice grunted a high-pitched grunt at Benalla and transferred his attention to some more relevant business of the day.

Before the week was out, isolated events occurred that were to have a marked influence on the imminent climax of two years' battle. Tired and worn out from cold and lack of sleep, Senior Constable Kelly's party watching the Kelly home was withdrawn from the Glenrowan barracks, leaving Constable Bracken in sole charge. On Thursday afternoon, "the ornamental Queensland sub-inspector and his niggers"—to use the words of Standish—left Spencer Street en route to Brisbane. The same afternoon, the Diseased Stock Inspector appeared at Benalla barracks to tell Hare that the gang was entirely out of funds. Hare snorted and dismissed him from service, remarking to Sadleir, "If this is the sort of person Nicolson and you have been depending on, it's no wonder you haven't caught the Kellys!"

At 9 o'clock the same night, Sherritt and a trooper entered the pub on the Chiltern road out of Beechworth and found Maggie, the barmaid, for whom Sherritt had an affectionate regard, leaning across the bar and talking confidentially to a miner. Stung with jealousy, Sherritt remarked as they took their seats at the upper end of the counter, "That girl often sees Joe Byrne."

"When?"

"Every Saturday night."

"Are you sure?"

"Well, I heard so."

Nothing further was said when Maggie took their order, and the trooper left soon afterwards. Convinced Sherritt knew where the gang were hiding, he had bought him drinks at several of the Beechworth pubs that night, and now he had a clue; Sherritt had raised his guard too late. He took a turn down the road; then retraced his steps and re-entered the bar.

When Maggie came for his order, he said, "Is it true you see Byrne on Saturday nights?"

"A devil of a man could have told you that but Sherritt," exclaimed Maggie.

Such then was the kiss of Judas Sherritt for his schooldays mate.

29. The Death of Sherritt

NO ONE WILL EVER KNOW quite what considerations influenced the outlaws during these few final days. If the shroud that surrounded so much of their lives was dark, then the pall of reticence that fell on their relatives and friends following the terrible climax of their story was darker still, and death has long sealed the lips of so many who could have spoken, but who shut their teeth to spite the world which dragged the name of courage through the mud of official execration and public lies.

Why had the outlaws not struck while the iron was hot? Why had they let things drag on for sixteen months until the entire organisation was beginning to go into debt? In the months in the Yackandandah road mine workings when they studied the daily papers and came to realise that the forces backing Berry were so split by old-world hates that no one could afford to give them a hearing, did their deepening frustration tarnish the comradeship of earlier days? Did the sharp-minded Dan, who had seldom been encouraged to believe that anything but naked class interest conditioned the affairs of men, ever resent the authority of his older brother, who, in his pride of race, had lifted the world on to their shoulders? Did police intimations of a pardon for the betrayal of his mates ever disturb Joe's dreams at night? Was it true that Ned and Joe had to watch Steve for fear he might sell out?

The answer is that any single one, or all of them, could have saddled up and ridden north across the border to work out a new life in New South Wales or Queensland, but chose to remain true to their relatives and friends and the cause they espoused. If courage were needed in the bright days of Euroa and Jerilderie, what steadfastness was required when life itself, emaciated by suspicion, sometimes seemed a ghoul feeding on the happiness of men's souls!

Some say Ned thought the ultimate solution was to spirit off His Excellency the Governor, Lord Normanby, from the pleasaunce of his holiday residence at Mt Macedon and lay before him over a bottle of three-star brandy in the hills the justice of the Kelly cause and the mutual advantage of a little bloodless reciprocity. After all, the New South Wales Governor, Sir Hercules Robinson, had pardoned Ben Hall's mate, Gardiner, on condition he leave the colony and Gardiner was now running a saloon in San Francisco. It is certain that Ned and Joe gave a lot of study to derailing and robbing the gold-train from Beechworth, and no doubt they studied many other alternatives.

The gang had been seeking favourable opportunity to strike for months, but now — with the sale of Maggie to the tender mercies of a greedy trooper, and the likelihood that she and those around her would be pressured to reveal the whereabouts of their

151

headquarters — their plans suddenly crystallised. Sherritt must be executed and his execution would be the tool for drawing the police special force from its base and laying open the banks in Benalla. It would be necessary to isolate the town by cutting the rail links north and south, and the plan was assisted by the fact that the moon was approaching the full and the Broken River at Benalla's southern entrance was brimming.

To cut the line from Melbourne was simple. The rail bridge at Benalla would be blown, and the road bridge too, if necessary. But where to cut the line from points north? The answer was where they had their maximum force — at Glenrowan right in the midst of their staunchest support, where the police watching party had just been withdrawn and where there was no telegraph station and no rail traffic on Sundays.

It is not easy to reconstruct the scene on the twenty-level off the Yackandandah road on the Friday and Saturday following the Chiltern pub incident. Men came and went — miners, cockies who couldn't rub two bob together, members of the Greta Mob, perhaps even Maggie herself — many of them young and Australian-born. Steve had been dispatched early to sound the tocsin in many a gully and creek flat in the greatest ride of his life. Dan came and went, but spent most of the time on top with his cattle dog, acting cockatoo; none of the others were as tough in their judgements or as discriminating in their choice of friends. In the centre at an old table sat Joe Byrne, the fine glow of Irish beauty on him, busily writing out instructions, checking maps and times and ticking off items on a list, while beside him stood Ned, warm and genial, shaking old friends by the hand and referring now and then to an annotated sketch map, the light of confidence in his eye.

Piled on the dray at the head of the drive were weapons, harness, kegs of gunpowder and four new suits of armour proof to rifle bullets. There had been endless debates about the armour, especially as the breastplate prevented accurate aim with a rifle. Byrne pointed out that extra horses were needed to carry it, it had to be put on and off which was difficult in the best of conditions, its great weight reduced speed of movement and impaired mobility — worst of all, success of any tactical plan depended on covering all possible contingencies and it introduced an incalculable factor. The gang now had the support of several score men who were ready to take up arms. The opinion of these men had finally swung the argument, and to compensate for the inaccuracy of aim, Ned had bought four rapid-fire Winchester repeaters and shortened the barrels.

152

Ned, Joe, Dan and Steve, encased in armour, would serve as shock troops. They would derail the police special on the bend just north of the hamlet, hand the survivors over to the Greta Mob with instructions to make for the hills, and then ride the hop, step and jump into Benalla to blow the bridge and rob the two banks. With a minimum of £4000 or £5000, they could then keep their organisation together and hold Hare and his men hostage until the gaolers in Melbourne saw fit to release Mrs Kelly, Bill Skillion and Bricky Williamson. This, at any rate, was what Kelly indicated after the event.

On the Friday, a freakish storm scurried down from the hills over the Woolshed, stripping the bark and shingle roofs off a few old shacks. On Saturday, the cloud flotillas rode across the blue on the back of the south-westerly, while below, the shadow squadrons charged over the ridges and fled down the valleys.

On this day the party in Sherritt's hut had rarely been gloomier. After a few hours sleep they got up and moped about indoors. Sherritt told Armstrong that young Denny Byrne had twice looked in at the rear, and now it appeared beyond doubt the outlaws knew they were there. Perhaps he remembered the evil dream his mother-in-law, Mrs Barry, had had a few days earlier, for he said, "They can set fire to the hut and shoot you one by one as you run out." Armstrong replied for that matter they could shoot them any night on the way to Byrne's and he was going into Beechworth that evening to tell Ward they were discovered and any further watch was futile.

As night set in and lights began to quiver down the valley, the candle was lit and logs piled on the fire to last until morning, so that when the troopers sat down to tea with the Sherritts, the shadows gesticulated against the rough plaster walls as if to give form to their fears. Mrs Barry arrived from her home up the valley to spend the evening with her daughter who was pregnant — some said to Detective Ward — and then Armstrong and two of his men retired through the wooden partition into the bedroom, leaving Constable Duross with the Sherritts.

The minutes sauntered by in the soughing of the wind in the gums. Then came a knock at the back door — knuckles on the rough hardwood palings, as happened many a Saturday night when people moved to and from the pub, visiting neighbours, or coming and going from Beechworth, eleven kilometres away.

"Who's there?" called Mrs Sherritt.

A man's voice answered — a small voice with an accent.

"Anton Veeks, I have lost my vay."

"Who is it?" asked Sherritt.

153

"Anton Wicks," his wife replied.

"Who?" repeated Duross.

"It's only Anthony Wicks, a German who lives over the creek," replied Aaron, making no attempt to go to the door. "He's in the habit of going astray when he's drunk."

Still he made no move.

"Go and show him the way, Aaron, Don't keep him waiting out there," said Mrs Sherritt.

Aaron unfolded his long legs, motioned Duross to the bedroom, eased himself over and removed the door-prop. As the light spilled into the darkness he took a short step forward and spoke in a whimsical tone, "Do you see that short sapling over there? Climb that . . ."

He stopped abruptly. "Who is that?" He stood framed in the doorway confronting the night as a figure emerged from the shadow of the chimney and the hut was shaken by the crash of a rifle shot. A second explosion shattered the enclosed space, and as Aaron swayed and fell back on to the boards, a voice rang out, "Bail up!" and Mrs Barry recognised the frightened German, Wicks, in handcuffs, and beyond him, Aaron's schoolmate, Joe Byrne, rifle smoking in his hand.

The echoes flew across the valley and rebounded into the hut, the women screamed and rushed forward, while outside, Aaron's dog howled and snapped forward on its chain. Mary Sherritt, fifteen years of age, knelt by her husband — Aaron lay in his death agony from wounds in heart and brain.

Mrs Barry had once slept in the same bed as Joe and his mother; she had known him since boyhood. "Oh, Joe, Joe, why did you do it? Why did you shoot poor Aaron?"

"The bastard will never put me away again," cried Byrne as he withdrew into the shadows. "Who was that went into the bedroom?"

Mrs Barry hesitated and replied, "A man called Duross."

"What is he?"

"He's looking for work about here."

"Go and tell him to come out."

She went to the bedroom door, but Duross could not be enticed. "He won't come."

"I'll soon make him; come out of that place!"

The fears that had menaced the police since that October day twenty months before, when the drizzle had fallen on their dead colleagues at Stringybark, scurried in the door on the cold night wind and clutched at the throats of the four troopers. Duross, who had dropped the calico curtain over the entrance to the bedroom, fumbled around for cartridges, while Dowling climbed a sack of flour in the vague expectation of getting a shot over the partition if the outlaws entered. Armstrong and Alexander tried to load their shotguns and peeped around the curtain, but were unable to see anything more than Sherritt, who was now lying quiet. Armstrong asked his men if they were willing to sally out. With one breath, they answered in the affirmative, but advised against it.

In response to instructions, Mrs Sherritt opened the front door and found Dan there. Dan glanced at the body, smiled at her and said softly, "Good evening, ma'am!"

Meanwhile Byrne had ordered Mrs Barry outside. "You've known me since I was a boy, Mrs Barry. They tell me you haven't a good word to say for me nowadays. Your daughter goes around blowing what her husband would do when he caught me."

"I never said anything about you, Joe, except when I heard you were with the Kellys, I said I was sorry you hadn't more sense."

The outlaws then ordered Mary to join her mother outside and began to fire into the bedroom. A lump of plaster struck Dowling and he dropped and hid behind the sack of flour.

"How many men are inside?" asked Byrne.

"Two."

"Is that all?"

"Yes, only two."

"What are their names?"

"I don't know — one is Duross."

"How green you are!" Byrne jeered. "If you be telling me lies I'll murder both of you!"

He turned to the girl. "Go in and tell them to come out."

As Mary went inside the sound of whispering and the click of firearms could be heard plainly.

"Do you hear that?" cried Byrne scornfully. "Come out or I'll riddle the bloody place! If you don't come out I'll shoot you down like bloody dogs!"

When the girl reappeared, Byrne again asked how many men were inside, but Mrs Barry nudged her and she burst into tears. Byrne turned from the girl in disgust and fired again. "Go in and bring them out or I'll shoot the both of you."

The men in the hut could hear Dan and an assistant gathering bushes and piling them against the wall; and when Mary entered this time, they grabbed her, placed a hand over her mouth and pulled her under the bed.

When the minutes passed and it became apparent she was unlikely to reappear, Dan knelt beside the pile of twigs and struck a match which the wind blew out.

155

"If you set fire to the house and she gets shot or burned, you can just kill me along with her," said Mrs Barry, in tears.

"Well, call her out."

But the girl answered that they would not let her go and ceased to reply.

"Let her go, you cowardly dogs, screening yourselves with women," cried Byrne, reloading his rifle. "I've got any amount of ammunition; I'll riddle the bloody house!"

Mrs Barry again begged the outlaws not to shoot.

"Don't be frightened; I only want the men in the house," said Byrne. He proceeded to unlock the German's handcuffs. "Here is a man who tried to lag me for shaking his horse, but I'm not going to shoot him."

"Send her inside to see if the slugs have penetrated the wall," said Dan.

"There's no use me going in there to be burned with the rest."

"We'll see about that."

Inside, Mrs Barry found Armstrong and Alexander flat on the bed, while Duross and Dowling hid under it, pressing Mary securely to the wall with their boots.

"Oh, my God, Mrs Barry, I was near shooting you," said Armstrong, while Duross seized her by the legs and pulled her to the floor. Dowling whispered, "If you don't keep quiet we'll have to shoot you."

It must have been about nine o'clock, and as nothing more could be achieved, the outlaws, leading a packhorse, struck across the valley towards the southern ranges which straddled their path to the Oxley Plains and a bigger mission beyond. Wicks had already run home and barred the door.

For the next three hours, the troopers stayed where they were, listening to the dog whimpering and the leaves of the gums clashing like warriors in endless battle. About midnight, Armstrong pushed the doors to with his gun, rolled the log off the fire and threw some cold tea on the coals in case the outlaws should look in at the window. Then he shifted Aaron, covered him with a blanket and returned to the bedroom. The Kellys had spent several days at Jerilderie, he whispered, and it was unlikely they had finished with them yet. The pall of fear still on them, the troopers continued to lie in the cold until dawn when they peered out and saw nothing more unusual than a local Chinese.

Alexander opened the door gingerly, and, guns at the ready, the troopers reconnoitred, after which Armstrong returned inside and wrote a note which he gave to the Chinese with instructions to take it to the police in Beechworth. The Chinese had scarcely left when he returned, saying he was frightened; so Armstrong sent him to fetch the local schoolmaster, who likewise took the note but returned, saying his wife would not let him deliver it because the outlaws were waiting in the ranges.

At last Armstrong plucked up courage to set off for Beechworth himself, wondering how he could get hold of a horse. Paddy Byrne came towards him at a fast gallop, but just as rapidly veered off and disappeared. On the long slope from town he met a farmer on a hack, ordered him off and spurred up the slope. Beechworth was at Sunday dinner and one o'clock struck from the Post Office tower when he reported to Senior Constable Mullane events which had occurred seventeen hours before, and which now were to be flashed to Superintendent Hare in Benalla.

30. At Glenrowan

AT AROUND 10 P.M. on Saturday, 26 June 1880 — after the shooting of Sherritt and after the echoes of the last train for the weekend had fled Morgan's Lookout — Ned and Steve, accompanied by supporters leading a string of horses, rode into Glenrowan from the Greta hills.

In the early days, the gap where the line and road took a twist in their thirty-seven kilometre run from Benalla to Wangaratta had reminded some Scots overlander of home, for it was known as The Glen. With the discovery of gold on the Ovens in 1852, this pleasant wooded spot with its mineral spring and single steep height had changed little; then it had grown and reached its peak in the early seventies on the custom of the fettlers laying the Great Northern Railway. When the line opened, trade flowed to the towns on either side so that all that remained in 1880 were a handful of scattered shacks, a general store, a weather-beaten blacksmith shop and two bush hotels, one each side of the railway station. The police barracks, post office and school were a kilometre away in the direction of Benalla.

It was from these barracks that the police had conducted their watch on Mrs Skillion's, while it was at McDonnell's on the Greta side — rebuilt ten years before — that the Greta Mob had the habit of gathering and which Ned and his party now entered.

Despite occasional comings and goings of police and rowdiness at McDonnell's, life usually went on quietly as the farmers grew their crops on the alluvial flats and carted their produce in to be loaded onto the goods train for Melbourne. Yet it was true that a certain cultural cleavage became evident at weekends and holidays, when the weather was fine, and picnic parties rode in from Wangaratta and the surrounding countryside. Some of the best horsemen in the district could be seen at McDonnell's where it was liable to be 'The Wearin' of the Green', 'The Ladies of Brisbane', or even 'The Bull of Kerrymore', while at the smaller Glenrowan Inn across the tracks, you were likely to hear the concertina, the tread of dancers and:

> Now Robin my boy, this is not a gavotte,
> 'Tis a polka we're wanting and that pretty hot,
> For the mailcoach from Hobart Town must not be in late,
> So polka, my Robin, and you too, Miss Kate.

It was here, at the Glenrowan Inn, that the Kelly gang was to make what was soon to be known as the Last Stand. Built of stringybark boards, roofed with corrugated iron, lined and ceiled with calico sheet, the building resembled a thousand other grey bush pubs amid the twisted gums across a continent. It was somewhat high in the old style, with twin gables running the width of the veranda in front, and under the front gable a bar and parlour, separated by a passage which ran through to the older part behind. Separated from the line and station by a paddock scored by a watercourse, it faced the stationmaster's house and adjoining railway gates. A horsetrough rough-hewn from the butt of a large tree stood outside, along with a lantern atop a post and a signboard which displayed the legend:

The Glenrowan Inn
Ann Jones
Best Accommodation

The building was rough, but why shouldn't the accommodation be good, for Mother Jones was thirty-five and of happy disposition, and few, they said, could roast a leg of lamb better.

Having outlined their intentions and the assistance required in what promised to be a lengthy engagement, Ned and Dan crossed the line directly from McDonnell's to some tents occupied by platelayers and their families. Once satisfied no detectives were present, they crossed to the gatehouse, but becoming impatient, broke in the door and found the stationmaster, Stanistreet, climbing into his clothes. What could he do to stop a police special? Ned was given an indifferent answer. Who could tear up the line, then?

When told only the platelayers, the outlaws retraced their steps; and while Steve shepherded the women and children to the gatehouse, Ned set off with several linesmen along the ballast towards Wangaratta. En route, he got them to open a box alongside the track for the necessary tools and said he had been at Beechworth the previous night, had shot several police, was expecting a train from Benalla with police and black trackers and was going to kill each one of the bastards.

They had not far to go. At the end of a cutting not far from the station, the line took a sharp curve over a gully, and here he set the men to work. "Look sharp, or I'll tickle you up with this," he said, brandishing his revolver. After two hours, two lengths of line had been taken up and the party was marched back to join their families.

Now began the wait for the police special. Neither Ned nor Joe bargained on the time it would take Armstrong to carry the news of Sherritt's death to Beechworth, nor how long it would take after that for the police to set out in pursuit.

Ned went ahead with preparations. He questioned Stanistreet closely on the use of lamps, instructed him to give no signal in event of a train approaching and took over an inner room at the Glenrowan Inn to serve as armoury. Soon afterwards, Dan and Joe arrived wet from the ride over the Oxley Plains and joined Steve at the gatehouse to swap notes as the sky paled beyond the distant Alps.

When daylight came, the outlaws began to bail up passers-by and send them to the pub. Mrs Jones was greatly excited and chatted with Joe while her sixteen-year-old daughter Jane prepared breakfast. With his fine long head and curly brown hair and beard, Joe looked neat and gentlemanly as he sat at the table in his blue sack coat and tweed riding breeches, thoroughly at home. When Jane called out, "There's not enough bread in the house," the plump, lively mother told her where she would find a loaf and observed, "I have plenty of bread, but I'm keeping it for you, Joe."

The girl liked Ned best. When she brought him ham and eggs, he asked how old she was. "I thought you would be eighteen," he said. He gave her his revolvers to look at and she slipped one in her pocket and said she would keep order for him.

Dan and Steve spent most of the morning bailing up people on the road and sending them inside and were then relieved by Ned and Joe. The growing crowd of prisoners was greatly entertained at the sudden improvement in attitude of irritated new arrivals, when—after refusing to say who he was for some time—Ned put his revolver away and announced modestly, "Well boys, I'm Ned Kelly; you must come!"

As the day advanced, the life of the hamlet was increasingly drawn into the maelstrom. Around noon, Curnow, the local schoolmaster, drove up with his wife, sister and child, accompanied on horseback by his brother-in-law, David Mortimer. Noticing the crowd, he remarked, "Mrs Jones must be dead; she's been very ill lately," and when he reached the level crossing to be told by Stanistreet, "The Kellys are here; you can't go through," he took it for a joke.

A horseman blocked his path and said, "Who are you?"

Curnow saw the revolvers in his belt and concluded it was Ned Kelly himself. He recognised a second man as a local called Delaney. Now he noticed a third man, who like Kelly, was armed and proved to be Byrne.

"Oh, you're the schoolmaster, are you? And who are they?" asked Kelly, indicating the women and Mortimer.

"Where are you going?"

"I'm sorry, but I must detain you."

The outlaw ordered them to step out of the buggy and turned again to Delaney, while Stanistreet told Curnow what had happened. Kelly was accusing Delaney of taking a horse to oblige a policeman and of seeking admission to the force. He declared he would have the life of anyone who aided the police in any way, or had friendly feelings for them; he could and he would find them out. A law had been made, he said, rendering it a crime to help him and his mates, and he would make it a crime for anyone to aid the police. When he drew his revolver, the schoolmaster's wife and sister were prompted to intervene, and Delaney, who was one of the gang's telegraphs and must have been highly amused by the harangue, duly promised to watch his step.

"I forgive you this time, but mind you be careful for the future," said Kelly, telling one of the admiring boys who had collected to run Mr Curnow's buggy into the yard. To relieve tension, Byrne produced brandy and a tumbler and poured drinks, finally giving Delaney the bottle.

At that, the womenfolk went into Stanistreet's where Steve was still managing to keep a weather eye although suffering exhaustion from his long ride. The rest crossed to the hotel where there were already forty people, and Kelly told them to make themselves at home, but not to go outside the yard without permission.

After a time, Dan got talking to Curnow and asked him to have a drink, and they joined some prisoners in the bar. Curnow mentioned he had been told they had been to Beechworth the previous evening and shot several police. Dan replied that they had been near Beechworth, done some shooting and turned the devils out — by which he meant the special force in Benalla. Byrne joined them, and glancing at Dan's glass, said, "Be careful, old man," to which Dan replied, "All right," and added water.

"What puzzles me is why you've stuck up Glenrowan," observed Curnow. "Well, we're here to wreck a special train of inspectors, police and black trackers which will pass through to take up our trail from Beechworth," replied Byrne. "We rode hard across country, often up to our saddle-girths in water to get here. We've had the line taken up at a dangerous part, and we're going to send the train and its occupants to hell."

Curnow was a personable man on a good income but had no special sympathy for the selectors of the district, particularly the Irish; he felt he must do something to prevent the outrage planned. He was standing in the yard after lunch when Dan approached and asked him inside to have a dance, so he replied that he had on the wrong boots. When Ned said, "Come on, never mind your boots," he replied that he was lame, but would be pleased to dance if Kelly accompanied him to the school to get his dancing boots; it had occurred to him that Bracken, the trooper, who had been stationed at Greta and knew Ned, might see them and give the alarm. His heart jumped when Ned agreed to the proposal, but someone remarked that his house was near the barracks and Kelly turned and asked, "Is that so?"

"Yes, I had forgotten that."

"Well then, I don't think I'll go."

Curnow had lost the first round. He entered the crowded parlour, where the furniture had been pulled back and someone was playing a concertina, and allowed himself to be talked into dancing. When he heard Ned mention that he intended to visit the barracks and bring back Constable Bracken and Reynolds, the postmaster, Curnow laughed and said, "I'd rather you did it than I; but when you go, can I come with you and take my wife and child and sister home?"

Once bitten, Kelly made no answer.

Curnow was to write later:

> The intention to do something to baffle the murderous designs of the gang grew on me, and I resolved to do the uttermost to gain the confidence of the outlaws and to make them believe I was a sympathiser. I saw clearly that unless I did this, I would be unable to get permission to go home with my wife, child and sister, and consequently, be unable to stop the destruction of the special train. The outlaws kept a very sharp watch on their prisoners without seeming to do so.

Meanwhile the sun shone, the day moved on and Morgan's Lookout stared down on the rough buildings in its lap. In mid-afternoon, some of the younger sparks held a jumping contest. The outlaws were like boys at a picnic. Ned joined in the hop, step and jump; but one of the prisoners beat him, so he made three or four more attempts to better the distance. When he took off his coat and failed again, Byrne remarked, "You seem a bit off today, Ned."

"Yes, I'm a bit handicapped," said Ned, glancing at the revolvers. "These fellows are a little too good for me."

Seeing Kelly in a good humour, Curnow took the opportunity to ask if he could visit the gatehouse, and Kelly consented on the understanding there would be no funny business. As he approached the line, he noticed the red llama-wool scarf around his sister's shoulders and thought, "What a splendid danger signal that would make!"

Inside, Hart was lying on the ottoman, three revolvers by his side, complaining of swollen feet. "I've not had my boots off for several days and nights," he said.

Curnow immediately became solicitous. "You should bathe them with hot water." He called, "Can you let Mr Hart have some hot water in a basin, Mrs Stanistreet?"

While the women attended to Hart, Curnow went behind the house to be immediately joined by Stanistreet who said, "We must sound the alarm somehow." At that moment, Mrs Stanistreet appeared. Curnow's suburban conscience was worrying him, so he asked if they thought it would be wrong to break his word to Kelly. "No," they replied.

"Did they take the department revolver from you?"

"No."

"Let's go inside; we don't want to be seen talking together like this."

As it happened, they had no sooner re-entered the gatehouse than Dan arrived, looking for a bag. He searched the house and crossed the line to McDonnell's, but returned empty-handed. Curnow sympathised with him and accompanied him back to the inn. As soon as Ned appeared from the kitchen, he said, "Mr Stanistreet possesses a loaded revolver from the railway department; someone might get hold of it."

Kelly thanked him, and he saw he had in a great measure won their confidence.

The outlaws let more than twenty prisoners go home during the afternoon and might well have let Delaney go too, had it not been for Mrs Jones who declared, "No he must stop; revenge is sweet!"

As dusk fell and the air sharpened, most of the prisoners came inside, and Jane Jones, revolver in pocket, counted the women and children. Curnow watched, but still no opportunity presented itself.

At last he overheard Ned tell Mrs Jones he was going down the road to capture Bracken and would take Jane to call him out of the house. As Mrs Jones did not want the girl to go, he seized the chance and told Kelly his brother-in-law, Dave Mortimer, would be better as he boarded next door with the postmaster and knew Bracken well. After a pause, Kelly agreed, so Curnow waited until he disappeared to the stables, then followed and asked if he could take his party home at the same time. "You have no cause to fear me; I am with you heart and soul," he said.

"I know it and can see it, but you'll have to wait until I'm ready to go," replied Kelly.

Some of the prisoners were enjoying themselves around a log fire in the yard, while others were playing cards inside, numbering altogether about sixty. Curnow and his womenfolk arrived back at the kitchen to find Mrs Jones trying to get a ring off Joe's finger, but it was two or three hours before Kelly turned up and told him to get his buggy and wait in front.

In the interim, Ned and Joe had decided on a variation of their plan. What had seemed just and right in a moment of indignation when Sherritt had compromised Maggie and their whole operational structure, now seemed unnecessarily brutal. Back amongst the warmth and frailty of people at the inn, they realised again that even the police were human. Their plans had worked out well to date despite the lateness of the special, and their force was secure and intact. Rather than send the special into the gully, with the misery of broken limbs and injured horses and all other untold consequences, they decided to draw the special force to the barracks.

So Ned and Joe had been to McDonnell's to rebrief the bush telegraphs and the Greta Mob, and Ned had taken a picked man to the gatehouse, instructing him in the use of the signal lamp. This man would stop the train down the line and the police would hurry to the barracks, leaving the train free to proceed to the station, the only place the mounts could be unloaded. Safe in armour, the gang would then drive the police into the barracks where fire from the Greta Mob would keep them cooped up. While the police mounts were driven off into the hills, the gang would ride the special back to Benalla.

After what seemed an interminable wait, Ned, Joe and party reappeared on horseback about 10 p.m., picked up Curnow's party and set off down the road. Apart from Dave Mortimer, two other young men who lived with the postmaster — one of them the postmaster's son, Alex Reynolds — were in the cavalcade. The outlaws wore light-coloured overcoats and each carried a bundle on the pommel. Curnow was amazed at their bulky appearance.

On approaching the block of government cottages, Ned pulled up in the darkness and dispatched the man with the signal lamp. Then he dismounted and tied his mare to the fence outside the barracks and ordered Mortimer in the gate. Mortimer knocked while Kelly levelled his rifle from behind an angle in the wall, but no reply came despite repeated loud knocking and calling at Kelly's command.

What was wrong? Ned held a brief consultation with Joe; then disappeared down the side with young Reynolds, to return finally, leading the trooper. Bracken had come to the door, shotgun in hand, but had been forced to drop it, and had then dressed while young Reynolds was catching his horse. Ned had warned the trooper's wife that his life depended on her silence.

When he rejoined the party on the road, Kelly put a halter on the policeman's horse. "I can't trust you with a bridle, Bracken," he said.

"If I hadn't been ill in bed all day, you wouldn't have taken me so easily," grumbled Bracken. "If this horse I'm on is what it used to be, it would take more than you to keep me prisoner."

Kelly did not seem willing to contest the claim and again mentioned to Joe that he had expected the special before this. When Curnow asked if he could take his family home, Ned replied, "Yes; go quietly to bed and don't dream too loud. There'll be someone down during the night to see that you're all right."

At last Curnow had his opportunity.

31.   Surrender be Damned!

WHILE CURNOW, keyed up with his resolve to warn the police, returned to his home a few steps down the road, the outlaws conducted the trooper back to the hotel, now crowded with over forty persons. All doors were locked. Ned was more puzzled than ever by the nonarrival of the police train.

Despite the fact that they were well into their second night without sleep, the outlaws were in a jolly mood. Hunted as they had been for so long and cut off from free-and-easy relationships with ordinary people, it was as if their time had come at last for a little fun. Whether their prisoners were friends or enemies made little difference; they were all human beings adrift together for a few hours on a scrap of spinning globe. After the enforced secrecy of so many months, Kelly seemed to want to take everyone into his confidence. Against the forces that had cut him off for so long from the ordinary contacts of peaceful existence, he poured dire and bloodthirsty threats. Yet, with Bracken, stiff-necked and resentful, he was lenient. When Dan wanted to handcuff him to the sofa, he said, "Let him be."

Now the gang brought out their armour forged from the stolen ploughshares, and showed it to the amazed prisoners. The iron was as thick as a dinner plate and had been quilted inside. Kelly declared he would be on the spot when the train ran over the culvert and would shoot all those who were not killed.

Upon request, Mortimer brought out his concertina and drew it apart while someone sang a Scottish reel. Then Mrs Jones offered her son sixpence to sing 'The Wild Colonial Boy', and the defiant spirit of the old convict days lived again amid the shadows cast by the broad fire;

> He took a pistol from his belt
> And waved it like a toy,
> "I'll die but not surrender,"
> Cried the wild colonial boy.

Someone must have the Kelly song. Now come the plaintive words Ned speaks to Kate:

> Farewell to my home in Greta,
> My sister, fare thee well.
> It grieves my heart to leave you,
> But here I must not dwell.

. . . now his complaint against authority:

> They placed a price upon my head,
> My hands are stained with gore,
> And I must roam the forest wild
> Within the Australian shore.

. . . now his threat of vengeance:

> But if they cross my cherished path,
> By all I hold on earth,
> I'll give them cause to rue the day
> Their mothers gave them birth.

. . . and finally, after half-a-dozen stanzas, the parting words of Kate:

> *See yonder ride four troopers —*
> *One kiss before we part.*
> *Now haste and join your comrades — Dan,*
> *Joe Byrne and Stevie Hart.*

Mrs Jones was delighted. Kelly was a darling man, she told prisoners. She wouldn't mind if he stayed a week.

So Sunday wore into Monday, and still there was no sign of the special. Then nothing would do but they have a dance; as Mrs Jones said later, the devil was in them. The chairs were cleared away and Dave Mortimer struck up. They danced a set of quadrille — Ned with Jane, Dan with Mrs Jones, Byrne with one of the menfolk and several other couples joining in. The centre of attention, Ned was laughing and entertained all around him. When he eventually declared he was no dancer and would have to knock off, Mrs Jones encouraged others to get up.

"Something is troubling me besides dancing," said one of the platelayers whose wife and children had had little sleep. Mrs Jones replied, "We will all be let go soon and you can thank me for it."

The rumour went around: the Kellys were sick of waiting for the train and had the idea the police might have got wind of them and be coming from a different direction. Despite the fun, many were longing for a good, sound sleep. One of the prisoners asked Ned if it were true they were going.

"Yes, my boy," said Ned. "We're off directly and when we are gone you can clear out as soon as you like."

It was 2 a.m. when the outlaws commenced preparations to leave. Soon after, Dan entered the parlour and said: "Now you can all go home." The prisoners roused themselves and their families and started to congregate near the door. They were about to leave when Mrs Jones ran up the passage and barred the way. "You are not to go yet," she said, "Kelly is to give you a lecture."

Almost immediately Kelly entered. "Everyone come into the dining room," he said. "I have something to say and want everyone to hear it."

The prisoners crushed after, wondering what was coming. As the outlaw was about to speak he turned to a platelayer whom he heard called Sullivan, and asked him if he had ever been to New Zealand. "Yes," came the reply.

"Are you Sullivan, the murderer?" asked Kelly.

"No, I am not."

Kelly had not attended his Pentridge seminars for nothing! Sullivan had turned Queen's evidence in New Zealand fourteen years before after a series of thirty stranglings; but instead of being hanged along with the three accomplices he had betrayed, was given a Governor's pardon and a ticket to Melbourne.

When the Victorian Government refused to invoke the Criminals' Influx Prevention Act, the people had answered in their own way and shouted his deeds in his face from North Wharf where he landed, to Sandhurst, where 3000 people met the train and hooted him out of town. Bitter because everyone shunned him, he had been given succour by an old deaf Irish woman at Wedderburn who saw his name on a letter and thought he was from Paddy's Land.

The prisoners in the parlour, half-ready to go with their shawls, their babies and their bundles, looked on amazed as Kelly's voice bounced from the walls and the fire flashed from his eyes. If Ned Kelly was a murderer, he said, then Ned Kelly's accusers, who had all the education and wealth to set an example, were the accomplices of murderers, for they had hoodwinked the people and the police of Victoria by spiriting Sullivan off so that now no one knew where he was.

Ned cooled down just as rapidly as he had burst into flame. After a few preliminaries such as mounting a chair and getting off again amid barracking, he began:

> First I wish to tell you that if I should hear any one of you present here tonight telling the police of any of our doings or sayings, or showing the way we left, or in fact, telling anything whatever about us, I shall make it my duty to visit them some day and have a settling with them. And I can promise you it will not be such a settling as I had this day with young Delaney here. I let him off, but by God, I'll not let any more off the same way; so you know what to expect from me if any of you let out any of our plans that you have heard here.
>
> I am not a bit afraid of the police and know if they alone hunted me I would never be taken. But what I'm really afraid of is those damned black trackers. Those boys I honestly fear, for I know what they can do. They can track me over bare stones and a white stands no chance with them at all. It was mainly to kill those bastards that I tore up those rails down there — and in fact, what brought me here. I knew very well when they heard we were down at Beechworth they would pack those incarnate devils after us, and I was prepared to meet them half-way.

I can't make out what has delayed that train, and think they must have taken a different route. But again I don't see how they are to get there, especially as they are not accustomed to the country. No, I think they have got information of our being here and are leaving it till they are positive. Well, anyhow, let them come when they like; we are ready for them even now.

I suppose some of you people would like to know what I have been doing lately, and how I managed to escape capture so long. Well, I don't mind telling you a little. It can't do any harm and it will pass away a few minutes.

Kelly was beginning to enjoy himself and commenced leg-pulling.

A lot of people imagine that after robbing Euroa bank and before sticking up Jerilderie, we were out of funds and had to stick up the Jerilderie bank to supply ourselves. Nothing of the kind! I had no more intention of robbing the Jerilderie bank a fortnight before, than I have now of flying.

What brought us to Jerilderie was this: I was after that infernal scoundrel Sullivan that turned Queen's evidence in New Zealand. I had heard that he came up the North-Eastern, and was told of his being at Rutherglen. I followed him there, but he was too quick for me and had gone on to Uralla. Up to Uralla we went, and found he had gone to Wagga, and there we lost sight of him. We thought he had gone up Hay way from there, but abandoned the chase, and when coming home through Jerilderie . . .

Here the outlaw closely watched his audience . . .

It struck us to stick up the bank, which we did, as you all know.

I don't know how much money we took from either Jerilderie or Euroa, but a considerable deal more than they told in the papers. Anyhow we lost sight of Sullivan, and I would sooner have met him than robbed a dozen banks. I consider him to be one of the greatest villians unhung, and moreover, the first time I come across him the Lord pity him. I won't shoot the hound — it is too good for such as he — but I will hang, draw and quarter him — kill him by inches. I have not given him up yet and will hunt the bastard till I die. I will give five hundred pounds to the man who tells me where he is. I would follow him to England if I knew he was there.

After coming down from Jerilderie I took a trip to Melbourne and bought some firearms — these revolvers and some Winchester rifles—besides as much ammunition as we wanted . . .

Through the still night came the shrill whistle of a train. "By God, that bastard Curnow has deceived us," exclaimed Kelly. At once jumping down from the chair, he disappeared down the passage, rode over to the gatehouse and alerted Steve. In a few minutes he reappeared and told the prisoners, "Yes, Curnow has stopped the train and they're coming here."

The outlaws hurried out to their strange toilet and had no sooner turned their backs than Bracken, who had noted where the key to the front door was hidden, walked over and slipped it in his boot. ' From the rear, the frightened prisoners could hear smothered curses and the knocking of armour, and from the front, the sound of the train steaming into the station and the cries of the officers. Then came the thud of feet towards the back of the inn, at which Bracken unlocked the door and made for the station. Behind him, excitement waxed intense at the clatter of horses being unloaded and the sound of police making their way towards the veranda in whose shadow, cast by the harvest moon, the outlaws were now waiting.

There was silence.

Then, according to one of the more artistic accounts the police cried: "Surrender in the Queen's name!" and, like the Wild Colonial Boy himself, "Surrender be damned," cried the outlaws hitting the muzzles of their revolvers on their iron breasts, "you can shoot for six months and never hurt us!"

32.   A Shambles

THE OUTLAWS had been in possession at Glenrowan twelve hours when Superintendent Hare was disturbed from an after-lunch Havana in the smoking room of the Commercial by a messenger from the telegraph office. Well, well! Poor old Aaron! The Kellys had made a move at last—the very moment the trackers had returned to Melbourne. Hare was expecting a "told you so" but Sadleir was more than usually tactful. Together they went to the telegraph office to communicate with Standish.

The message buzzed along the wire to distant Melbourne, and in due course was delivered by foot messenger through the Sunday streets, but Captain Standish was out. It was not until 4.30 that he read of the murder of Sherritt and Hare's request that O'Connor and the trackers return at once to Beechworth. He immediately ordered his gig and drove to the G.P.O., where he dispatched notes by hansom to O'Connor and Chief Secretary Ramsay, and sent a telegram to Hare. He then returned to the Melbourne Club to find Ramsay waiting. Standish told him he was not certain O'Connor would go. Nevertheless, taking the sanguine view, the two gentlemen left to obtain an order for a special train, and on return, found O'Connor had arrived in the cab which had delivered the note.

O'Connor felt satisfaction to find the Commissioner now forced to ask a favour; while Standish found O'Connor condescending. O'Connor observed he could see no objection to going to Beechworth and would be ready that evening. He asked that the special pick him up at Essendon. So as darkness fell, both gentlemen left — O'Connor for Flemington to prepare his trackers for the journey, and Standish for Spencer Street to order the special.

But when the call was made all engines were cold. Standish had wired Hare to expect the trackers soon after midnight; but it was not till 10.15 p.m. that the train with five reporters aboard steamed out of Spencer Street. O'Connor and his wife and sister, in holiday mood, climbed aboard with the trackers at Essendon. Luckily for the occupants, as things were to turn out, a further delay of half an hour ensued when the train crashed through the crossing gates at Craigieburn and damaged its brakes. It was not until 1.30 a.m. that they arrived in Benalla.

Hare was waiting at the station with eight men and seventeen horses, and as the horses were being boxed a consultation was held and more time was lost. Perhaps someone remembered Kelly's threat to blow up the line, for it was suggested the gang had been at work with dynamite between Benalla and Beechworth. As the moon was shining brightly, Hare proposed a constable be strapped to the brass handrail near the front of the engine. But this plan was abandoned for a better one. The engine from Melbourne was sent ahead as pilot, and a second engine which Hare had under steam in case the special was further delayed, was hooked to the carriages and ordered to follow closely behind. With Inspector O'Connor and Superintendent Hare to entertain the ladies in one compartment, the reporters in another and the trackers in a third, the train was to proceed at full steam to Wangaratta, where a short stop would be made before turning off to Beechworth, forty-two kilometres further on.

As pilot engine and special steamed towards Glenrowan, Curnow was having trouble with his wife and sister. They had no sooner left the outlaws than he announced his intention of going to Benalla, but the women were anxious. They said it was unlikely that they would be allowed to return home unless some agent of the gang were watching. If he attempted to reach Benalla he would be shot on the road by spies, and if his plan succeeded he would be hunted out and shot. The discussion continued as supper was prepared, and the women became more alarmed as Curnow quietly collected candle, matches and his sister's red llama-wool scarf. Eventually, he offered to take them all to Mrs Curnow's mother's farm nearby and his sister consented. But Mrs Curnow worked herself into a pitch, declaring that if he went she would stay there and the three of them would be murdered.

At last she consented to go along. Curnow left the doors unlocked and a note on the table stating where they had gone and why; Mrs Curnow was ill and needed medicine. So they left, with Miss Curnow wearing the red scarf at her brother's request. However, the farm was no sooner reached than Mrs Curnow's fears broke out afresh and she wanted to return home.

Curnow scratched his head and tried another tack; he said he had given up going to Benalla. Immediately, Mrs Curnow quietened down and when they arrived home, she went to bed. While Miss Curnow engaged her attention, Curnow went outside to harness his horse. Hearing a noise in the distance which he recognised as the train, he grabbed buggy lamp, matches and scarf and ran for the line. He reached a straight stretch, lit the lamp and held the scarf in front of it.

The pilot engine slowed down, the van drew level and the guard called out, "What's the matter?"

"The Kellys," cried Curnow.

The engine groaned to a halt with a shrill blast of the whistle to warn the special, and the guard, jumping down, rushed over to him.

"The line has been torn up half a mile past the station, and the Kelly gang is lying in wait at the Glenrowan Inn," said Curnow.

"We'll take the train to the station, then stop."

"No, no, don't do that or you'll get shot."

"All right, I'll go back and stop the special. Who are you, anyway?"

"I'm the schoolteacher. My name's Curnow. Don't let anyone know who warned you; I'm doing this at the risk of my life."

"All right, I'll keep your name secret. Jump in the van."

"No, I can't; I've got to get back. My wife and sister are without protection."

From the moment it had pulled up, the pilot engine had been

sending warning blasts along the colonnade of trees bordering the line so that when Curnow reached home he found his wife almost out of her mind. Five minutes before, a man had come to the door and they had been terrified until they realised that he was a stranger just arrived in Glenrowan. When Curnow suggested they go outside and hide, Mrs Curnow refused to budge, so Curnow blew out the lights, hid the scarf and his clothes, which were wet from the long grass, and got ready to deny he knew anything about the stopping of the train.

The mixed party of twenty-three aboard the special had scarcely settled down after Benalla when they were startled by the blasts from ahead. They stuck their heads out of the windows and saw a red light waving from the pilot engine; then the special jerked to a standstill. Hare tried to get out, but had to cool his heels while one of the reporters climbed out the window to get the key from the guard; then he seized a rifle, clambered down and stumbled forward. The guard recounted what had occurred and explained that the schoolmaster had refused to stop, saying he must return to his wife. Hare received the news that the Kellys were in Glenrowan with suspicion; and as it was not clear where the line had been pulled up, he ordered the trains to be coupled together and the troopers to ride on the engines.

As the trains steamed up to the platform, the pressmen extinguished the light and piled the seat squabs against the windows to stop stray bullets; they realised they were on the edge of sensational developments. The railway buildings stood out clearly but were in total darkness and the other buildings lay in the shadows. Hare gave the order, and troopers, trackers and pressmen rapidly climbed out while O'Connor reassured the ladies. Not a soul was to be seen.

"The schoolmaster might be right," said Hare. Seeing a light at the gatehouse, he hurried down and tapped on the window. Mrs Stanistreet could be seen in the glow of the candle sitting up in bed with her children and the bedclothes huddled around her.

"Who's there?" she called.

"The police; where is your husband?"

Mrs Stanistreet opened the window, but Hare could get nothing further from her. "My good woman, do calm yourself and answer me; I will see no harm will come to you."

Mrs Stanistreet eventually pointed to Morgan's Lookout and to the inn, and Hare said, "Who took him away?"

"The Kellys."

"How long ago?"

He learned that Hart and another man had disappeared with

the stationmaster perhaps ten minutes before. Hare returned to the station and had barely given the order to unload the horses when he heard his name called and Bracken climbed on to the platform, pointed to the inn and told him if he didn't go immediately the outlaws would be gone. Hare shouted, "Come on boys," and started to run.

"What shall I do with the horses?" cried one of the troopers.

"Let them go. Come on men; they will be gone."

Two men followed him; those with the horses could not find their weapons immediately and straggled after across the broken ground.

In his excitement, Bracken had failed to mention that the inn was packed with innocent people, and police accounts as to who opened fire are contradictory.

Hare claimed that before the outlaws disappeared and he gave the order to stop firing, his men fired fifty or sixty shots and the outlaws thirty or forty. He said he was close to the inn when he saw the flash of a rifle and felt his left hand go limp, after which three flashes followed from the veranda. The man who had first fired then stepped back and began to fire again. A voice cried, "Fire away you beggars, you can do us no harm," and a trooper by his side said, "That is the voice of Ned Kelly."

Kelly claimed he arrived opposite the station as the train drew in and was dismounting to bail up the police when a bolt in his armour failed; by the time he had adjusted it the police were firing into the inn. Hearing screams, he thought they came from Mrs Stanistreet and that Hart had been cornered, and he was half-way between the gatehouse and inn when he received a bullet in the foot, and immediately after, another in the left arm. It was only then, he declared, at the third volley, that he and his mates replied to police fire. As the armour required him to hold his rifle at arm's length to get anything of a sight and his arm was smashed, he fired at random at the flashes through the wraiths of gunpowder smoke drifting across the field — two shots to the front and two to the left.

By now he was close to the hotel from which echoed the crash of bullets and the screams of women and children. People were running to and fro past the lighted windows. He shouted, "Put out the lights and lie down!"

He walked towards the back door. There was someone nearby in the darkness. "Is that you, Joe?" he asked.

"Yes. Is that you, Ned? — Come here!"

"Come here be damned! What are you doing there? Come here and load my rifle. I'm cooked!"

"So am I. I think my leg is broke."

"Leg be damned—you've got the use of your arms. Come on, I'll pink the beggars."

"I'm afraid it's a case with us this time."

"Don't be so excited. The boys will hear us and it will dishearten them."

"Well, it's your fault. I always said this bloody armour would bring us to grief."

"Don't you believe it. Old Hare is cooked and we'll soon finish the rest."

What was that?

Through the gloom appeared Dan and Steve. Ned sent them inside and Joe followed. They clanked up the passage. As the bullets hummed off their armour, they pulled up the bar counter and partitions, barricaded the walls, and cursed the police. To the prisoners Byrne seemed completely reckless—as though he did not care whether he lived or died.

It was a shambles. In the front foom were thirty-five people, most of whom were lying face down on the floor. The women were screaming, children were whimpering, some cried out to the police to stop firing, many were praying, one young fellow exhausted by long hours of excitement lay snoring on his back. Someone suggested rushing to the door and calling on the police to hold their fire. Someone else suggested borrowing arms from the Kellys and retaliating.

"You are better off where you are," cried Byrne.

George Medcalf lay in the parlour, a bullet through the eye. From the back room came screams of agony from young Johnny Jones as he lay bleeding from the mouth with a bullet through his belly, and the cries of Mrs Jones asking the menfolk to help shift him. At last an old labourer called Martin Cherry rose and helped her.

Then Jane—no revolver now—but with a candle, appeared in the front room. "All women and children are to come out," she said. The women roused their little ones and a large party ran out the back door and down the Wangaratta side of the house. They were about to cross the drain close to the gatehouse when a voice from under a culvert cried, "Who comes there?"

"Women and children," they answered.

A fusillade of shots passed their faces and they broke and turned and made their way back to the hotel. It was apparent that the police, unused to battle and schooled in dread of the outlaws, would fire in panic at anything on two legs.

But Johnny Jones had got through on the back of Neil McHugh. The rest had to lie down again on the floor while the bullets continued to drum through the walls. A shot hit the clock on the mantelpiece and set it striking. It struck a hundred times before another laid it on the floor in pieces. Now a bullet wounded Jane in the stomach.

Every now and then the outlaws went to a door or window or into the open to fire; but for the most part they stood in the passage or kept to the room they used as an armoury. They began to call out for Ned.

What had happened? Soon after Ned had sent them inside one of the prisoners heard him cry, "Come on, boys, follow me!" Did he want them to go out shooting? Did he intend them to escape? Kelly said later that he set out to get help from some of his mates who were waiting outside the perimeter of battle.

Constable Gascoigne claimed that the battle had been in progress for about ten minutes when Ned came out again towards the railway, exchanged shots with him and called out, "You bloody cocktails can't hurt me; I'm in iron," before he disappeared in the smoke. From Gascoigne, perhaps, Ned received a bullet through the right thumb preventing him from cocking the revolving rifle he had kept from Stringybark and thus from breaching the police cordon — in which event the course of the battle might have proved different. The Greta Mob probably saw the exchange with Gascoigne, for it was at this time that two rockets went up behind McDonnell's Hotel, summoning from afar eyes already turned towards Glenrowan by the sound of rifle fire. In the hours remaining before dawn there would be much galloping over the bright, tree-shadowed hills between Glenrowan and Greta.

33. Death of Byrne

During his career in the Victorian police force, no one had ever laid a hand on Hare — why, he didn't waste time trying to discover. In fact, Francis Augustus Hare had been lucky all his life, and now, by the sheer cussedness of fate, after less than a month in charge, he had defied all Grandma Nicolson's fears and cornered the gang. But a bullet had pierced his wrist, he had uttered the famous words, "Good gracious, I'm shot!", and had turned back. He reached the station just as Constable Bracken clattered off along the sleepers to summon help in Wangaratta; but the reporters tied a tourniquet on the wrong side of the wound, so that when he attempted to return to the battlefield he was unable to climb through the post-and-rail fence.

"Poor Mr Hare," said the ladies as they watched him being assisted on to the platform. They opened their picnic hamper and handed him some sherry through the window, while the reporters urged him to return to Benalla for medical aid and to rouse the men at the barracks. The train was ordered and shunted a short distance towards Wangaratta, then reversed and disappeared rapidly with the ladies, so that the pilot engine had to pick up Hare and chase after it.

This comedy had scarcely ended when a man walked boldly from the hotel. Immediately he was challenged he shouted, "Stanistreet, stationmaster!" He came over and told Senior Constable Kelly, whom Hare had left in charge, about the situation at the inn. Shortly after, Neil McHugh turned up with the dying Johnny Jones in his arms and said there were thirty people in the hotel. He added soon afterwards, "For God's sake, don't go near the hotel as they intend shooting you all in the morning; they are in armour," and as a result, some of the troopers envisaged thirty desperate men preparing to sally forth and attack them.

After the first exchange of fifteen minutes before, the fire had become desultory and the people in the hotel had quietened down. Thin high cloud blurred the edge of the moon. Senior Constable Kelly placed his men; then set out to reconnoitre, taking with him his best bushman, Constable Arthur, who had escorted Ned to Beechworth the time Hall had beaten his skull with a revolver. They crawled behind what shelter they could find, making for the base of Morgan's Lookout to the right of the hotel, and kneeled beside a tree. Arthur found his hand resting on what proved to be a revolving rifle. It was wet and sticky, and close beside it was a knitted skull cap. Arthur was so startled he could not speak; the rifle was covered in blood. Hearing a curious ringing sound, the troopers listened, but in the absence of anything further, returned to the station, where Senior Constable Kelly told the reporters he feared one of the outlaws had escaped. For a time, everything was quiet, and the police lay on the ground trying to keep warm and listening to the horses as they whinnied and moved uneasily behind the hotel.

This was the hour, when, if the outlaws wanted to retreat, they could have done so. Their mounts were saddled and ready, the police cordon was thin and extended along two sides only, and they had plenty of friends across the line. But they merely called for their wounded leader and discussed what they should do as they stood in the passage in their sombre iron. No doubt, with the weight of steel added to the accumulated tiredness of more than three days and nights of nonstop activity, some of the gloom of their sixteen hunted months had come over them again. A prisoner asked where Ned was. "He's gone," replied one. "I suppose he's done for." When advised to surrender, Byrne replied, "We will never surrender, but most likely we will leave directly."

About this time a disturbance was heard at the rear of the inn. Having been driven back by Constable Gascoigne, Ned, perhaps, was still intent on getting help at McDonnell's, for a figure was seen to move amongst the horses and attempt to mount, and an animal reared and broke through the sliprails into the bush on the Benalla side. By now, Senior Constable Kelly had returned to his former position, accompanied by Constables Arthur and Phillips.

At Wangaratta, meanwhile, Steve Hart's old enemy, Sergeant Arthur Loftus Maul Steele, finding the special to Beechworth was overdue, had taken a walk down the railway track towards Glenrowan and heard the faint sound of volley firing. Soon afterwards, Bracken had appeared and told him amongst other news that the outlaws were wearing tin cans on their heads. Steele took five men and galloped nonstop to join Senior Constable Kelly. He suggested to Kelly and his men that they get closer to the inn, while he himself took up a position behind a tree about ten metres from the back door.

Half an hour passed. Then a train could be heard approaching from the direction of Benalla and a commotion commenced in the inn accompanied by talking and the rattling of iron plates. When Sadleir climbed out of the train accompanied by nine men and a doctor, two volleys fired at rapid pace came from the front veranda. When the balls tore up the dirt, it occurred to the doctor that the fire was random, but the troopers replied with hot fire.

Events were now to occur which threw a curious light on police concern for civilians and in particular on the enthusiast, Steele, whose spiritual home was the scullery of Buckingham Palace. It must have been obvious that, with the force of police doubled, the fire would become heavier, so the prisoners decided to make another attempt to leave. Mrs Reardon spoke to the outlaws as they stood in the passage. "Yes, you can go," said one, "but the police will shoot you. Ten to one they'll take you for one of us."

A prisoner put a white handkerchief out of the window. Immediately three shots struck it and he threw himself on the floor. When things grew quiet, a party of a dozen, mostly children, gathered at the back door. Dan spoke to Mrs Reardon. "If you escape . . ."

"What shall I do?" she asked.

"See Hare, tell him to keep his men from shooting till daylight to allow all these people to get out, and that we shall fight for ourselves."

When the party ran out, fire blazed from all directions. Reardon distinctly saw O'Connor pop his head out of the drain and shout, "Who comes there?" and they were forced back into the inn.

"I wish to heaven we were out of this," said Mrs Reardon.

Dan said, "Mrs Reardon, put the children out and make them scream, and scream yourself."

Mrs Reardon went outside with her baby girl and called to the police to have mercy. "I am only a woman," she cried. "Allow me to escape with my children. The outlaws will not interfere with us — do not you."

The moon was setting. She could see men behind the trees. A voice said, "Put up your hands and come this way or I'll shoot you like bloody dogs." It was Sergeant Steele.

She tucked her baby under one arm, held up the other, and ran forward followed by her nineteen-year-old son leading his younger brother, and by her husband leading the two young ones. "Let my husband come with me," she cried.

Steele fired and immediately flashes followed from the police in front of the hotel.

"Mother, come back or you will be killed," cried young Reardon, turning back.

"I will not be back. I may as well be shot outside as inside. I don't think the coward can shoot me!" Steele had his rifle pointed at her.

"Don't shoot; can't you see it's a woman with a child in her arms?" cried Constable Arthur.

Mrs Reardon felt the concussion of a bullet on her arm and screamed, "Oh, you have shot my baby!" while Arthur cried angrily to Steele, "If you fire again I'll bloody well shoot you!"

Steele, apparently mistaking Mrs Reardon for Mrs Jones, said excitedly as though it were a feather in his cap, "I've shot Mother Jones in the bum!" He turned his gun towards Reardon and his son who were returning again to the inn with the children, and cried, "Throw up your hands!" Young Reardon lifted his free hand over his head and his father threw himself to the ground. Steele fired, and fired again. Young Reardon threw up his arms and screamed, bullet through the shoulder, and fell against the doorpost. "I've wounded Dan Kelly," cried Steele.

The people in the inn pulled the wounded lad inside, while the father, child on each hand, crept into the back room and put the children between his legs. A bullet scraped the breast of his coat, passed the faces of two other men and embedded itself in the sofa. In the passage, the outlaws, rifle butts on the floor, had been holding their fire. Byrne entered the back room and asked how everyone was. Several appealed to him to get them out, but he replied, "Stop where you are; you are a great deal better off than we are," then marched up to the bar and had just poured himself a nobbler of whisky when he received a bullet in the femoral artery through the gap of his armour.

"Many more years in the bush for the Kelly gang," he cried, and turning around twice, fell to the floor with a clang, the blood gushing from his groin.

Mrs Jones redoubled the abuse she had been hurling at the police. Above the crack of rifles her voice could be heard screaming, "Murderers! Ned Kelly is good enough for any of you murderers!"

Soon too could be heard the voices of Dan and Steve calling again for their absent leader. When they passed into the armoury, Reardon heard one ask the other, "What shall we do?"

Mrs Reardon, meanwhile, had hidden behind a tree. As she lay on the ground, four or five bullets whizzed past her head, and then a railway guard named Dowsett crept up, calling softly, and helped her to the station. She had scarcely discovered that Steele's bullet had passed through the shawl leaving the baby unharmed when she was pounced on by reporters.

Dowsett returned to the inn and took up a position between Senior Constable Kelly and Sergeant Steele. As the outlaws were now firing rapidly from the rear window, he feared an attempt to escape, so called out, "Why not shoot the horses!" One by one they picked them off and the mounts screamed and plunged, filling the glen with horror.

At last, for the first time in three long hours of battle, the officer in charge attempted to ensure that the innocent civilians in the inn should not be struck by more bullets than could be helped. Sadleir gave Constable Dwyer instructions for the men: No fire until one blast of the whistle—two blasts, cease fire—fire to be directed above the height of a man's head—civilians to go unmolested if they approach. He then put his head over the edge of the drain where he stood with O'Connor and called out, "All you innocent people throw yourselves flat on the ground and you will not be shot."

Something like a titter was heard among the police as they watched Dwyer pass from post to post. His progress comprised a series of short dashes, sudden halts and strange, nervous leaps, by which, he explained, he was clearing the bullets. Senior Constable Kelly remarked to Steele, "You should see O'Connor down the drain; if you gave him a thousand pounds he wouldn't stick his head up!"

So the battle drifted as spinelessly as any before or since — Dan and Steve relishing neither escape nor surrender, fearing that Ned as well as Joe had been killed, and the police, still awed by the fabulous name of Kelly, waiting for daylight, the arrival of new reinforcements, or some plan from their leaders.

34. The Bunyip

DAWN CAME clear and beautiful, with frost on the ground and smoke from the guns curling over the field and mixing with the fog. The glen lay in the shadow, and the sun had scarcely turned golden the top of Morgan's Lookout when everyone's attention was attracted to a disturbance in the bush on the Wangaratta side of the hotel. Constable Arthur was lighting his pipe when he heard someone behind him. He turned, and the sight so surprised him he let it drop from his mouth. Advancing through the light timber from the Lookout was a figure dressed in a grey cotton coat reaching past the knees. Most extraordinary of all was the head. Arthur goggled for some seconds before he concluded it was some madman who had conceived the notion of storming the hotel with a nailcan on his head. "Go back you damn fool; you'll get shot," he shouted.

The apparition, no more than thirty metres off, replied "I could shoot you, sonny;" no sooner said than he lifted a revolver, placed it across his forearm and fired. The bullet went wide. Someone pointed towards the figure and shouted, "Look at this!" With big head and shoulders looming through the mists of dawn it looked like a huge blackfellow wrapped in a blanket.

"Challenge him and if he does not answer you, shoot!" cried Senior Constable Kelly.

Arthur lifted his Martini and fired at the helmet, thinking to knock it off. The figure no more than staggered and continued to advance, slowly putting one foot forward after the other with a macabre lurching motion and edging towards the rear of the inn. An opening in the helmet looked like a huge mouth so Arthur fired a second shot. The figure staggered again but still came on. He fired again and heard the bullet spin off.

Amazed cries came from the other men. Someone shouted, "It's a ghost!"

Dowsett exclaimed, "It's old Nick himself!" Senior Constable Kelly shouted, "Look out, boys, it's the bunyip. He's bullet-proof!"

Ned had been lying on the rising ground in sight of the inn, exhausted and bleeding in his cold mountain of iron, with who knows what thoughts, what bitterness racking him. Earlier, he had been close to the tree when Arthur had found his revolving rifle and had refrained from shooting Steele in the back. Tom Lloyd had found him and helped him to adjust his armour. Now, feeling somewhat revived, he was out to join his brother and Steve or die in the attempt. He rapped on his breastplate with the butt of his revolver to summon them, and Dan and Steve came to the rear and commenced firing. "Come out, boys, and we'll whip the lot of them," he cried, his voice echoing loud from behind the visor.

The police poured bullets at him. Arthur fired, Phillips fired, Healy discharged both barrels of his shotgun. A chorus of shots broke out from all over the ground. Those who could not see the outlaw fired into the inn from which the screams of the women broke afresh. Ned, in spite of wounds to his foot, arm and right hand, continued to advance, laughing derisively, bearing his great weight of iron, staggering under the impact of the shots, and firing deliberately but without accuracy at the inner ring of the police.

Arthur, in the centre and closest to the outlaw, fell back some metres to better cover. The others on each flank pressed in, while Ned squatted in a clump of saplings to reload and rest. Dowsett moved in from tree to tree and got behind a log a little to the right of the outlaw's path. Steele moved in on the left flank. Dowsett yelled to Senior Constable Kelly, "Come over here and you can get a shot at him"; and Senior Constable Kelly advanced to join Dowsett and fired twice at the outlaw's hand which projected from behind a tree.

Then Ned rose, fired deliberately at Steele who was wiping from his eyes dirt flung by a bullet from the hotel, and headed towards Dowsett. He had approached within fifteen metres when the railway guard cried, "You'd better surrender, old man, you're surrounded."

"Never, while I have a shot left," replied Kelly.

"How do you like that?" asked Dowsett, cocking a revolver over the log and firing at his helmet. The bullet bounded off like a parched pea.

Kelly levelled his revolver over his wounded arm, fired and countered, "How do you like that?"

But he could not hold his gun level and the bullet tore the turf in front of the log.

As though to warn of danger, the outlaw's grey mare passed by a few metres to the rear, and Kelly turned to find Steele advancing at a run, swinging his gun as if to club him. He tried to bring his revolver to bear. Steele fired at his knees, and he staggered back a yard. At point blank range, Steele fired a second time, scoring his hand and hip with a charge of swanshot.

The outlaw tottered. His voice boomed under the helmet. "I'm done, I'm done!" He could sustain the weight of armour no longer. He sank on to his haunches, then fell back against the log, fifty metres from Dan and Steve, who had now advanced into the yard.

Steele and Dowsett were on him in a flash. Even as he fell he struggled to bring his revolver to bear, but they seized his arm and the discharge merely blew Steele's cap off. As they grabbed the weapon, blood spurted from his shot-peppered hand and a voice rumbled from under the helmet, "Steady, do not break my fingers." At that moment, Senior Constable Kelly landed on his shoulders and wrenched his helmet off and Steele seized him by the beard and throat. Wild and wasted, the outlaw cursed the Englishman with hate.

"It's Ned Kelly," cried Senior Constable Kelly.

Cried Steele, "You bloody wretch; I swore I'd be in at your death." He drew back his hand to shoot.

"Take him alive," cried Dowsett.

"You shall not shoot the man," cried Constable Bracken, leaping the log and seizing Steele by the wrist.

"Let me live as long as I can," Kelly said.

Half a dozen pairs of hands held the outlaw down. Dwyer, who had been leaping the bullets shortly before, rushed up with a war-whoop and kicked him in the groin; then hopped away cursing and rubbing his shin where it had caught the edge of Kelly's steel apron. Bullets from the rear of the hotel reminded the police the fight was not yet over, and they picked up their rifles and let fly with a volley which splintered the post-and-rail and tore the slabs around the door. "Fire away you bastards; you can't kill us," cried Dan and Steve as they retreated inside.

A cluster of officials had joined the troopers around the fallen outlaw and already the spate of questions which were to be asked him until the final hour of his life had begun. Where was Kennedy's watch? He did not care to say.

"Leave him alone," said Sadleir, who then inquired if he could get his mates to surrender.

"It's no use trying; they are now quite desperate," Ned answered.

Steele and Senior Constable Kelly unscrewed the fastenings and cut the straps and wire which held the armour together. Dr Nicholson, who two years earlier had treated Fitzpatrick's wrist, helped them remove the plates from the outlaw's body. Kelly was then carried to the station and laid in a room under a guard of six troopers.

By now, hundreds of people had collected—locals, railway officials from Benalla and Wangaratta, farmers who had ridden in from the surrounding hills. They pressed around the door. Inside, the outlaw lay bloodless and wasted, hair and beard matted with sweat, hands tied and blood-covered, conversing with one or other of his captors in a calm matter-of-fact way in a tired voice. Dr Nicholson examined and dressed his wounds.

It was soon found he was utterly disabled. He had bullet wounds in the right leg, left foot and arm, and two in the region of the groin, and his thigh and hands were badly mauled by swanshot. Dressed in buff whipcord trousers and waistcoat and a slate-coloured coat of cross-barred pattern, he wore an ordinary workman's Crimean shirt of white flannel with large black dots. When the doctor wished to treat his foot he was forced to slit the riding boot and particularly noted the fine quality leather, thin soles and high heels. The outlaw wore them without socks; apparently he was proud of his neat feet.

Exhausted though he might be, and on the edge of death, Kelly had now to go through an experience most of the great or fraudulent of the earth have to submit to at one time or another—he was interviewed by the press. Every word which fell from his lips was hurriedly taken down in notebooks to be worked into stories for newspapers in whatever part of the world the name of Kelly was known. He answered briefly and sometimes not at all.

"What I intended to do, and in fact was just about doing," he said, "was to go down with some of my mates and meet the special train and rake it with shot. The train, however, came before I expected, and I had to return to the hotel. I thought the train would go on, and on that account I had the rails pulled up so that these bloody black trackers might be settled."

"Then you must have wanted to kill the people in the train," said one of the police.

"Yes, of course I did. God help them, they would have got shot all the same. Would they not have tried to kill me?"

One of the reporters asked him what brought him to Glenrowan.

"It does not much matter what brought me to Glenrowan. I do not know or I do not say. It does not seem much anyway."

"Why didn't you make your escape?"

"If I liked I could have. I got into the bush with my grey mare and lay there all night. I had a good chance but I wanted to see the thing end. When the police fired the first round I got wounded in the foot. Shortly afterwards I was shot in the left arm in front of the house."

"Are you aware that people say you tied Kennedy to a tree before you killed him in cold blood and that you shot Scanlon while he was kneeling?"

"I don't care what people say about Kennedy's death. I have made my statements as to it and if they don't believe me I can't help it. At all events I'm satisfied Scanlon was not shot kneeling; that is not true as he never got off his horse."

"Were you the one who shot Hare in the wrist?"

"At the commencement of the affair this morning I fired three or four shots from the front of the hotel, but I don't know who I was firing at. I only fired when I saw flashes. I then cleared for the bush. Two constables passed close by me talking, and I could have shot them before they had time to shout if I liked. I could have shot several constables at one time. Why don't the police use bullets instead of duckshot?"

"What was it like when the bullets struck your armour?"

"Just like blows from a man's fist. One of the policemen firing at me was a splendid shot; I don't know his name."

Evidently Kelly had not been able to recognise his old friend, Constable Arthur; and so the talk went on until the pressmen thought they had sufficient to satisfy their editors. The outlaw was then left alone with his guards and Sadleir, who appeared to have forgotten he was in charge of a battle and lounged before the fire cutting tobacco and smoking.

Then Dwyer, who had been acting as Sadleir's runner throughout the morning, entered with the remains of a bottle of brandy. A spark shot into the outlaw's eye and he lifted his head. "You cowardly dog; you kicked me when I was down."

"You are the cowardly dog," said Dwyer uneasily. "You killed my poor comrade."

"Who was your comrade?"

"Poor Lonigan."

"Dwyer lost his temper; that's all there is to it," interposed Sadleir.

"Look, old man, when you were out there did you not try to shoot me?"

"No," replied Dwyer.

"Then you had no business there. What's your name?"

"Dwyer."

"Where are you from?" Bloodless and worn, yet the old note of

184

power was in the voice.

"That is no matter to you."

Kelly grunted.

"You are right; you do not matter to me!"

He lay back, interested in the conversation no longer, eyeing the bottle in the policeman's hand.

"Will you have a drink of brandy?"

"Yes, please, if you'll give me one."

"Why wouldn't I?"

"Put it to my lips. My hands are tied."

Dwyer emptied the bottle into the nobbler and held it to the outlaw's lips. He swallowed it eagerly. Drops fell from his lower lip and he sucked the spirit from his beard.

"Give me a bit of bread, I'm hungry."

Sadleir spoke: "Go, Dwyer, and see if you can get him a bit of bread."

Dwyer turned to the door. Kelly still sucked his beard.

"Fetch another bottle of brandy," said Sadleir.

The peppering of police rifles sounded in the door and the first rays of the sun struck in on to the far wall through the small high window. Kelly regarded the bound wrists that life had brought him—Sadleir also, who for so long had hunted him.

Dwyer entered. "Here you are," he said. Sadleir took the brandy and filled the nobbler. He raised the outlaw's head, arranged the pillow under it, and put the glass to the outlaw's lips. Then Kelly ate the new-baked scone which Dwyer had brought him. Perhaps now as his jaws worked he felt the hostile world beyond the border had its kindness, too, that he had forgotten in many months.

"Thank you, Mr Sadleir," he said. "This is more kindness than I ever thought to get."

"You shall have every care and attention, Ned, don't fret. Just keep yourself quiet."

The noise of the shooting and the cries of the growing crowd came in. Sadleir spoke again: "Ned, the fate of the other two men is certain. Do you think if you sent a message to them they would surrender?"

It was some seconds before Kelly answered.

"They will not mind what I say," he observed wearily. "The heart's gone out of them. They won't come out fighting like men . . . they're only boys . . . they'll stay in there until they're finished . . .

"Yes, when I saw Byrne my best friend fall, from my place in the bushes up there, the heart went out of me too."

35. Enter Dean Gibney

NOT EVEN ARGUS with his hundred eyes could have foreseen the disruptive effect of Armstrong's cowardice, and that of his men, on the outlaws' plans. Now, with the police team dominating the field, the surviving captain and coach were set to immolate the remaining opposition and cut the goalposts down.

Shortly before Kelly was taken, twenty troopers arrived from Beechworth and Benalla, almost doubling the winning side. For two hours during which their captain attended the outlaw chief and smoked plug before the fire, the team stood about, hands in pockets and breech-loaders against the trees, looking occasionally towards the station as though expecting the second advent. The crowd was finding things slow. Finally about 10 a.m. Sadleir withdrew from the fascinating company of the outlaw and ran out determined to get the spectators off the ground so the game could proceed in the traditional manner.

Inside the hotel the prisoners could hear someone calling from the drain. It was Sadleir saying they would be given ten minutes to leave. After earlier experiences some were terrified at the idea. Argument waxed high. Then one of the railwaymen cried, "Well, we may as well be shot outside as in, and I for one am going." So saying, he opened the door and made for a hollow in front of the hotel.

The rest soon followed and were called on to lie down and hold up their hands. A couple of unfortunates ran too far and jumped fairly into the middle of O'Connor's trackers who immediately cocked guns to their ears. They explained vehemently they were not bushrangers and appealed to O'Connor who ordered them back to join the men, women and children who were now lying on the ground under the police guns, in mortal fear lest firing break out afresh.

One by one the prisoners were questioned by Sadleir and O'Connor. Delaney and the two young McAuliffes were handcuffed on suspicion of being Kelly sympathisers, and Reardon junior was taken to the station for medical treatment. The others were left to their own devices, to be interviewed by reporters and given something to eat. From them it was learned that Byrne had been killed and that old Martin Cherry had received a bullet in the groin and was sitting behind a sack of oats in the back room.

But the battle could not be delayed for one wounded old Irishman and the order to fire high was revoked. The prisoners had no sooner been herded off the field than fifty police commenced firing, the fire starting at one end of the cordon and circling the hotel. Whenever Dan or Steve appeared, there was the crack and whine of many bullets.

The firing was still heavy when the noon train arrived from Melbourne carrying many passengers, chief among whom was the Very Reverend Dean Gibney, Vicar-General of the Catholic Church of Western Australia. He had been in Benalla on his way to Albury when told that Kelly had been taken and was gravely wounded. He had inquired if there was a priest at Glenrowan, and being told there was not, decided to stop off there.

Because of the press of people around the room where Kelly lay, Dean Gibney found himself unable to get near; but after making inquiries he met Dr Nicholson, who told him the outlaw was very low, and arranged for him to go in.

The Dean spent the best part of an hour in the room and called Nicholson in several times to ease the outlaw, who was in a fainting condition. He asked Kelly if it would be safe for him to approach the hotel and get Dan to surrender. "I would not advise you to go; they would certainly shoot you," was the reply.

"They would not shoot me if they knew I was a priest."

"They will not know who you are and they will not take time to think."

Dean Gibney had the room cleared and prepared the outlaw for his last hour. He found him penitent, and when he asked him to say "Lord Jesus, have mercy on me," Kelly repeated the words most reverently and added, "It is not today I began to say that." The Dean heard his confession, and after anointing him, proceeded outside. He had scarcely left when he heard people saying the outlaw was cursing and swearing. He said to himself, "My labour is lost if such is the case." He made his way back and asked the trooper in charge if Kelly had been making use of bad language. The trooper replied, "No." He asked Kelly himself and Kelly said, "No." He went outside and challenged the parties. "The man is bad enough without you repeating lies about him," he remarked. But the damage was done; the reporters had already heard the rumours.

Dean Gibney then watched the storming party at work. The fire was desultory now, and most were of the opinion the outlaws had retreated behind the chimney into the safest corner of the building to wait until darkness to escape. How to bring matters to a climax was Sadleir's preoccupation. He did not wish to rush the place for fear lives would be sacrificed; but to continue firing was a waste of ammunition.

The problem had occurred to him earlier in the day. Shortly after Dr Nicholson dressed Ned's wounds, Sadleir had asked if he thought he was justified in making a rush on the hotel. Nicholson said no, the day was young, and it would be better to wait as there was no possibility of escape. "It is a pity we have not a small cannon with us. It would make them give in pretty quick, as their armour would be no protection to them, and the chimney would be knocked about their ears."

Sadleir had replied that Captain Standish was starting from Melbourne, so he would immediately send him a telegram.

As if 2000 bullets and fifty troopers were not enough to suppress two teenagers! But if Glenrowan could show imagination, so could Melbourne. Colonel Anderson, Commandant of Garrison Artillery, had no sooner received a request from Standish for a small cannon than he wired for particulars of the building. Sadleir wired back, "Weatherboard, brick chimney, slab kitchen. The difficulty we feel is that our shots have no effect on the corner, and there are so many windows that we should be under fire all day. We must get the gun before night or rush the place."

Colonel Anderson gave orders. A twelve-pounder field piece and sufficient ammunition to knock a hole in a fortified city was dragged down Collins Street. At 2.20 p.m. Lieutenant Nicholson and detachment set off from Spencer Street by special train, the gun behind in a truck, with order to proceed at the scheduled speed of sixty-four kilometres an hour to reach the scene before nightfall.

In addition, the Colonial Secretary advised Sadleir by telegram that a wooden bullet-proof shield should be constructed to be fitted on a dray or wagon, under cover of which the gun crew might approach sufficiently close to the building to ensure its destruction by a broadside. Chief Secretary Ramsay was willing to go still further to ensure success. Fearing darkness might set in before the cannon could be brought to bear, he communicated with Professor Ellery, government astronomer of the colony, asking his advice as to the practicability of sending an electric light apparatus to the seat of war. But the professor replied that even if the apparatus were placed on the ground it would take quite twenty-four hours to get it in working order.

So Mr Ramsay advised by wire that huge bonfires be lit as night set in to prevent escape and to show clearly to the gunner the object at which he should aim. It is creditable to the mind which could plan so destructive an attack that it should also instruct that care be taken to ensure that the only occupants of the building were members of the gang.

While the station telegraph was ticking out messages to and from headquarters, the officers in charge of the attacking party were finding themselves greatly embarrassed by the barracking of spectators. Hundreds of people had collected, including not a few of the outlaws' relatives and friends. Wild Wright and his brother Tom, Steve's brother Dick, Kate Kelly and several of the Lloyds were watching events from a ridge on the Greta side of the station.

When the prisoners came out they said they had left Dan and Steve standing cowed in the passage, so when the rumour went round about a cannon to destroy the two lads it was taken as a joke. People were saying to one another, "Why don't they rush the hotel? Why don't they put on the armour?" and several working men were heard to say, "I would do it myself if I had firearms; I would rush the hotel myself."

The police were finding this sort of conversation extremely galling and approached Sadleir who replied, "It is not time for the rush yet; stand back and hold your ground." Sadleir found himself plagued by suggestions from his men, including one from Constable Johnston that he be allowed to fire the hotel.

So matters dragged on till 2 p.m. when Kate Kelly and Mrs Skillion rode across the line. Mrs Skillion was the focus of attention. Dressed in a handsome black riding habit trimmed with scarlet, she had a scarlet underskirt and wore a jaunty Gainsborough hat adorned with a conspicuous white feather. Everyone watched as she was stopped by Senior Constable Kelly and dismounted. The policeman asked her if she would go into the hotel and ask her brother to surrender. "I'd rather see them burn first," she replied. Then Dean Gibney, who was standing nearby, stepped forward and asked her to go to her brother and tell him there was a Catholic priest anxious to visit him. Mrs Skillion finally allowed herself to be moved by the priest and walked boldly towards the hotel.

A cry went up.

"Come back before we fire," shouted the police.

"You had better come along with me and see Mr Sadleir," called Senior Constable Kelly. The police were in a wide horseshoe, gathered in groups behind the trees. Mrs Skillion rejoined Dean Gibney and the trooper and they hurried from tree to tree inquiring for Sadleir, who was at last pointed out standing near the gatehouse.

"Go on now and ask him," said the Dean. As Mrs Skillion headed towards Sadleir, there was a sudden burst of firing and renewed shouts from the crowd, and Dean Gibney turned to find the hotel alight.

Constable Johnston had persuaded Sadleir to agree to his suggestion a few minutes earlier and had been returning from a homestead on the Benalla side with a bottle of kerosene and some straw when he had run into four bushmen, all armed. "Did you see two horses, a grey and a chestnut, pass here?" he asked them. The men replied gruffly they had not, and he had made a run for the hotel and set fire to the corner while the police continued to shoot at the front and the rear.

As Johnston ran back to join Sadleir, the fire speedily gained hold, and within a few seconds the flames were playing up to the roof. Still the outlaws made no sign. Suddenly someone realised what the police had apparently forgotten. The cry was raised. "Old man Cherry is still inside!" A wave of revulsion swept through the crowd and Kate Kelly ran to Mrs Skillion, crying, "Oh, my poor, poor brother!"

Dean Gibney stepped forward and walked rapidly towards the burning building. He was not half-way when there was a cry from Sadleir telling him not to go without orders. Gibney turned. "I am not in the police service," he shouted. "I am going to do my duty and there is no time to lose." There was a burst of clapping from the crowd. He stepped forward, bareheaded and crucifix aloft, and entered the building amid cheering.

36. In the Hotel

DEAN GIBNEY hurried on to the veranda of the Glenrowan Inn and entered as the flames were taking over. "I am a Catholic priest come to offer you your life. For God's sake speak to me," he cried.

The bar was deserted. He turned into the central pasage, and there in a doorway, lying on his side as though he had just fallen, was Joe Byrne. He knelt and found the body quite stiff. Ahead, the parlour was in flames, so he turned, hoping to get through to the rear by a small room opening off the bar, but found there was no passage. The only way was to make a dash past Byrne, so he blessed himself and rushed through to find the rest of the passage clear of flame. Coming to the room the outlaws used for their armoury, he cried again, "I am a Catholic priest come to offer you your life!"

There was no answer so he looked in. Dan and Steve lay stretched side by side full-length on the floor with bags rolled up under their heads and their armour laid to one side. The fire was beginning to run through the end of the room. Gibney took the hand of the man nearest to him and found it cold and limp and noted the settled looks on their faces. He examined the eyes of one and felt the pulse of the other. Their beards were scarcely grown. Beside them lay a cattle dog shot through the head.

As he hastened from room to room, looking for Cherry, he concluded they had laid themselves out to let the world know it was not by the police they had died. They had no weapons in their hands, nor was there trace of blood. Perhaps each had put his pistol under his vest and pulled the trigger.

The smoke and flame were thicker at the front now, almost obscuring the body of Byrne. There was no sign of Cherry, so he walked out the back to find the police advancing at the run. One constable carried a revolver as though determined to have a shot, so he laid his hand on his arm and said, "Do not fear, they are both dead." Around the corner of an outhouse he found a private citizen helping police to lift Cherry, now on the edge of death.

The crowd, which was continuing to swell as people rode in from all directions, had scarcely lost sight of Gibney when the whole structure appeared to explode, masses of flame simultaneously rushing out of the sides and roof. A shout of horror went up, and immediately several troopers and civilians ran forward and disappeared in the pall of smoke. In the meantime, one of the Aboriginal trackers had dragged the body of Byrne on to the veranda.

Cheers broke out as Gibney reappeared, accompanied by groups bearing Cherry and the body of Byrne towards the station. The crowd surged around. Were the outlaws alive? Dean Gibney had no time to answer. Old Martin Cherry — immigrant, gold-miner, railway fettler — had been bleeding for hours from the groin and could not last much longer. He seemed conscious but was unable to speak as Gibney administered extreme unction; and soon he passed away.

There was nothing for it but to wait till the fire had burnt itself out. Inspector O'Connor leaned against a tree reading the *Argus*. The crowd and the police collected in groups, talking. For a moment there was alarm as shots were heard again — but it was merely cartridges exploding in the armoury. Mrs Skillion sought out Mr Sadleir and got permission for herself, two sisters and Tom Wright to see Ned. They came into the little room already crowded with police and officials watching the pale and dishevelled outlaw and hanging on his every word. Kelly's eyes brightened. Each leant over and kissed him. Although he was excessively weak he seemed to be rallying, if only from the brandy with which the police had been plying him. When they left he talked freely, nevertheless regarding with suspicion the strange faces about.

"Since the Jerilderie affair we thought you had gone to Queensland," one remarked.

"It wouldn't do for everyone to think the same way," he replied dryly.

"It looks as though Dan and Steve will be burnt to death," volunteered a constable.

"No fear," replied Ned. "If they were alive they would have finished one another when they found the game was up. We had all sworn to shoot each other rather than surrender to the police."

"Why didn't Byrne and the others leave the hotel and join you?"

"Ah, if they only could have there would have been a different story to tell," he replied.

"Why couldn't you reach the hotel?"

"I was at last surrounded and only had one revolver with which I fired four shots. I had plenty of ammunition but it was no good to me. I had half a mind to shoot myself. My arm was broken in the first fire and I told Joe and Dan so. I loaded my rifle but could not hold it. I could have got off, but when I saw them pounding away I told Dan I would see it over and wait until morning. I got away into the bush and found my mare and could have rushed away to beggary, but I wanted to see the thing out. I had a chance at several policemen during the night but declined to fire."

"What on earth induced you to go to the hotel in the first place?" inquired one of the spectators.

"We could not go anywhere else," replied the outlaw. "I would have fought them in the train or else upset it if I'd had the chance. I did not care a bugger who was in it, but I knew on Sunday morning there would be no usual passengers. If I were right again I would go to the police barracks and shoot every one of the bloody traps and not give one a chance."

So he spoke and the traps listened. Meanwhile Sadleir was becoming increasingly apprehensive because the growing crowd contained many known Kelly sympathisers. Johnston had told him of four armed men; Constable Gascoigne had seen three men; a selector had been caught hiding behind police lines; the reporters had information of an armed party at the base of Morgan's Lookout; Dick Hart had been caught driving the police horses off; an armed party was reported in a nearby gully, and other men were under observation at McDonnell's. And that was apart from the many relatives who kept moving around, talking to one group and then another, and the discovery of a bag containing a keg of gunpowder and fuses.

Eventually, the outlaw was carried to a nearby guard's van to make the journey to Benalla. As he lay bandaged and helpless, his face marked by the heavy bruises where police bullets had struck his helmet, everyone was surprised by his gentle expression. A fireman blackened from work on the engine attempted to look at him. A startled expression of wild passion swept over the outlaw's face, and he cried to send away the black devil who was leaning over him.

He uttered no complaint about his wounds. As the train beat over the rails Dr Nicholson asked him what the armour meant. He replied he had intended to fight it out and paste as many of the traps as he could before they got him. He was sick of his life as he was hunted like a dog and could get no rest and didn't give a damn what became of him.

The outlaw's sisters returned to the scene of the fire. Scene, indeed! In front stood the sign:

Glenrowan Inn
Ann Jones
Best Accommodation

Behind it — all else standing were the brick chimneys scarred by hundreds of bullets. The old inn of the pioneers was now grey ashes, sheets of bullet-rent corrugated iron, twisted iron bedsteads, a sewing machine and a few tin cans. As the heat subsided, the Kellys and their friends moved over. From the smouldering embers were raked the remains of Dan and Steve. Wild Wright led Mrs Skillion to the horrible object that so shortly before had been her brother. She bent over it, raised a dirge-like cry and wept passionately.

The police felt somewhat loath to act when they were ordered to bring the remains of the two outlaws to the station. How? They looked at the ominous faces of the bushmen standing about. One spark, and blood would flow afresh and a new gang would be in the hills. Before the police could summon their forces, some of the outlaws' party wrapped the remains in blankets and took them over to McDonnell's where Steve's brother Dick issued the ultimatum: "Tell the police to keep their hands off. If they want the bodies, tell them they'll have to fight."

Night fell as the party returned in grief over the ranges to the Kelly homestead with their terrible burden.

So Glenrowan returned to its peaceful winter nights. It would flame for a while longer in newsprint; its name would be on the tongue of half the world. But soon it would sink over time's horizon to become little more than one other of a thousand

Australian hamlets where wheat and farm products were loaded at the sidings and a few score farmers collected in a pub or bought provisions at the general store. And yet it would be remembered too — a name on a printed page, a pinpoint for airmen, a place where travellers would point out of train windows, or a motorist might pull up, take a look around and observe as though savouring it on the tongue, "Old Ned, hey? So this is where!"

The siege of Glenrowan where the Kelly gang made its last stand! What sort of a battle was that? Did great generals fight with large armies and clever tactics? Was it here these raw Australians evinced that fabulous quality of toughness, uncalled for in meat, rebellious farmers or striking workmen — but admirable in leather, business men or the front line of Empire? Perhaps.

If a full dress finale were needed to illustrate the slovenliness of two years of police pursuit, perhaps Glenrowan might claim some distinction. The only moment of the whole sprawling Kelly drama in which the police could claim achievement had been made suspect by the very callousness the outlaws contended had driven them into opposition — the wanton killing of Johnny Jones, George Medcalf and Martin Cherry and the wounding of several women and children by the very force which should have been their protectors.

And as if that were not enough, Justice, which for so long had brought upon itself the mistrust of thousands of common folk throughout the country, was again cast under suspicion when the police, to cover their guilt spread the reckless lie that Ned had shot Cherry early in the battle when Cherry had ignored his command to hold aside one of the window blinds.

37. Melbourne Gaol

IN THE DAYS THAT FOLLOWED, reports of the siege of Glenrowan appeared wherever the English language was spoken. The authorities heaved a sigh of relief. According to the aristocratic principle, "Unto everyone that hath shall be given", the Chief Secretary, Superintendent Hare and Commissioner Standish received complimentary telegrams from Lord Normanby in Melbourne and Lord Augustus Loftus, Governor of New South Wales. A spate of messages leapt across the continent. From London came a comment from a young medical student, Arthur Conan Doyle, who praised the imagination of the outlaws and recommended armour for use by infantry. Military chiefs occupied with extending the borders of Empire observed in enlightened moments that the Kellys would have made fine soldiers.

Back in Greta the outlaws' relatives held a wake over the corpses of the two lads they had sheltered and fed, and for whom they had lived and dreamed so long. What threats and bitter tears, what expressions of pride and regret sprang that winter night from the pent-up hearts of these hot-blooded Irish-Australians?

The *Herald* correspondent wrote out of a fetid imagination:

> The scene at Greta was indescribable. The people seemed to flock from the gum trees. There were some of the worst-looking people there I ever saw in my life. The two bodies were carried into Mrs Skillion's hut amid the wailing and groaning of over 200 people. They were laid down on the table side by side — a dreadful sight. Their friends rushed to the hut to get a glimpse of them, but Mrs Skillion took down a gun and threatened to blow out the brains of the first person that entered the house without her permission. She then allowed only three at a time to enter. The first who went in were two girls and an old man, a relative of the Harts. He cried like a child. Then Tom Lloyd and Quinn went in. They looked at the bodies for a moment and then Tom Lloyd took hold of Kate Kelly's hand, and lifting his right hand to heaven swore a most dreadful oath that he would never leave their deaths unavenged.
>
> All day long scenes like this continued. Drink was brought over from O'Brien's Hotel and they were all more or less in a state of intoxication and dangerously inclined. Lloyd went out into the clearing at the back of the hut with Mrs Skillion and the two kept in conversation for a long time. A number of papers were passed between them. Then Lloyd got on his horse and rode to Benalla to beg the body of Byrne.

The *Melbourne Sketcher* came out with a cover drawing showing the mourners wild-eyed and with wild, tangled hair and beards, clad in rough dress, holding beakers aloft around the funeral bier of the dead in the dim light of the rough bush home at Greta. The artist, lucky for him, poor hired devil, was 225 kilometres away in Melbourne. Perhaps as he worked with his pen and ink in these days before the printer had learnt to reproduce the photograph, he remembered the druids, the mistletoe, the blood-offerings of the ancient Celts, who 2000 years before had peopled the whole of the English, Scottish, Welsh and Irish lands until driven over sea and mountain by the Anglo-Saxon invader and the Norman.

Sadleir seems to have at last realised the explosiveness of the situation. A squad of sixteen police dispatched to retrieve the corpses of Dan and Steve was recalled. So, without inquest, the remains of the two boys were lowered into the grave at Greta cemetery in the presence of a large crowd. The coffins bore brass plates on which was simply recorded:

Dan Kelly, died 28th June, 1880,
Age 19 years;
Steve Hart, died 28th June, 1880,
Age 20 years.

The train which carried Ned to Benalla also bore the corpses of Byrne and Cherry. On the dead outlaw's right hand was the topaz ring he had taken from Scanlon, and on the left another gold ring with a white seal on it. In one pocket of his jacket was a prayer book, and in the other some bullets and a brown-paper packet marked Poison. Friends applied for the body to be handed over, but the police refused bluntly, giving no reason; Standish had instructed that he be buried rapidly at Benalla.

On Tuesday morning, the body was brought from the lock-up and slung erect on the door to be photographed by an enterprising artist from Melbourne. The features were composed in a natural way and easily recognised. The face had full, fine forehead, regular features, blue eyes, downy moustache, and a bushy beard covering a full chin, whilst the hair was curly and had recently been cut. The figure was of a tall, lithe young fellow.

The spectacle, however, was repulsive. The hands were clenched in the agony of death and covered with blood. Blood also covered the blue sack coat and strapped tweed trousers, which, even in death, he wore with a loose grace. Officers, policemen, trackers and civilians who had been present at the previous day's encounter were gathering to have their photograph taken also when a young woman ran up weeping and threw her arms around the body.

Who was she? Perhaps one of Joe's barmaids. Perhaps some half-silly country lass or hysterical servant girl who had never known him, but had made the gang her heroes. Perhaps Maggie herself!

At least the *Herald* wasted no such sentiment on him. It mentioned that Byrne had been the idol of the girls of the district, so handsome and so mild-mannered—then recounted how on one occasion when his sister had been unable to stop some horses passing through a fence, Byrne, foaming at the mouth, had rushed up, seized her by the hair with one hand, and struck her over the face with the other. "So much for the ladies' man!" said the *Herald*.

The inquest was held so quietly that no one in the town was aware of it until it was over. Only three attended the courthouse, where Standish sat on the bench with fellow Melbourne Club member, McBean, who had tried to buy the Kelly selection ten years before. A verdict of justifiable homicide was immediately returned. Next morning, the remains were sneaked out of the rear of the police station and buried in a corner of Benalla cemetery not far from where the clay lay yellow over the bones of Martin Cherry.

"He has made his own bed; let him lie on it!"

But Mrs Byrne, quiet, nice woman who kept her counsel, was not there to tuck him in.

Ned was taken to the Benalla barracks where a heavy guard was placed on him. He slept heavily during the night. Senior Constable Kelly claims to have spoken to him in the morning in the presence of Sergeant Steele and Constable McIntyre, and to have recorded the following brief conversation later used in court.

"I said, 'Look here, Ned, now that it's all over I want to ask you a question before you go: Did you shoot Fitzpatrick at Greta when he went to arrest your brother?' Ned replied, 'Yes, I shot him in the wrist, and the statements made that Fitzpatrick inflicted the wound himself are quite false.' I then asked Ned if he had got a letter from Kennedy for his wife before he died. Ned replied, 'I got no letter. He never said a word after he was brought down except God forgive you. I shot him. He kept firing all the time, running from tree to tree and tried to kill Byrne until his ammunition was done.' "

About 8 a.m. on Tuesday, a springcart escorted by eight armed foot police emerged from the barracks yard, and was driven at a slow pace over the Broken River into Benalla. Inside, the wounded outlaw lay on a stretcher. A small crowd followed to the railway station where he was carried carefully to the brake van and laid on a mattress under heavy guard. One of the Lloyd girls, a cousin of the outlaw, was the only relative present. She was allowed to speak to him, and as the train moved out, she cried without restraint.

A reporter who made the journey wrote as follows:

He looked terribly emaciated, his spare countenance rendered more wan by the terrible bruises with which it was covered — the effect of the bullets which struck his helmet. As he lay on the floor there was something horribly pitiful about his appearance. He maintained a reticent and sullen demeanour during the journey, answering questions gruffly.

At each station on the way there was a great rush of people anxious to get a look at him. Senior Constable Walsh said, "Do you mind them looking into the van?"

"No," said Kelly, "I've no objections." He seemed refreshed by his sleep of the night before.

And Dr Ryan, who attended the outlaw's wounds, recorded:

He spoke little, seemed like a man in a trance and glared at strangers. Most men wounded and lacking sleep as he was would have been far more prostrated, but he has a splendid constitution. His body looked as if it was well nourished. His skin was as clean as if he had just come out of a Turkish bath. I attended to his wounds and now and then gave him some brandy and water. He seemed grateful, but gave the idea he wished to die.

The only other piece of recorded conversation was with Senior Constable Armstrong. Ned said to him, "Was Senior Constable Johnston in the hut when Sherritt was shot?"

"No, why do you ask me that, Ned?"

"What men were there?"

"I'm sorry to say I was."

"To have gone out in yon light would have been foolhardihood," observed the outlaw. "You would all have been shot but one. It was not our game to shoot you all; we wanted one man to go in and draw the police away from the barracks."

During the battle, crowds had blocked the streets outside the newspaper offices in Melbourne and editions came off the press every hour. As soon as it was known that Kelly was on the 2 o'clock train, a crowd commenced to gather at Spencer Street. The police cleared the platform and the yards, and erected elaborate barriers. The people congregated, climbing on stationary vehicles and lamp-posts, and crowding the windows on the opposite side of the street.

But it was all a hoax! The train stopped at North Melbourne. Here only fifty persons had gathered. They crowded around the van, but plain-clothes police quickly cleared a passage. The outlaw was placed on a stretcher and carried shoulder-high to a four-wheeled wagon on the roadway. The reporter recorded: "The lower-class portion of the crowd pressed around and gave exclamations of pity."

Instructions were given to drive on, and the vehicle, followed by others containing police, moved up Victoria Street to the old

Melbourne gaol. All along the route folk ran to their doors or leaned over their fashionable balconies of iron filigree, hoping to catch a glimpse of the man whose deeds of blood and defiance had sent such thrills of horror and admiration across the continent.

Outside the gaol a tremendous crowd had gathered. An attempt was made to raise a cheer for the wounded hero. The large iron gates were thrown open, the way cleared. Without stopping, the cavalcade rattled through into the courtyard; and the strong body of police which had assembled outside to guard against a rush by sympathisers marched in, and the gates clanged behind.

Such pomp and circumstance!

Within the gaol, Kelly was received by the Governor, Mr Castieau. Prisoners under the direction of warders removed him from the wagon and carried him into the hospital where he was placed on a water bed prepared for his reception. Dr Shields, the gaol medical officer, took over from Dr Ryan. Both gentlemen examined the outlaw. They recorded:

> Healthy and exceptionally clean. Most serious wound in left arm. Ball struck when arm was bent, entering mid-way between wrist and elbow, passing through arm and piercing it again above the elbow. Four slug wounds in right thigh and leg. Slugs in right hand near thumb prevented him from using rifle. Shot in left foot near big toe, bullet passing through instep. Kelly suffering from mental depression.

The Reverend F.J. Aylward, of St Patrick's Cathedral, was introduced to the outlaw and agreed to inform Mrs Kelly of the fate of her sons. He had not far to go for she was in the same building. When she was taken from the workroom and heard that Ned was in the gaol hospital, she became extremely anxious to see him. She had not been surprised at the outcome of the Glenrowan battle because on the night of Sherritt's death she had dreamed of a clash in which the bobbies were victorious. A few days later, by which time Ned had gained some strength, the mother spent half an hour with her son in the presence of Castieau, and left him reluctantly, assured she would see him again when his health improved further.

Kelly's wounds healed rapidly. He was a model prisoner. At last Dr Shields announced he was fit to undergo the ordeal of trial. On Sunday 1 August, almost five weeks from that black day at Glenrowan, Kelly was aroused, given a blue serge suit and told he was to appear at the Beechworth Court of Petty Sessions. A few minutes later he was helped from his cell into a wagonette and driven to Newmarket station.

As he stood waiting with his escort and a few railway officials he hailed three boys riding racehorses.

"Give your horses to me, and I'll show you how to ride them," he cried.

"What do you know about it?" they replied.

On the journey up, Kelly held court. There was the Englishman Steele who had wounded young Reardon and finally brought the outlaw down. There were Bracken and Faulkiner, the latter one of the three troopers Hare had sent in disguise to the Whorouly races the previous year. Immediately they found Kelly would not allow himself to be questioned, but would, however, volunteer information. There was some discussion of the Glenrowan fight. One remarked there was only one man in it.

"Byrne and Hart were plucky and trustworthy fellows," said Kelly.

"Hart was a mere boy. None of them were such good shots as they thought they were," interjected Steele.

Kelly acted as though stung. "What the hell do you know about it?" he cried in a nettled tone rising towards Steele. "I'll knock your bloody head off."

"Come, keep your coat on," cried Mathieson. They pushed him down and he glowered at Steele.

As the train rattled on, Ned lay on a platform chair, right leg stretched out stiffly, talking occasionally, and looking out on the quiet country. Passing through Donnybrook he pointed out a hut on the left and remarked, "That is where I first drew breath."

The train stopped at Seymour.

At Euroa he remarked that he had never found anyone so hard to get on with as Scott of the National Bank. He added, "But I got on all right with her." Glancing towards the Strathbogies, he sighed, "There they are; shall I ever be there again?"

When the train passed through Glenrowan, he gazed intently at the scene of battle, remarked that a good man had fallen there and pointed out the log at which he himself had fallen. He argued that he was illegally in custody as he had not seen any warrant and that he could never be hanged on the evidence held by the police. He nodded towards Bracken and observed, "There is a man I did not have the heart to shoot."

There was some discussion of the Chinese. Several of the constables observed they should be kicked out; they didn't want yellow men in the country with their dirt and crime. "If I had a pigtail," observed Ned, "I'd go home to China. One Chinaman is worth all the bloody Europeans living."

Faulkiner spoke of the police excursions in the Warby Ranges. "The idea of Hare being a picked man sent up to catch me," snorted the outlaw. "I can tell you every place his party used to camp and who used to get up the horses."

"In the morning?"

"Yes! We knew the movements of the police. We knew the police hid at Sherritt's in the daytime and watched Byrne's at night. But Joe got through! Same at Wangaratta—Steve visited his mother! And didn't we laugh when we saw it in the *Wangaratta News* afterwards. It was true, too, and the police didn't believe it! I would have liked to have caught that fat bastard Hare—and Nicolson, too. What was Nicolson doing up in Benalla pulling my friends into his office and giving them money to do your lazy devil's work? The Government could have given them all the money it possesses and they wouldn't have sold me."

They asked him why he hadn't stuck up more banks.

"After Jerilderie," he replied, "I was told all branch banks sent their receipts to Melbourne almost daily, and it wasn't worth sticking up any more."

At Wangaratta a few people who happened to be on the platform caught a glimpse of the outlaw. During the final leg of the journey through the low ranges towards the May Day Hills and Beechworth, Kelly sang the verses of Joe Byrne's parody:

> *We have mates where'er we go*
> *That somehow let us know*
> *The approach of every foe*
> *To the bold Kelly gang.*

Beechworth was ready to receive him. Waiting at the station was an augmented force of troopers and a few score spectators who had been tipped off by friends; the journey had been accomplished with a maximum of secrecy. As the outlaw was hurried to the waiting hansom, he lunged forward, kicking one of the police horses on the leg and causing it to rear under its rider. A few minutes later the cortege rounded the post office corner into the street where Harry Power had hailed his crowds ten years before, passed the cab rank and the courthouse, and rolled through the stone gaol gateway where iron gates had been substituted for the old wooden ones.

38. The Trial

Two days before Kelly had been sent to Beechworth, Mrs Skillion and Tom Lloyd journeyed to Melbourne where Mrs Skillion briefed Mr David Gaunson M.L.A. Then, discovering the venue had been switched, Gaunson and Mrs Skillion took the train to Beechworth and applied to see the prisoner.

They found that although Kelly had every legal right to interview witnesses before the trial, his relatives were not allowed to see him, the pretext being that one of them might provide him with the means of cheating the gallows. Kelly complained to Gaunson in the presence of gaol officials: "It seems to me unjust when I am on trial for my life to refuse those I put confidence in to come within cooee of me . . . All I want is a full and fair trial, and a chance to make my side heard. Until now the police have had it all their own way. If I get a full and fair trial — I don't care how it goes — the public will see I am not the monster I have been made out. What I have done was under strong provocation."

On Friday, 6 August, the Beechworth courthouse was besieged at an early hour. The doors were scarcely opened before the court was crowded and the gallery filled with ladies, while hundreds packed the entrance unable to gain admittance. It was a square building, like the gaol and the police station constructed out of hewn stone by the prison gangs. The courtroom was lofty, dominated at one end by the public gallery and at the other by the bench, to the left of which were the dock and witness box.

A strong police guard took up position near the dock lest some weapon or poison bottle be handed to the prisoner. William Henry Foster, P.M., who had played such an undistinguished part as police tool in the persecution of the Kelly sympathisers eighteen months before, took his seat on the bench. He had already considered Gaunson's application for an adjournment on grounds of insufficient time to prepare the defence, and opened proceedings by refusing it.

The prisoner had been taken secretly from the gaol to a cell adjoining the courthouse at 8 a.m. As he was assisted into the dock and placed on a chair all eyes turned towards him. He nodded and smiled to Mrs Skillion, Tom Lloyd, Dick Hart and several other friends in the body of the court. On behalf of Her Majesty the Queen on the information of Thomas McIntyre, Constable of Police, he was charged with the "wilful murder of Thomas Lonigan at Stringybark Creek in the Northern Bailiwick of the Colony of Victoria on the 26th day of October, 1878."

The case opened with the calling of McIntyre, who deposed a statement on the shooting at Stringybark, his conversation with Kelly, and his escape. As McIntyre entered the box, Kelly turned to glance at him. He was questioned by Mr C.A. Smyth for the Crown and gave his evidence clearly and calmly. Occasionally Ned gave him a penetrating look. The first sitting ended with the trooper still giving his account of the death of Lonigan.

Next morning McIntyre continued in evidence. Gaunson asked him if he thought Fitzpatrick was an upright and truthful man, to which witness replied: "If he had possessed these qualities I don't think he would have been dismissed. I know it was on the evidence of Fitzpatrick that Mrs Kelly, Skillion and Williamson were convicted."

"Upon the evidence of a man who was not good enough for the force?" inquired Gaunson.

"I never saw anything wrong with Fitzpatrick," replied the witness.

Gaunson asked him why he had been scouring the country in plain clothes, and if it was not true that the moment Kennedy had jumped off his horse, witness had taken it and left him in the lurch. He questioned him regarding the feeling of the police towards Kelly, and witness answered: "Many of the men want to see him hanged; I can't say what the feelings of the others are."

George Stephens, the groom, made a statement containing remarks concerning the death of Lonigan made by Kelly at Younghusbands'. Gaunson asked witness as to the police attitude to Kelly. Witness replied he had heard nothing of police anxiety to see Kelly acquitted and thought Ned would hang. At this point Ned was observed to smile.

Samuel Reynolds, medical practitioner, of Mansfield, gave evidence on the inquests of Lonigan, Scanlon and Kennedy. The clerk spent an hour reading depositions, during which time Mrs Skillion, Lloyd, Hart and several friends left the courtroom. Mr Foster then expressed the opinion that McIntyre had given evidence in an honest and intelligent manner, to which Mr Gaunson retorted it was certainly unusual to make such a statement before the prisoner had been dealt with.

The final hearing took place on Monday. Many witnesses appeared for the prosecution. Not a single witness was called for the defence. In spite of a little skirmishing, Gaunson had done nothing to discredit the prosecution, let alone establish any sort of defence. Mr Foster committed the prisoner for trial at Beechworth General Sessions on 14 October.

So ended the preliminary trial of Edward Kelly. The prisoner was apparently recovering health, but appeared listless and seldom displayed interest in proceedings — suggesting by his attitude the hopelessness of defending a case of which his own counsel knew next to nothing. Pale and self-contained though he was, he was still the most arresting figure in the court. During the hearing he frequently exchanged nods and smiles with his relatives. To a young woman in the gallery who seized sly opportunities to respond, he threw kisses on several occasions. He replied to a number of modish young ladies who stared at him from the front seats by staring back until they were compelled to look away. On which he smiled quietly and looked to see where the flies had gone in winter. The following day he was returned to Melbourne Gaol.

Although the trial had been set down for Beechworth, reported threats by the Kelly relatives caused it to be transferred to Melbourne. The case was listed to come before the same Judge Sir Redmond Barry who had sentenced Tipperary Jim and Ellen Kelly and offered to give Ned himself fifteen years for wounding Fitzpatrick. Barry's family, in fact, had been oppressors of the Welsh and the Irish since the time of William the Conqueror.

On 15 October, under instructions from Mr Gaunson, application was made to Judge Barry for an adjournment to the next sitting. The affidavit declared that friends and relatives had been denied usual access and the prisoner thereby had been embarrassed in preparing his defence; and furthermore, that the efforts of Mrs Skillion to raise fees for counsel had so far been blocked by refusal of the Lands Department to grant title to her husband's property although rents had been paid under a seven-year lease.

In the early days of Port Phillip, His Honour, while posing as a radical, had supported continuance of the convict system and advised Governor Latrobe against making land available to free-holders in the squatting district, so his refusal of Mrs Skillion's application was in line with his history as a Tory in liberal clothing.

On Monday, 18 October, an immense crowd collected early in Russell Street outside the old courthouse, where the Central Criminal Court was to sit. The doors and the gates leading into the courtyard at the rear were kept shut and order maintained by a strong posse of police. Mrs Skillion was allowed in and made her way through the gloomy stone passages to the southern gallery and sat in the second row. Jurors, witnesses and those connected with the case were admitted by back ways, leaving the crowd clamouring outside. The partly filled courtroom regarded

Constable McIntyre curiously and picked out Senior Constable Kelly and others who had been connected with the drama.

Precisely at 10 a.m. Mr Justice Barry entered. The Hon. Wisdom, Attorney-General of New South Wales, and Mr Cowper, High Sheriff of the same colony, were accommodated on the bench to the right of His Honour. The crier declared the court duly open. A flutter of excitement passed across the chamber as the order was given to place Edward Kelly in the dock, and Kelly appeared, having been conducted along a connecting passage from the gaol. But apart from the efforts of the prisoner to circumvent the attempt of a newspaper artist to sketch him, those present were to be denied any further excitement.

Mr Bindon rose as counsel for the prisoner and asked for an adjournment on ground that it was necessary for himself and Mr Gaunson to study depositions of witnesses for the prosecution extending to eighty-five pages of brief paper, and hence that it was also necessary to read the voluminous newspaper accounts of the Euroa, Jerilderie and Glenrowan affairs referred to in such depositions. The affidavit also stated appeal had been made to the Crown to supply counsel's fee of fifty guineas, and that the sheriff had replied instructing Mr Gaunson to undertake the defence on the usual conditions, viz., seven guineas for both attorney and counsel. The Crown Law officers would decide on further remuneration, if any.

When Mr Bindon resumed his seat, Mr Smyth, for the Crown, after a lengthy preamble, said that although he opposed the application, he was loath to do anything which would convey the impression the prisoner had been improperly treated and would withdraw opposition if His Honour thought counsel for the defence had made a case. So once more the court disbanded.

When the time came to return the prisoner to the gaol, it was found that part of the crowd had scaled the fence at the rear. While some were driven back, a row of constables, revolvers drawn, held back others lining the path to the gaol entrance, and the cry of "Hats off!" went up when Kelly appeared. The reporter who recorded the incident at first took this to be a gesture in honour of the outlaw, but then ingratiated himself with his editor by adding it was probably rather that those at the back wanted a clearer view.

At last on Thursday, 28 October, the case got under way. The same crowd assembled outside. In the heavy courtroom built in the early days of Melbourne — reminiscent in its severity and yet curious ornament of feudal church and castle — the same assembly gathered. This time Tom Lloyd and a young unknown woman from Greta had joined Mrs Skillion in the body of the court. Both women were heavily veiled. His Honour arrived ten minutes late, refused Mr Bindon's application for a further adjournment, then granted application for a chair for the prisoner, who, as before, sat pale and self-contained, looking like a selector in Sunday clothes, his dark, silky bushman's beard in sharp contrast to the shaved faces about.

Mr Smyth opened by sketching the events of the drama. Detective Ward produced warrants dated April 1878 for the arrest of Edward and Dan Kelly on charges of horse-stealing. He then produced a warrant to apprehend Kelly for wounding with intent to murder Alexander Fitzpatrick.

Then came McIntyre to tell of the events of Stringybark and the murder of Lonigan . . . "Dear, dear, what a pity the bastard tried to run!" . . . "I'm glad it's Lonigan; that bugger gave me curry in Benalla one day!" . . ."There are not three men in the force a match for me!" . . . "Mind you give no alarm or I'll put a hole through you!" As witness on witness appeared, other memories from the past crowded after each other.

George Stephens, former Younghusbands' groom: "The prisoner said in my hearing, 'If there was any shooting at Stringybark, I did it.' "

Henry Dudley, government printing officer: "In the yard he got hold of me by the collar of my coat and said, 'If you don't hold your tongue I'll blow your bloody brains out. Is it not bad enough to be a proscribed outlaw without having to take cheek from an old man like you?' "

Robert McDougal, government bookbinder: "Taking out a double-cased gold watch, he said it belonged to poor Kennedy. 'Which would be best—for me to shoot him—or for the police to shoot me, and take my mangled corpse into Mansfield?' "

James Gloster, draper and hawker, of Seymour, spoke up for his old sparring partner: "My impression was that he took the shooting on himself to screen others. He said, 'My mother struggled up with a large family. I am very much incensed with the police. It is not murder to shoot one's enemies. The police are my natural enemies.' "

So passed the first day. The *Herald* reporter recorded, "It is understood His Honour will sit up to midnight so as to get the trial finished as soon as possible. His Honour is averse to having the jury locked up during race time."

39. Kelly Speaks Out

THE SECOND DAY of the trial began still and sultry, but by 10 a.m. a hot north wind was blowing clouds of dust into the faces of the crowd off the roads leading from Carlton. At the entrance the press was so great that several gentlemen in frock coats arrived late in court and had to tip-toe to their seats in squeaky boots. The prisoner wore a flowered silk handkerchief around his throat, and as the case commenced and he stirred as with impatience, it seemed there might be dramatic events before the day was out. Mrs Skillion, Tom Lloyd and the unknown girl had been joined by Mrs Lloyd and Denis McAuliffe. The prisoner smiled at them.

As evidence for the prosecution proceeded the prisoner became increasingly restless, repeatedly conferring with Gaunson. Then a stir, as of a little wind, passed over the courtroom when it became apparent that he wished to take over from Bindon and himself conduct the cross-examination — an unheard-of procedure, especially as prisoners had no right under law to give evidence on their own behalf but must stand silent in the dock until the case had been proved or disproved by witnesses. Gaunson whispered animatedly, wagging his head in the negative, and the prisoner eventually gave up. Throughout the morning he paid close attention to evidence, sometimes sitting, sometimes standing, and occasionally leaning over the front of the dock. His health had greatly improved.

As certain of his exploits were mentioned a smile passed over his face. As an artist present recorded — he seemed to take credit that neither he nor his mates were wholesale murderers, and to regard the affair as a vendetta. During the previous sittings of the court one would have been almost tempted to say he had a poker face. His face did not say anything it did not want to say. Looking at him, you would think: There is a man who knows his business! But today he was different. Was it that the north wind stirring over the cobbles of the gaol had brought him a message from Greta? His conduct was quiet and respectful, but the listlessness had gone and his eyes were dark and restless.

Robert Scott, bank manager of Euroa, took the stand and recounted the events of that Euroa Sunday, long past. As he told how he had threatened to strike Kelly if he attempted to enter Mrs Scott's room without knocking, the prisoner seemed greatly amused. Scott mentioned how in the cart, en route to Younghusbands', prisoner had remarked, "Oh, I shot Lonigan."

When witness replied to Mr Bindon that Kelly had personally behaved well to him and had not used a single rude word before the ladies, the prisoner chuckled and winked at the jury, which, however, solemnly aware of its dignity, did not respond.

Then appeared Trooper Richards and Living, the accountant. Then Tarleton, who recounted the outlaw's speech at Jerilderie. Then came the clang of iron as Senior Constable Kelly displayed the armour and headpiece. He declared that the prisoner had admitted at the Benalla lock-up he had shot Fitzpatrick in the wrist.

Sergeant Steele: "Prisoner said, 'Yes, I shot him, right enough.'"

Under cross-examination, Steele denied he had told Mrs Jones that if she would say prisoner had shot her son he would forward recommendation that she get portion of the reward. Finally came Samuel Reynolds, surgeon, of Mansfield, to testify once again that Lonigan was dead.

So closed the case for the Crown. It rested on the direct evidence of McIntyre, who had endeavoured to show that prisoner had murdered Lonigan in cold blood, and on the word of half a dozen other witnesses using Kelly's remarks in evidence against him. Bindon's minor sallies had done nothing to shake it.

The court adjourned for lunch. As on the previous day, refreshments were supplied to the jury who were not permitted to mix with the public.

At 1.15 p.m. Mr Bindon commenced the case for the defence. He called no witnesses, but contented himself with an effort to have the case referred to the Full Court. "The only thing with which the court should be concerned," he declared, "is the shooting of Lonigan. I object to all other points in evidence. I ask that such points be reserved, and a case stated for the Full Court."

"What points do you allude to?" asked His Honour.

"All the transactions which took place after the death of Lonigan which were detailed in evidence."

"I think," said His Honour, "that the point is a perfectly good one if you can show any authority in support. However, I regard the conduct of the prisoner during the whole afternoon after the killing of Lonigan as important to show what the motive was. I must therefore decline to state a case."

So Mr Bindon retired from his second defeat, leaving Mr Smyth to address the jury. The prosecutor for the Crown spoke strongly:

"When you find one man shooting down another in cold blood, you need not stop to inquire his motives; it was of malignant hatred against the police. The prisoner had been leading a wild, lawless life and was at war with society. I have proved abundantly by witnesses who were scarcely cross-examined that the murder of Lonigan was committed in cold blood.

"So far as I was able to gather anything from the cross-examination, the line of the defence was that the prisoner considered himself justified in going about the country with an armed band to revenge himself on the police because he considered he and his family were injured in the Fitzpatrick case.

"Another point in the defence has been that because Sergeant Kennedy and his men did not surrender themselves to the prisoner's gang, the gang was therefore justified in what they called defending themselves."

He turned to the jury.

"How long will you allow this state of affairs to exist gentlemen? Such behaviour is not to be tolerated. I have almost to apologise to you for discussing the matter.

"Even admitting prisoner's defence that the charge of attempt to murder Fitzpatrick was a lie, which I do not for one moment consider, it is perfectly idle to say this would justify prisoner in subsequently killing Constable Lonigan.

"I think it is not an unfair inference to draw that McIntyre on that terrible day was kept alive till his superior officer arrived, only to be murdered afterwards, so that not a living soul would have been left to tell the sad tale of how these unfortunate men met their death at the hand of this band of assassins.

"The prisoner wants to pose before the country as a hero, but he is nothing more than a petty thief, as is shown by the fact that he rifled the pockets of the murdered men. The prisoner has shown himself a coward throughout his career . . ."

So continued the prosecutor for the Crown, facing the jury, occasionally turning towards the bench or the prisoner who sat quiet and unsmiling in the dock, measuring him with his eyes as insult followed insult.

Then Mr Bindon rose. "It was not my intention to refer to, or introduce, a number of matters which have nothing to do with the present trial for the shooting of Lonigan. Unfortunately, my intentions have been rendered futile by the Crown. The question still remains: How far is this material to be used by the jury in arriving at a verdict? According to all principles of fairness and justice, these matters should not have been brought forward. The only thing you are concerned with, gentlemen, is the shooting of Lonigan. With the shooting of Kennedy and the proceedings at Glenrowan you have nothing whatever to do at present, and I therefore request you to keep these things from your minds."

The police had appeared at Stringybark not in uniform but in plain clothes, he said. An unfortunate fracas had occurred which resulted in the shooting of Lonigan. The evidence of McIntyre showed signs of deliberate and careful preparation, and was that of a witness who, under the peculiar circumstances at Stringybark Creek, could not be expected to distinguish what actually did take place. Of course, it was nonsense to say Lonigan was not shot; but the point was by whom was he shot? It was a most dangerous doctrine to rely on the evidence of one man, more especially when the charge was that one man had shot another deliberately and in cold blood. As for the confessions prisoner had made at various times, they were uttered either for the purpose of intimidation or in order to screen others, and therefore were of no use whatever in corroboration of McIntyre's evidence.

"Only McIntyre and the prisoner can say anything of the affair," concluded Mr Bindon. "The prisoner's mouth is shut; but if he could be sworn, then he would give a totally different version of the transaction . . . There is no ground for saying the police fell in with a gang of assassins. The whole career of the prisoner shows that he is not an assassin, a cold-blooded murderer, or a thief. On the contrary he has shown himself to have the greatest possible respect for human life. I ask: will the jury convict a man on the evidence of a single witness and that a prejudiced witness? If you have the smallest doubt, gentlemen, I trust you will give a verdict in this case different from that which the Crown expects."

Now as the light streamed in through the high window of the western wall, little more remained than for Judge Barry to sum up, and the jury to reach its verdict. The case had produced little excitement. The exchanges that marked the earlier cross-examination had given way to dull speeches. The defence had done nothing more than skirmish. The audience sat quietly; but the prisoner showed renewed signs of the restlessness that had marked his behaviour earlier in the day.

His Honour, portly and red-faced, irritated by a large carbuncle which sweltered under his long peruke, at last commenced the summing up in the full voice and dominant manner of one who had been trying for years to live down the fact that he had been a failure until his arrival in Melbourne. In fact, the big event of his year was the dinner he gave every 13 November to mark the day he had stepped off the boat.

He declared that if two or three men made preparations with malice aforethought to murder a man, even if two out of the three did not take part, all were equally guilty. The fact that the police were in plain clothes had nothing to do with the case. No person had a right to stop or question them. The counsel for the defence had told the jury to receive the evidence of McIntyre with great caution; but he would go further than that and hope that the jury would receive and weigh all evidence with caution. It was not necessary to have McIntyre's evidence corroborated and he asked the jury to note the behaviour of McIntyre in the witness box and say whether his conduct was that of a man who wanted to deceive.

The charge against the prisoner was the murder of Lonigan. The object of admitting evidence subsequent to the shooting was to give the jury every opportunity to judge the conduct of the prisoner and his intentions on that particular day. With regard to the confessions made by the prisoner at various times, the jury must realise they were not made under compulsion, but when the prisoner was at liberty; and if he had made them in a spirit of vainglory or to screen his companions, then he had to accept full responsibility.

The prisoner's mouth was not closed. True, he could not give sworn testimony, but he could have made a statement, which, if consistent with his conduct for the past eighteen months, would have been entitled to consideration. But the prisoner had not done so.

His Honour concluded: "Whether prisoner shot Lonigan or not is an immaterial point. The prisoner was engaged in an illegal act. He pointed a gun at McIntyre's breast. That circumstance is enough to establish his guilt.

"The jury will, however, have to regard the evidence as a whole and say accordingly whether murder has been committed. It cannot be manslaughter. Your verdict must be either guilty of murder or an acquittal."

So at 5.10 p.m., with this injunction, the jury retired.

The officers of the court, the police, the pressmen, the small crowd in the public benches, the outlaw's relatives, the prisoner himself, waited idly and silently, yet with rising tenseness as the heavy minutes ticked by. At 5.35, the jury filed in. Gaunson in his blue robe, the periwigged attorneys and frock-coated reporters, stately Sir Redmond, red-faced in his red mantle and white wig, the outlaw's relatives and the outlaw himself, turned towards the leader who stood forward and announced a verdict of guilty. The sound of quiet sobbing ran through the court as the words they had long awaited struck the two women. The outlaw showed no sign.

The Judge's associate then asked the prisoner if he had anything to say why sentence should not be passed upon him. Kelly, for so long silent, rose and addressed the court in a quiet, conversational tone as if quite at home, yet so as to be heard distinctly throughout the courtroom.

"Well, it is rather late for me to speak now," he remarked. "I thought of speaking this morning and all day, but there was little use. There is little use blaming anyone now. Nobody knows about my case except myself, and I wish I had insisted on being allowed to examine the witnesses myself. If I had examined them I am confident I could have throw a different light on the case.

"It is not that I fear death; i fear it as little as to drink a cup of tea. On the evidence that has been given, no juryman could have given any other verdict; that is my opinion. But as I say, if I had examined the witnesses, I would have shown matters in a different light, because no man understands the case as I do myself.

"I do not blame anybody—neither Mr Bindon nor Mr Gaunson; but Mr Bindon knows nothing about my case. I lay blame on myself that I did not get up yesterday and examine the witnesses, but I thought that if I did so it would look like bravado and flashness."

(Very apt to the moment was some comment by Ned, made previously to an *Age* reporter in Beechworth: "I do not pretend that I have led a blameless life or that one fault justifies another; but the public, judging a case like mine, should remember that the darkest life may have a bright side, and after the worst has been said against a man, he may, if he is heard, tell a story in his own rough way that will lead them to soften the harshness of their thoughts against him and find as many excuses for him as he would plead for himself.")

"For my own part I do not care one straw about my life, nor for the result of the trial; and I know very well from the stories I have been told, of how I am spoken of—that the public at large execrate my name. The newspapers cannot speak of me with that patient tolerance generally extended to men awaiting trial, and who are assumed, according to the boast of British justice, to be innocent until they are proved to be guilty. But I don't mind, for I am the last that curries public favour or dreads the public frown. Let the hand of the law strike me down if it will; but I ask that my story be heard and considered—not that I wish to avert any decree the law may deem necessary to vindicate justice, or win a word of pity from anyone. If my lips teach the public that men are made mad by bad treatment, and if the police are taught that they may exasperate to madness men they persecute and ill-treat, my life will not be entirely thrown away. People who live in large towns have no idea of the tyrannical conduct of the police in country places far removed from the court. They have no idea of the

212

harsh, overbearing manner in which they execute their duty, how they neglect their duty, and abuse their powers."

Writing in later years a gentleman recorded: "It was an unforgettable moment when the prisoner ceased to speak. For two days his case had been in retreat and had scarcely scored a point. Now, breaking the utter silence of the old Criminal Court, came a stir of sympathy from a few of those present and a trace of annoyance on the part of others. Mr Justice Barry coughed and proceeded to pronounce sentence of death; but as he did so there came interruptions from the prisoner, and what amounted to an argument ensued, increasing in tempo and warmth until His Honour was obviously nettled."

"Edward Kelly, the verdict pronounced by the jury is one which you must have fully expected."

The prisoner: "Yes, under the circumstances."

"No circumstances that I can conceive could have altered the result of your trial."

"Perhaps not from what you now conceive, but if you had heard me examine the witnesses it would have been different."

"I will give you credit for all the skill you appear to desire to assume."

"No, I don't wish to assume anything," replied Kelly. "There is no flashness or bravado about me. It is not that I want to save my life, but because I know I should have been capable of clearing myself of the charge and I could have saved my life in spite of all against me."

His Honour: "The facts are so numerous and so convincing not only as regards the original offence with which you are charged, but with respect to a long series of transactions covering a period of eighteen months, that no rational person would hesitate to arrive at any other conclusion but that the verdict of the jury is irresistible and that it is right. I have no desire whatever to inflict upon you any personal remarks. It is not becoming that I should endeavour to aggravate the sufferings with which your mind must be sincerely agitated."

"No; I don't think that," replied Kelly. "My mind is as easy as the mind of any man in this world, as I am prepared to show before God and man."

"It is blasphemous of you to say that. You appear to revel in the idea of having men put to death."

"More men than I have put men to death," replied the prisoner in strong and calm tone, "but I am the last man in the world that would take a man's life. Two years ago, even if my own life was at stake — and I am confident, if I thought a man would shoot me I

213

would give him a chance of keeping his life — I would have parted rather with my own. But if I knew that through him innocent persons' lives were at stake I certainly would have to shoot him if he forced me to do so. But I would want to know that he was really going to take innocent life."

"Your statement," said His Honour, moving forward in his seat and looking more closely at the prisoner, "involves a cruelly wicked charge of perjury against a phalanx of witnesses."

"I dare say; but a day will come at a bigger court than this when we shall see which is right and which is wrong. No matter how long a man lives he is bound to come to judgement somewhere, and as well here as anywhere. It will be different next time there is a Kelly trial for they are not all killed. It would have been for the good of the Crown had I examined the witnesses, and I would have stopped a lot of the reward, I can assure you, and I don't know that I won't do it yet if allowed."

Kelly's remarks had opened up a whole series of perspectives, so that Judge Barry hardly knew what to say. Eventually he replied, "An offence of this kind is of no ordinary character. Murders have been discovered which have been committed under circumstances of great atrocity. They proceeded from motives other than those which actuated you. They had their origin in many sources. Some have been committed from a sordid desire to take from others property they have acquired, some from jealousy, some from desire for revenge. But yours is a more aggravated crime, and one of larger proportions, for with a party of men you took up arms against society, organised as it is for mutual protection and respect for the law."

"That," said Kelly, "is how the evidence came out here. It appeared that I deliberately took up arms of my own accord and induced the other three men to join me for the purpose of doing nothing but shooting down the police."

It seemed that at last His Honour was giving up his attempt to reason with the prisoner. He sat back and commenced a lengthy homily on the folly of crime.

"Unfortunately," he said, "in a new community where society is not bound together as closely as it should be, there is a class which looks upon the perpetrators of these crimes as heroes. But such unfortunate, ill-educated, ill-prompted youths must be taught to consider the value of human life. It is hard to believe that a man could have sacrificed the lives of his fellow creatures in this wild manner. The idea is enough to make one shudder.

"It is remarkable that although New South Wales joined Victoria in offering a large reward for the detention of the gang, no person came forward to assist the police. There seems to have been a spell cast over the people of the North-Eastern district which I can only attribute to sympathy with crime or dread of the consequences of doing their duty. For months the country has been disturbed by you and your associates, and you actually had the hardihood to confess having stolen over two hundred horses."

"Who proves this?" interrupted Kelly.

"That is your own statement!"

"You have not heard me. If I had examined the witnesses I could have brought it out differently."

"I am not accusing you. This statement was made several times by the witnesses. You confessed it to them and you stand self-accused. It is also proven that you committed several attacks upon banks and you seem to have appropriated large sums of money — several thousands of pounds. It has also come within my knowledge that the country has expended about £50 000 in consequence of the acts of which you and your party have been guilty.

"Although we have met with such examples as Clarke, Gardiner, Melville, Morgan and Scott, who have all met ignominious deaths, still the effect has, apparently, not been to hinder others from following in their footsteps. I think that this is much to be deplored, and some steps must be taken to have society protected.

"Your unfortunate and miserable companions have met deaths which you might envy.

"I will forward to the Executive Council notes of evidence which I have taken, and all circumstances connected with your case; but I cannot hold out any hope to you that the sentence I am now about to pass will be remitted. I desire not to give you any further pain or to aggravate the distressing feelings which you must be enduring.

"Edward Kelly, I hereby sentence you to death by hanging. May the Lord have mercy on your soul!"

If Kelly was, in fact, enduring those distressed feelings of which the learned judge spoke, his uncreased brow did not show it. There may rather have been a spark of anger and contempt in that same clear, level voice as he looked at Sir Redmond Barry across that small gulf of courtroom which divides worlds, and replied: "Yes, I will meet you there!"

As the Court was being cleared, Kelly, en route to the gaol, talked animatedly. "They're not all dead yet. It will take forty thousand police to get rid of them. I will return from the grave to fight!"

The sun was setting as they locked him in his cell. The north wind still blew from distant bushlands. The prisoner sat on his bunk singing bush songs and popular ballads until a warder told him it wasn't right for a condemned man, and he'd better shut up.

40. The Gallows

THE TRIAL occurred at the height of the spring racing carnival which served as the grand finale to the Melbourne season — that round of dance-giving, vice-regal levees and evenings at the theatre which occupied the fashionable set during the months of winter and spring. The year 1880 had been marked by the usual distinguished round to which the opening of the International Exhibition had brought additional festivities. The verdict of the Criminal Court struck a sombre note in the midst of rejoicings, reminding those with eyes to see that marvellous Melbourne for all its boasts was not without its seamy side — showing on the averted face of Justice her scowl for her victims.

On the Monday following the verdict, Mr William Gaunson, who had joined his brother David in seeking a reprieve, saw Chief Secretary Mr Berry, and asked when the Executive Council would meet to consider the case and fix date of execution. Berry replied, "In a week's time from now." The brothers Gaunson and the outlaw's friends immediately set about organising a public demonstration for the following Friday evening and had petition forms printed and distributed. From Ballarat, Bendigo and Geelong — from towns stretching across the colony came news that similar meetings were being organised.

But for a day or so, the Kelly affair was to be pushed into the background. Tuesday was Cup Day. Flemington, one of the world's three great racecourses, was the magnet for a land of half a million horsemen. The four- and six-in-hands that trotted along Flemington Road shone brightly. The heavy horse omnibuses they passed were tightly packed with crowds of artisans, frock-coated clerks and shop assistants and their brightly gowned lady companions. On the lawns, the ladies had never dressed more expensively nor the gentlemen bowed so gallantly! Melbourne's nineteenth cup classic was won by the two-to-one favourite, Grand Flaneur, who came home with a weight of 43 kilograms, a clear length ahead of Progress.

The following day, the Gaunsons learned that Executive Council would meet that evening; the authorities had apparently decided the sooner Kelly was in the grave, the sooner agitation would cease. William Gaunson protested at the unseemly haste and pointed out the meeting had been arranged for Friday and the announcement made that signatures to the petition were to be in by Monday so that such matters might be weighed when Council came to deal with the case. Mr Berry replied that the matter was out of his hands; Executive Council would consider the case that evening.

Gaunson then saw the Attorney-General, Mr Vale, who likewise declined to make a move. As a last resort he interviewed Captain Le Patourel, private secretary to the Governor. He informed him support for reprieve was pouring in. Plans were well advanced for the meeting. Ladies in every direction had asked for tickets for the stage and reserved seats. It had been decided to hold a procession to Government House to present the prayer of the meeting, and support was so great they would have to march eight abreast. The good captain replied that His Excellency was completely in the hands of the Council, and could not assume responsibility for postponing either meeting of Council or consideration of the case.

At Melbourne gaol, the prisoner had been placed in a cell in the old wing. He was dressed in gaol clothes and ate the prison fare. Irons had been riveted on his legs and leather pads attached to his ankles to prevent chafing. The inner door of iron bars was closed, the outer door of solid iron kept open. A lamp continually burned overhead; and night and day a warder watched. Regularly each morning Kelly walked for a time in the adjoining yard with a warder on each side. He spoke about what he had done and could have done.

Immediately following the trial he seemed resigned to his fate. Sometimes he sang to himself. Other times he seemed morose and would not speak. Then he was visited by Mrs Skillion, Tom Lloyd, Denis McAuliffe and his sister, and his cousins Kate Lloyd and Patrick Ryan. He expressed his desire to see Kate and his sister Grace, now fifteen years old. The visitors told him of the efforts for his reprieve and he began to hope against hope.

On Wednesday morning he was informed Executive Council would meet that evening and requested permission to write a letter. As his right hand was still stiff from wounds, they sent a fellow prisoner to whom he dictated at length some features of his case, signing with a cross. The answer which came back was much more to the point. He was to be executed on Thursday, 11 November. He remarked it was very short notice.

The press had already noted the efforts to gain a reprieve. The

Herald, under its slogan *Impartial Not Neutral,* recorded, "It is quite evident that an effort is being made to work up spurious sympathy for the condemned Kelly with a view to inducing the Executive Council to commute sentence of death passed upon him . . . Considering the state of mind of the prisoner, it is the worst thing that can be done. It is a most painful subject to write upon."

But not all pressmen had such fine consideration for the condemned man. The *Ballarat Star* said, "No man or woman who has seen a wild beast or viper destroy human life would extend compassion to the murderous brute or reptile."

On Friday afternoon Captain Standish as Chief Commissioner of Police called on Mr Gaunson and requested him to drop the idea of a deputation as no procession could take place without permission of the Mayor. Gaunson replied he could not undertake to check the people in the exercise of their right to see the Governor. Then Captain Le Patourel called to state that His Excellency was unable to receive the deputation that night, but would see them at 10.30 a.m. the following day. He asked for the number to be restricted to three or four.

During Friday, the condemned man dictated another letter to the Governor—this one being concerned mainly with the events at Glenrowan. It concluded: "I should have made a statement of my whole career; but my time is so short on earth that I have to make the best of it to prepare myself for the other world."

That night the city's biggest auditorium, the Hippodrome, was packed with 4000 people. Outside gathered a crowd which the papers estimated variously between 2000 and 6000. The *Argus* reported they belonged to the larrikin classes, the *Herald* was revolted by the sight of so many respectably dressed citizens—women in particular—associating themselves with so dubious a cause. The *Age* said, "Such a meeting of thieves, prostitutes and foolish persons as the two Gaunsons got together . . . is absolutely dangerous to the Commonwealth."

The chair was taken by Mr A.S. Hamilton, president of the Society for the Abolition of Capital Punishment. The principal speaker was Mr David Gaunson, Chairman of Committees of the Legislative Assembly. Resolutions were unanimously carried calling for the exercise of the Royal prerogative of mercy, and for a procession to Government House on the following morning.

Next morning, such a small part of workaday Melbourne collected at the Town Hall that the Gaunsons, Mr Hamilton and Mr Caulfield, "the boy politician" who had lately come to espouse the cause of Kelly took one look, gave it the slip, and set off in a cab with Kate Kelly. They drove over the old single-arch bridge

218

which spanned the Yarra, passed the swamp and Victoria Barracks on the right, and came to the lofty iron gates beyond which could be seen the square tower of His Excellency's new residence. Kate Kelly, heavily veiled, and dressed in black, trimmed with jet beads, was pale but composed when the small party was ushered into the Yellow Room where at last His Excellency joined them. Mr Hamilton bowed and presented the petition of the meeting.

His Excellency, a portly gentleman, clearly regarded the affair as a waste of time and announced brusquely, "Mr Hamilton, I can but forward the document to the Government and tell you that it will come before the Executive on Monday. I regret, however, the case has already received careful consideration, and the decision arrived at was not come to without due care. I would be deceiving you and acting cruelly towards the condemned man if I held out any hope of mitigation."

David Gaunson, ready-tongued as usual, commenced to argue for clemency. He pointed out that the state of prisoner's mind on the occasion of the Stringybark tragedy deprived his actions of the character of murder in the legal sense. Now was a time of great national carnival. Victoria had as its guests representatives of many nations, and there could be no more suitable occasion for some great act of clemency and mercy. He reminded His Excellency that in the German Empire, save in political cases, there had been no exercise of the death penalty for seventeen years.

The Governor replied: "I cannot enter into arguments, sir. The duty I have to perform is the most painful a Governor can fulfil. The decision of the Executive Council has only been arrived at after the fullest and most complete consideration, and the matter can proceed no further." There was no mistaking the vice-regal tone. Mr Hamilton took Kate by the hand and conducted her forward. She knelt down in front of the representative of Her Most Gracious Majesty. Mr Hamilton explained she was the sister of the condemned man, and they hoped it would have some effect if she begged for mercy.

"No, no," said His Excellency in impatience and anger. "I have a painful duty to perform and I do not see that anything can be got by prolonging this interview."

He turned and left them.

At the Town Hall, meanwhile, the growing crowd had lost patience too and set out for Government House. It met the returning deputation at Princes Bridge, heard of the Governor's obduracy, and then dispersed.

During their stay in Melbourne, the condemned man's relatives and friends put up at the Robert Burns Hotel in Lonsdale Street west. It was perhaps no accident that the name of Scotland's champion of the common man, who had sent a gun to the Polish revolutionaries, should have become associated with that of Ned Kelly, another farmer's son. During the week, the hotel had been the scene of ceaseless activity. On the Saturday of the demonstration it became the centre of the great campaign for signatures. Men and women came and went all day. Petitions were filled in at many hotels throughout the city, at the races, and at the Exhibition. On the following day, signatures were obtained at churches and chapels of many denominations throughout the colony. When Monday came and it was time for presentation of the petition to the Governor, over 32 000 signatures had been collected and others were still coming in by rail and coach from country centres.

By 10 a.m. a small crowd had assembled at the Town Hall. William Gaunson with Mrs Skillion, Kate and Jim Kelly — younger brother of the outlaw, recently released from prison in New South Wales — arrived eventually and set off at its head for Government House. The police tried to push them back at Princes Bridge, but, unwilling to use violence, were forced to let them proceed and galloped off to guard the gates of the Governor's residence. After some discussion, Gaunson and the others climbed into cabs and went ahead to be met by Captain Le Patourel, who told them His Excellency would receive no deputations that day, but the petitions could be forwarded to the Treasury up to 2 p.m., the hour fixed for the meeting of Executive Council. So the deputation returned to the city leading the crowd — which according to the press, "regarded the relatives and Wild Wright as objects of veneration" — to the Robert Burns Hotel where as many as possible entered.

In the afternoon, William Gaunson, Mrs Skillion and Kate Kelly attended the Treasury to present the petition. As evening approached a great crowd collected in the gardens and along Spring Street opposite the Treasury. The word came out that the Executive was determined to adhere to its decision that Ned be executed the following Thursday morning. The crowd flooded down Bourke Street and returned to the hotel where James Kelly said, "It is not all over yet!" — a remark loudly cheered.

Next morning the press recorded: "The petition altogether is one to which no importance whatever can be attached. Many of the signatures appear to have been written by children or illiterate persons."

But if all was not yet over, time was running perilously short!

On Tuesday evening, several thousand people who collected in the Supreme Court Reserve near the gaol were forced on to the road by a posse of police. William Gaunson, Caulfield and others, who arrived on a horse-drawn lorry surrounded by men bearing torches amid the cheers of the crowd, were stopped and forced to move on to vacant land in Madeline Street. The same day a stir was caused at the Robert Burns Hotel when Ann Jones was arrested for harbouring Kelly. From Glenrowan came the news that David Mortimer, brother-in-law of the schoolmaster Curnow, was shifting to Ballarat as a result of threats to shoot him and burn his mother out of her selection.

The rage of the press was growing. The *Age*, great champion of tariffs, turned its guns on a political opponent, Mr David Gaunson, M.L.A. — "the precious attorney who has so vilely prostituted his profession". Its leader writer wrote: "Has he not disgraced his position as Chairman of Committees of the Legislative Assembly of Victoria? . . . Looked at critically there is not an incident of Kelly's career to plead a passing word of pity . . . Happily Mr Gaunson is not a Victorian, his instincts having been formed amid the associations of the sister colony of New South Wales — a fact which should be remembered by those distinguished strangers who will doubtless carry the story of his adventures with them to Europe."

On Wednesday — the day before the execution — the friends of the condemned man were at their wits' end. Fresh signatures to the petition kept coming in, but that card had been played. The only move that remained was to free the prisoner by fraud or violence — and who was capable of that?

Throughout the morning Ned occupied himself dictating another letter to the Governor. In it he dealt with various episodes of his career, and attempted to explain some of his motives. It said, "I can solemnly swear now before God and man that it was never my intention to take life, and even at Glenrowan I was determined to capture Superintendent Hare, O'Connor and the blacks for the purpose of exchange of prisoners; and while I had them as hostages I would be safe, no police would follow me. And in lieu of taking them I thought it might be as well to leave them surrounding their police barracks at Glenrowan, and get possession of their train and horses without an encounter . . ." The letter concluded, "I know it is useless me trespassing on your valuable time. Because of the expense the Government has been put to, which is not my fault, they will only be satisfied with my life, although I have been found guilty and condemned to death

221

on a charge of all men in the world I should be the last one to be guilty of. There is one wish in conclusion I would like you to grant me — that is the release of my mother before my execution, as detaining her in prison could not make any difference to the Government now; for the day will come when all men will be judged by their mercy and their deeds . . . "

The *Age* recorded: "At the end of the last document prisoner requests that his mother be released from gaol and his body handed over to friends for burial in consecrated ground. Neither request will be granted."

On this last day of his life the outlaw was informed by his gaoler that he must prepare for the worst as there was now no chance of a reprieve. He remarked, "Such is life!" when told the hour of his execution, and requested that his photograph be taken for circulation amongst his friends.

In the evening he was visited by Mrs Skillion, Kate and Grace. Through them a request was conveyed to the Premier that Mr. W. Gaunson might be allowed to visit him. Mr Berry refused the request, but offered Mr David Gaunson the opportunity to be present at the hanging — a pleasure which the latter refused, declaring: "The Executive Council consists of nine mortal men who have refused to grant the prayer of 60 000, signed in an incredibly short space of time."

Isaiah Wright made an unsuccessful attempt to see his old friend. Finally, Kelly was visited by his mother. Her last words to him were, "Mind you die like a Kelly, Ned!" At 1.30 a.m. the outlaw lay down on his bunk, and, after tossing for an hour, went to sleep. That night additional forces of armed police patrolled the city, while plain-clothes men kept up a constant beat in the vicinity of the gaol, closely watching passers-by warning off odd drunks and idlers who loitered in the vicinity.

Next morning a crowd collected early in Victoria Street, and as fast as the public arrived, new police were sent from the barracks. By 10 a.m., the hour fixed for the execution, fully 5000 people were assembled, including numbers of well-dressed women. Scores of carriages lined the kerbs. At first, the small groups which collected regarded each other as strangers or talked in desultory fashion. Then as the press grew, the discussion became animated and anyone looking like a bushman was liable to be taken for one of the outlaw's friends or relatives. As the dread hour approached the tenor of the conversation was, "He'll die game!"

Inside the gaol, the outlaw rose at 5 a.m., fell on to his knees and prayed for twenty minutes, then lay down again. He finally dressed about 8 a.m. and sang a few old songs. He appeared quite contented. At 8.45 the blacksmith was called to remove his irons. When the rivets were knocked out and his legs liberated, he was attended by Dean Donaghy, Catholic Chaplain of the gaol, and then conducted from the old wing into the garden leading to the main building and the gallows. A warm wind was blowing again from the distant inland, and as he passed the handcart on which his corpse would soon be trundled to the dead-house, he remarked how lovely were the flowers. He then stepped jauntily out of the early summer sunshine within the sombre bluestone. In the condemned cell priests intoned a litany for the dying.

A few minutes before the appointed time, Colonel Rede in his official dress of Sheriff, and Mr Castieau, Governor of the gaol, proceeded to the gallows chamber followed by thirty representatives of police, press and of the legal and medical professions on whom authority had smiled and given cards of admission. The latter filed into the basement and turned to look up at the gallery six feet above their heads, in the floor of which was the drop itself — a hinged trapdoor — now secured by the bolt the hangman would shortly draw. Above the drop, stretching from wall to wall was a single beam from which dangled the hangman's rope.

Now the Governor of the gaol climbs to the gallery with the Sheriff, who formally demands of him the body of Edward Kelly.

"Present your warrant!" says the Governor.

He takes it from the outstretched hand, and with a bow so gallant for ladies — a link with distant days when slave and serf crawled on their bellies before their masters — he hands over the life of the condemned man. Now Castieau taps at the door in the left wall of the gallery and Upjohn the hangman, recently committed for larceny, appears from the cell opposite. He steps across the scaffold and turns a repulsive countenance to the spectators. He is broad, burly, with white, bristling, close-cropped hair, heavy lips, and a huge nose with a carbuncle on the end. He enters the condemned cell and proceeds to pinion the prisoner, who surprised and mildly nettled, remarks, "There's no need for tying me!"

However, the prisoner quickly becomes accustomed to the thought as in these last days he has become accustomed to so much else. Who knows what he thinks — whether he remembers the old Sydney road, the blue of the ranges, the almond trees white with blossom, the sulphur-crested cockatoos rising in flocks. Perhaps he remembers his mother, who, like creation itself, had struggled up through poverty with all her children, or the smile of his friend Joe to whom he had so often listened, perhaps not well enough.

His arms are pinioned by a leather strap so that he cannot throw up his hands to grasp the rope when the bolt is drawn. A white cap is placed on his head. Preceded by the crucifix held aloft by a priest, he walks steadily on to the drop. While the priests recite the appropriate prayer the hangman takes the two-finger-thick oiled rope. The prisoner winces as it touches him, then moves his head to facilitate the tying of the knot. The final seconds of his life are wiped off time's slate like the years — without mercy.

Some have written in hate that before Upjohn drew the cap over his eyes, the outlaw's face became livid, his eyes frightened — that he hesitated, glancing down at the spectators as if considering even then the possibility of making an appeal for mercy. The newspapers simply recorded that he seemed calm and pale and made the remark, "Ah well, I suppose it had to come to this!"

Upjohn now steps swiftly to one side, bends, and draws the bolt. The trap falls, the rope whips tight. The mortal remains of Ned Kelly, last of the bushrangers, swing two metres below where he previously stood. For a moment the body seems quite dead. Then a shudder passes through the corpse. The legs are drawn up in a convulsive movement and dropped suddenly again. Again and again this is repeated, until at the end of four minutes, Edward Kelly hangs quietly — facing the uniformed police and frock-coated gentlemen of the law and press in death as he had in his short twenty-five years of life. One of the reporters will write today:

"I shall never forget the cool cynicism of the manager of a great London paper on whom I called in Paris . . . I asked him if he would care to come to watch the execution of three communists at Satory.

'I go?' exclaimed my able editor. 'I go? Good gracious no; but be sure you go and write us a graphic account.' "

As the fatal hour approached, the assembly outside the gaol thickened and drew around the gates in a dense mass. Police and detectives had taken up positions in heavy numbers. A minute or so before ten o'clock, a cart forced a passage through the crowd and a baker delivered a loaf at the door amid a chorus of uncomplimentary remarks. The stir and bustle went on without check, yet the crowd was singularly orderly and horseplay entirely absent. Then suddenly a clock struck from a neighbouring tower and a young woman, clad in black, fell on her knees in front of the entrance and prayed aloud. Everyone counted the strokes as they fell slowly on the ear.

One moment of complete silence in which the great crowd realised that a fellow creature had passed from the world.

The wind which had blown from the north all morning raising clouds of dust had dropped and was veering to the south. The buzz of conversation started again, and the crowd craned their necks towards each exodus from the gaol, as though Ned himself might stalk forth in his armour of ploughshares.

In the gallows chamber they cut the dead man down and wheeled him under the patch of sky into the gloom of the dead-house. There they removed the cap from his face and found he had taken the fall with his eyes open. The face was placid in its immortal sleep. Then the men of science got to work and shaved face and head. A certain Mr Kreitmeyer oiled the face and took a clay impression from which he later completed a death-mask. Mr Hamilton, phrenologist and president of the Society for the Abolition of Capital Punishment who had chaired the reprieve meeting, made measurements of the head. Then a number of medical men and students got to work, cut up the corpse, and severed head from trunk.

There was cause for celebration on the satisfactory conclusion of the Kelly affair in Melbourne's mansions and clubland that night, but perhaps some of the mighty felt a sense of awe. Who knows? The rich seldom record; they have nightmares, but seldom dream. They wish to forget such episodes and try to expunge forever the names of those who defy them.

An old man recorded in later years, "Bourke Street lit by gaslight — the crowds silent and subdued as if some debacle had occurred. The verdict of old residents is that he was a much injured man who would have made a brave citizen of the world if fate had allowed." And perhaps the old man was right — the great burden of public sympathy was with the outlaw — for when, eventually, after all the newspaper agitation, the petition for removal of David Gaunson from the position of Chairman of Committees came forward, it had no more than 666 signatures. But whether of ignorant persons or minors, the press did not record.

41. *The Summing Up*

As COLUMN AFTER COLUMN was devoted to accounts of the outlaw's death, and the *Age* in its philosophisings even admitted English misrule in Ireland, Australia relived the tragedy of another obstreperous son. Reports from spiritist circles of extraordinary disturbances in the spirit world with the arrival of the soul of Ned

Kelly gave rise to laughter; but not a few people caught their breath, when — ten days after the annual dinner party to celebrate his landing in the Port Phillip District and twelve days after the outlaw was hanged — Sir Redmond Barry passed away from the combined effect of his carbuncle and congestion of the lungs. Perhaps Ned had reminded Sir Redmond of what he had occasionally suspected, but been unwilling to admit — that the criminals he had built his career upon could be better men than he, and that, by posing as a patron of the arts and education for the common man, he was, in fact, a fraud. As Barry rolled to his last rest, followed by a long cortege, many an onlooker recalled how Ned had declared calmly to his face, "Yes, I will meet you there!"

But life reasserts itself; the grass pushes up between the cobbles. Melbourne returned to its Exhibition, its dress shops, its work benches and its wharves. At a demonstration of the wonderful electric light invention, the sudden illumination surprised a middle-aged gentleman in the act of kissing a lady. The consequences were such, so the papers said, that the gentleman became a confirmed believer in gas.

Melbourne, marvellous Melbourne, city of quarter of a million, Queen of the Southern Hemisphere, soon found a thousand new things to interest it — the challenge to a duel issued by a member of the German delegation at the Vice-Regal ball, the yacht races on Albert Park Lake, the penny-farthing cycle races, the new aquarium where multi-coloured fishes could be seen, the building of a railway to Frankston and the plans for a replacement for Princes Bridge.

During the latter part of 1880, little was added to the final chapter of the Kelly drama. Affairs in the police department were thoroughly disorganised. In addition to quarrels between the officers, trouble had arisen in the ranks because of the unwillingness of Senior Constable Kelly and others to serve at Greta. The Glenrowan affair, with its reports by Curnow and others of galloping horsemen and armed parties outside the perimeter of battle, had given the outbreak a new and larger dimension not unrelated to Ned's republican sentiments and his assertion at Glenrowan that the miners and cocky farmers were "all damn fools to bother their heads about Parliament at all, for this is our country". Such was the fear of another outbreak, that — inhibitions of the ranks notwithstanding — Greta station was reopened at double strength, the strength at Glenmore increased and a new station opened in the Kiewa valley to block any back exit for stolen stock.

At the same time, although Paddy Byrne and his mother were arrested for theft of a saddle on Detective Ward's instigation, Dick Hart was able to defy police attempts to search his place for weapons and a new mood in the police command prompted Sadleir — given some backbone by Inspector Montfort, the same who had presided at the capture of Power ten years before — to defy Nicolson and give Jim Kelly a guarantee that he would not be prosecuted under the Influx of Criminals Act. So was Acting Commissioner Nicolson saved from precipitating his second outbreak in the North-East!

Shortly after Glenrowan, the Kelly Reward Board was appointed by Order in Council to distribute the £8000 offered by the colonies of Victoria and New South Wales for the apprehension of the gang. But it was not until March 1881 that the Government judged things were quiet enough to order it to proceed. The three members of Parliament who comprised the Board went blithely to their job and called only five witnesses — former Chief Secretary Ramsay, three reporters, and a certain Mr Rawlins of Glenrowan, inventor of the railway cattle truck. They advertised for applications. Before long they had divided the blood money between sixty-six of ninety-one applicants.

The largest amount — £800 — went to Superintendent Hare, to whom, it was now revealed, Mr Ramsay had promised promotion to the Chief Commissionership and the placing of a substantial sum on parliamentary estimates should he succeed in destroying the gang. Then came Curnow, who received £550 for his action in stopping the police train. Third came Senior Constable Kelly, with the nicely estimated sum of £377 11s 8d for his part in the pursuit, the Glenrowan battle and the final capture. Over £1000 was divided between Sergeant Steele, Constable Bracken, Superintendent Sadleir and Inspector O'Connor. Jesse Dowsett, the railway guard who helped to capture the outlaw on that winter dawn, received £175 13s 9d. Amounts ranging from £165 to £50 were paid to some forty other police and a few railwaymen whose services had been regarded worthy of recognition.

The constables who had spent the night under the bed on the occasion Byrne shot Sherritt were each allotted the sum of £42 15s 9d; and 50s was awarded to each of Inspector O'Connor's black trackers, to be spent as the authorities saw fit as they could not be trusted with it.

Ironically, the only person resembling a police spy to receive a penny was one of Sherritt's brothers. The claims of Aaron's widow and mother and of several spies, including a saw-miller for whom

Ned had once worked, and the "stock inspector" who had first reported the armour were rejected along with those of several magistrates and a number of troopers, including Constable McIntyre on whose witness the outlaw had been hanged.

In the same month, letters patent were issued by the Governor appointing a Royal Commission to inquire into the circumstances of the outbreak and the efficiency of the force. Standish, Nicolson and O'Connor had all demanded an inquiry—O'Connor as an officer and a gentleman—and Nicolson had made grave charges against his superior. The bitterness and jealousy that had simmered in the force had boiled over following the Glenrowan battle, and the two-year spate of public, press and parliamentary criticism now demanded satisfaction.

The Commission sat for six months. It held sixty-six meetings and examined sixty-two witnesses at length. It visited Benalla, Greta, Glenrowan, Beechworth, Sebastopol and Wangaratta. A wealth of corroborative and conflicting evidence was accumulated. Standish and O'Connor had bitter passages. The dour Nicolson pressed his case against the popular Hare. Wheel within wheel, and intrigue beyond intrigue were revealed.

Investigation of the Detective Branch, to which Nicolson had devoted so much of his career, proved it to be riddled with corruption and the Commission recommended its disbandment. A wholesale system of blackmail of publicans, terrorism and victimisation was revealed in the City Police. Superintendent Winch, who had previously been in line for the job of Chief Commissioner, was accused of extortion, drunkenness, frequenting brothels and half a dozen other peccadilloes, while Sub-Inspector Larner was proved to have had bad debts with publicans and to have turned a blind eye to infringement of Sunday closing. Events of the police pursuit, the cave parties, the Euroa bank robbery and the battle of Glenrowan were recounted again.

Regarding the end of his old friend Sherritt, Superintendent Hare remarked: "It was doubtless a most fortunate occurrence that Aaron was shot by the outlaws. It was impossible to have reclaimed him . . . His wife is much better off without him."

Sadleir, who had written in an official report that Ned Kelly had shot Cherry for refusing to hold aside one of the window blinds during the Glenrowan battle, was confronted by sworn evidence to the contrary, and when asked the magisterial finding on Cherry was forced to reply: "Shot by the police in the execution of their duty."

It was estimated that the total cost of the Kelly affair to the country would be in the vicinity of £150 000.

As the sitting proceeded and revelations of witnesses penetrated to the Kelly country, ferment arose among the sympathisers, many of whom stood in danger of being forced off the land by the Lands Department's refusal of their applications—in some cases now current for two years. As the Commission accumulated evidence, were they—in addition to other troubles—to expect a new drive to track down all who had helped the gang?

The feeling of the time is well described by A.D. Hardy in his recollections of his father, John Hardy, who travelled between Alexandra and Mansfield for the monthly Land Board Hearings: ". . . the Land Officer was warned through anonymous letters that his policy would lead to trouble. He did not seek police protection, but instead of driving by the Gap went by another route, riding a powerful bay horse across the Puzzle Ranges and crossing the Delatite River by the ford, breaking his journey at Forsyth's station Maintongoon. The North-East had for months been tense with excitement . . . I well remember my father setting out. Last in his preparations he unlocked a drawer and transferred a Colt revolver from its case to the saddle holster, and in the cartouche which he wore under his coat put extra cartridges. On such occasions his homecoming was awaited with anxiety . . ."

Mrs Kelly and her baby were released from prison in February 1881. By April, the sympathisers were gripped by an anti-spy frenzy which led almost immediately to the wholesale resignation of the spy force Sadleir had recruited and was paying with funds supplied by the stock protection societies; some left without collecting their pay.

"We are almost completely in the dark," reported Sadleir from Benalla. "They are swearing vengeance and trying to trace our agents who are in deadly fear. They are all armed. An outbreak could be infinitely worse than anything before." Fearing his policy of moderation had failed, he applied for a transfer.

A few days later, the *Benalla Standard* reported: "There is not the slightest doubt but what the formation of another gang of bushrangers is being meditated in the Greta district . . . the Kelly sympathisers have recently spoken openly to this effect and . . . some secret work is occupying their attention."

And on 24 April two pit-saws disappeared from Acock's farm near Glenrowan—whether for armour or to line a redoubt, the police could not discover. Inspector Montfort told the

Commission behind closed doors that the Kelly outbreak was guerrilla warfare and that he was studying the area not to forestall a new outbreak but for the "purposes of defence"; what was required in the North-East was not a law-enforcement agency but "an army of occupation".

At the same time, Ned's old antagonist of the Ah Fook and bootshop episodes, Sergeant Whelan, refused in open session to answer a question as to the possibility of a new outbreak on grounds his answer would "interfere with the public interest".

Faced with the prospect of new trouble, the Government requested the Commission to advise it on means to immediately strengthen control in the North-East. Would it be advisable to keep the black trackers in Victoria and appoint O'Connor Inspector in the Victorian service? To this question the Commission answered in the negative, and Superintendent Chomley was sent to Brisbane to recruit trackers to the Victorian force.

The Commission recommended the immediate establishment of a system of police patrol. According to a police witness, Ned Kelly himself on the night before his execution had said, "If you want to keep the district quiet you will have men employed who know the place and the people. As long as strange police go among them they will laugh at them!" So it was decided that in future police should keep continually on the move along the roads covering the Kelly country, showing themselves everywhere, and speaking to friend and foe alike so that Kelly sympathisers would not know from whom they got their information. Fortunately for the police, Montfort was placed in charge and interpreted this as meaning that his men must be seen to enforce the law without fear or favour. In May he asked and received permission to vet land applications, and in succeeding months, by over-riding Melbourne objections where necessary, he managed by degrees to mitigate the anxiety which was giving such a powerful impetus to threats of another outbreak. Giving his approval to a Land Board application by Tom Lloyd senior he told Melbourne: " . . . where I can see my way clear to encourage such men by a little timely concession to abandon their evil ways, I always recommend the granting of their applications."

Despite this and a general improvement in economic conditions, affairs in the North-East progressed slowly and the police continued to go about their jobs nervously. At last the Commission came out with its report. In a brief history leading up to the outbreak, the inference was made that Dan was innocent of the charge that had given rise to the outbreak; the Commission noted that his companion, Jack Lloyd junior, whose name was also on the Chiltern warrant, had appeared in court and been discharged. Fitzpatrick was stigmatised as "a liar and a larrikin"; his conduct had been "unfortunate in its results". The Commission also noted the severity of the sentences Judge Barry had meted out to Mrs Kelly and Messrs Skillion and Williamson, but added, "No evidence has been adduced that the outlaws or friends were subject to persecution."

The Commission criticised the administration, number, distribution, arms, mounts and retrenchment of police prior to the outbreak. It rejected Hare's charges against Nicolson and criticised the Chief Commissioner's behaviour as "not characterised either by good judgement or by that zeal for the interests of the public service which should have distinguished an officer in Captain Standish's position."

It found Nicolson had evinced great zeal, but his conduct on several occasions had not been characterised by judgement or discretion. He had laboured under great difficulties through undue interference on the part of Standish. It recommended his retirement. It recorded that Hare's services had been praiseworthy, but that he should be retired because of strained relations with Nicolson. It recommended additional super-annuation of £100 per annum because of his wrist wound.

It recommended that Superintendent Sadleir, who had received £240 17s 3d of the reward, be placed at the bottom of the list of superintendents because of errors of judgement. It censured Brooke Smith for incompetence, and recommended his retirement on £100 per annum.

Sergeant Steele, who received £290 13s 9d of the reward, despite the fact that he had wounded young Reardon and fired at the mother, now received a censure because he had missed an opportunity to follow the outlaws when they passed through Wangaratta en route from the Murray. The eager Englishman was hardly dismayed, however, having been presented with a sword by the squatters of the Moyhu Stock Protection Society. Detective Ward, who had received £100, was found guilty of misleading his superior officers. The Commission recommended he be censured and reduced one grade.

As for the hut party, the Commission accused them of disobedience and cowardice, and recommended their dismissal from the service. Armstrong had already left the country to start a new life in the United States. Senior Constables Kelly and Johnston were praised for their actions at Glenrowan and recommended for promotion. The Commission commended

Curnow for special recognition and expressed appreciation of services rendered by the press and the Queensland Government. Curnow had fled to Ballarat and was living in fear of his life.

The report had scarcely been tabled when one member, Mr Dixon, tabled a minority report in an endeavour to vindicate Hare and reopen the way for him to become Chief Commissioner. The remaining members of the Commission immediately replied. Mr Dixon's protest, they declared, was no more than a paraphrase of Superintendent Hare's official report which was itself a mere tissue of egotism and misrepresentation. There was every evidence to suggest Hare had been in collusion with Standish in the persecution of Nicolson. Comparisons might be odious, but it was singular that while Hare left his post and returned to Benalla under the impression that the wound in his wrist would prove fatal, the wounded outlaw was able to hold his ground encumbered by iron armour until seven o'clock, when in an attempt to rejoin his companions he fell overpowered by numbers.

Superintendent Hare's bill against the Government for surgical attendance amounted to £607, about £408 of which was paid to his cousin, Dr Charles Ryan, lately returned from service in the Turkish army in the war against Russia. While Hare himself was being petted and coddled on all sides and a special surgeon dispatched almost daily some fifty kilometres to attend him, the Government had questioned the payment of four guineas for the treatment of a black tracker who had received a head wound.

So wrote a majority of the Commission under pressure. So under duress a little more of the truth came out! Beyond that the Commission did not go. No effort was made to apportion responsibility for the deaths of Cherry, Medcalf and Johnny Jones and the wounding of the other innocent inmates of the Glenrowan Inn. The Commission seemed quite unaware that the law had exceeded its rights. When Reardon recounted how his son was shot and how he himself escaped from the hotel, one of the Commissioners remarked facetiously, "That was hot work!"—to which unfeeling remark Reardon replied sharply: "Hot work! You would not like to be there, I can tell you."

Not one friend of the outlaws was permitted to give evidence. Kelly's own accusations regarding the Stock Protection Society and what amounted to flagrant prejudicing of the law were ignored. To the root cause of the outbreak—the subversion of a whole series of Land Acts by the North-East squatters—the Commission gave no attention; it merely reiterated old charges from which one might conclude the Quinns and Kellys had been stealing cattle by the herd and holding the North-East in terror.

By its every action the Commission revealed its unconscious approval for the official policy of neglecting the rights of poor people and elevating into a major crime any infringement of the property rights of the rich, thus helping to perpetuate class friction and waste the psychic forces of the population. As if to illustrate the point, Hare, who had emerged from the inquiry with little credit, had nevertheless done so with the fattest pocket.

Across the face of the suspended earth the cloud galleons rode in peace; and in peace each dawn and sunset, the sun struck a chord at the earth's edge. Below on the earth's face a thousand million men shoved at the trough of life like pigs — the big pigs in, body and all, fouling their own food, and the many little hungry ones squealing around the flanks. It was a great age!

The Nihilist agitation in Russia continued to assume alarming proportions. Gangs of prisoners continued to tramp their way across the sodden roads to distant Siberia. A band of robbers 200 strong was spreading terror around Paulowski in the south — its captain a peasant woman of singular beauty. Aristocratic writers, oppressed with a sense of guilt at the sprawling misery of their country, were forging the soul of revolution.

In the United States, with the crushing of the Southern Confederacy, the Sioux nation of the Great Plains and successive strikes by labour unions — the last by bringing in new waves of cheap labour across the Atlantic — the Yankees were accumulating capital and opportunity at an unprecedented rate; it was the Gilded Age and the dawn of empire.

The agitation for Home Rule in Ireland meanwhile continued to create uneasiness in the public mind, the mind, of course, being that of proud England, mistress of the globe, possessor of half the machine power on earth, that Dr Jekyll and Mr Hyde torchbearer of technical and social progress at the expense of backward peoples. In Athlone, the stage collapsed under the great Parnell. The supports had been sawn through, not by England's hand, but by the hand of a son of Ireland, "the old sow that eats her farrow" — such was the subtlety of the imperial policy of divide and rule.

In France, Pasteur was working on hydrophobia, Impressionism was being born, Zola was writing *Attack on the Mill.* It was the age of Darwin in which the theory of survival of the fittest had been elevated into justification for the crimes of civilisation. It was the age of Huxley, Haeckel, Tolstoy, Ibsen, Puccini. It was the beginning of forty-three years of peace of which

Count von Bismarck wrote to his friend Prince Orlov:

> The great powers of our time are like travellers unknown to
> one another whom chance has brought together in a carriage.
> They watch each other, and when one of them puts his hand in
> his pocket his neighbour gets his own revolver ready in order to
> be able to fire the first shot.

It was the age, too, in which Prince Kropotkin stipulated that
only by co-operation could mankind avoid the fate of the
dinosaur, and in which grandfather Marx from his London villa
was thundering that the accumulation of capital was creating the
army of labour—that, in fact, Dame Capital was pregnant with a
socialist son and would soon be screaming with birth pangs.

To the south of feudal Asia, a heterogeneous Australian
population was rapidly coming to terms with what their betters
still considered to be a hostile and inferior environment. An
alternative link with Europe had been established by the laying of
a cable to Sydney from San Francisco via the Sandwich Islands.
While the sickle sang in old Europe, the stump-jump plough was
jolting its way through the mallee scrub, and the combine
harvester, its wheels and levers controlled by those same uncouth
colonials scant removed from bog Irish, puffed over the first of
endless horizons. As new industries were founded, the era of
factory and wage began to eat up that of the small farmer, just as
the latter had eaten up the roaring days. Miners, small farmers,
factory hands—such were the men and women who were forging a
new and distinctive spirit that was soon to take flight in a score of
writers and in Federation.

Meanwhile, Ned's grey mare, Mirth, bought at auction in
Benalla, trotted between shafts in Melbourne, pulling popular
actor George Seth Coppin around; while at Sunbury, out of
Melbourne, Ned's armour stood on show for the social set, a
trophy of war delivered by Superintendent Hare to Australia's
richest squatter, Sir William Clarke, whose father had been a
Sydney butcher before he learnt to apply the tricks of the meat
market to speculation in the age of the land-takers.

While former Superintendent Nicolson, now Police Magistrate,
continued his existence imprisoned like a turtle in virtue and
hostility, and while Standish prepared to recant his Masonic
loyalties and return to the Catholic faith, Hare—between stints as
Police Magistrate—took life easy at Sunbury. His luck had never
really broken. Life also continued serenely for His Excellency the
Most Honourable George Augustus Constantine, Marquis of
Normanby, Earl of Mulgrave, and Baron Mulgrave of Mulgrave,

all in the county of York, in the Peerage of the United Kingdom; and Baron Mulgrave of New Ross, in the County of Wexford, in the Peerage of Ireland; a member of Her Majesty's Most Honourable Privy Council; Knight Grand Cross of the Most Distinguished Order of Saint Michael and Saint George; Governor and Commander-In-Chief in and over the Colony of Victoria and its dependencies, etc., etc., etc.

Skull on a shelf in the Penal Department, body facing west in unhallowed ground at Melbourne gaol, denied the reawakening to eternal life that is to be the lot of all without sin in the dawn of the last day, Ned too was at peace.

But throughout the broad land, his spirit had never been more awake.

Appendix 1: The Cameron Letter

The text is from the original held by the Public Records Office of Victoria.

Dear Sir,

Take no offence if I take the opportunity of writing a few lines to you, wherein I wish to state a few remarks concerning the case of Trooper Fitzpatrick against Mrs Kelly, W. Skillion, and W. Williamson, and to state the facts of the case to you. It seems to me impossible to get any justice without I make a statement to someone that will take notice of it, as it is no use in me complaining about anything that the police may choose to say or swear against me, and the public in their ignorance and blindness will undoubtedly back them up to their utmost.

No doubt I am now placed in very peculiar circumstances and you might blame me for it, but if you knew how I have been wronged and persecuted you would say I cannot be blamed. In April last an information was (which must have come under your notice) sworn against me for shooting Trooper Fitzpatrick, which was false, and my Mother with an infant baby and brother-in-law and another neighbour was taken for aiding and abetting and attempting to murder him, a charge of which they are as purely innocent as the child unborn.

During my stay in the King River I run in a wild bull which I gave to Lydicker who afterwards sold him to Carr and he killed him for beef. Some time afterwards I was told I was blamed for stealing this Bull from Whitty. I asked Whitty on Moyhu Racecourse why he blamed me for stealing his bull and he said he had found the bull, and he never blamed me for stealing him. He said it was —————— who told him that I stole the bull. Some time afterward I heard again I was blamed for stealing a mob of calves from Whitty and Farrell, which I never had anything to do with, and along with this and other talk, I began to think they wanted something to talk about. Whitty and Burns not being satisfied with all the picked land on King River and Boggy Creek, and the run of their stock on the Certificate ground free, and no one interfering with them paid heavy rent for all the open ground so as a poor man could not keep any stock and impounded every beast they could catch even off Government roads, if a poor man happened to leave his horse or bit of poddy calf outside his paddock, it would be impounded, I have known over 60 head of horses to be in one day impounded by Whitty and Burns, all belonging to poor men of the district. They would have to leave their harvest or ploughing and go to Oxley and then perhaps not have money to release them and have to give a bill of sale or borrow the money, which is no easy matter, and along with all this sort of work ——— the policeman stole a horse from George King and had him in Whitty and Jeffrey's paddock until he left the Force and this was the cause of me and my stepfather George King stealing Whitty's horses and selling them to Baumgarten and those other men, the pick of them was sold at Howlong and the rest was sold to Baumgarten who was a perfect stranger to me and I believe an honest man. No man had anything to do with the horses but me and George King. William Cooke who was convicted for Whitty's horses had nothing to do with them, nor was he ever in my company at Peterson's the German at Howlong. The brand was altered by me and George King and the horses sold as strait. Any man requiring horses would have sought them the same as those men and would have been potted the same and I consider Whitty ought to do something towards the release of those innocent men, otherwise there will be a collision between me and him as I can to his satisfaction prove I took J. Welsh's black mare and the rest of the horses, which I will prove to him, in next issue, and after those horses had been found and the row being over them, I wrote a letter to Mr Swannell of Lake Rowan to advertise my horses for sale, as I was intending to sell out. I sold them afterwards at Benalla and the rest in New South Wales and left Victoria as I wished to see certain parts of the country and very shortly afterwards as there was a Warrant for me, as I since hear the Police Sergeant Steele, Straughan and Fitzpatrick and others searched the Eleven Mile and every other place in the district for me and a man named Newman, who had escaped from the Wangaratta Police for months before the 15th of April. Therefore it was impossible for me to be in Victoria, as every schoolboy knows me, and on the 15th of April, Fitzpatrick came to the Eleven Mile and had some conversation with Williamson who was splitting on the hill, seeing my brother and another man, he rode down and had some conversation with this man whom he swore was William Skillion. This man was not called in Beechworth as he could have proved Fitzpatrick's falsehood as Skillion and another man was away after horses at this time, which can be proved by eight or nine witnesses. The man who the troopers swore was Skillion can prove Williamson's innocence besides other important evidence, which can be brought on the prisoner's behalf. The trooper after speaking to this man rode to the house and Dan came out. He asked Dan to go to Greta with him. Dan asked him what for and he said he had a warrant for him for stealing Whitty's horses. They both went inside, Dan was having something to eat. The trooper was impatient and Mrs Kelly asked him what he wanted Dan for, he said he had a Warrant for him. Dan said produce your Warrant and he said he had none, it was only a telegram from Chiltern. Mrs Kelly said he need not go unless he liked without a warrant. She told the trooper he had no business on her premises without some Authority besides his own word. He pulled out his revolver, and said he would blow her brains out if she interfered in the arrest. Mrs Kelly said, if Ned was here, he would ram the revolver down his throat. To frighten the trooper Dan said, Ned is coming now. The trooper looked around to see if it was true. Dan dropped the knife and fork which showed he had no murderous intention clapped Heenans Hug on him, took his revolver and threw him and part of the door outside and kept him there until Skillion and Ryan came with horses which Dan sold that night, the trooper left and invented some scheme to say he got shot, which any man can see it was impossible for him to have been shot. He told Dan to clear out that Sergeant Steele or Detective Brown would be there before morning, as Straughan was over the Murray trying to get up a case against Dan and the Lloyds as the Germans over the Murray would swear to anyone and they will lag you guilty or not. Next day Skillion, Williamson and Mrs Kelly, with an infant were taken and thrown into prison and were six months awaiting trial and no bail allowed and was convicted on the evidence of the meanest man that ever the sun shone on. I have been told by Police that he is hardly ever sober, also between him and his father they sold his sister to a chinaman, but he seems a strapping and genteel looking young man and more fit to be a starcher to Laundry than a trooper, but to a keen observer, he has the wrong appearance to have anything like a clear conscience or a manly heart. The deceit is too plain to be seen in the White Cabbage hearted looking face, I heard nothing of this transaction until very close on the trial I being then over 400 miles from Greta. I heard that I was outlawed and £100 pound reward for me in Victoria and also hundreds of charges of Horse Stealing was against me, beside shooting a trooper. I came into Victoria and enquired after my brother and found him working with another man at Bullock Creek. Heard how the police used to be blowing that they would shoot me first and then cry Surrender. How they used to come to the house where there was no one there but women and Superintendent Smith used to say. See all the men I have today, I will have as many more tomorrow and blow him into pieces as small as the paper that is in our guns and they used to repeatedly rush into the house revolver in hand upset milk dishes, empty the flour out on the ground, break tins of eggs, and throw the meat out of the cask on to the floor, and dirty and destroy all the provisions, which can be proved and shove the girls in front of them into the rooms like dogs and abuse and insult them. Detective Ward and Constable Hayes took out their revolvers and threatened to shoot the girls and children, while Mrs Skillion was absent, the oldest being with her, the greatest murderers and ruffians would not be guilty of such an action. This sort of cruelty and disgraceful conduct to my brothers and sisters who had no protection coupled with the conviction of my Mother and those innocent men certainly made my blood boil as I don't think there is a man born could have the patience to suffer what I did. They were not satisfied with frightening and insulting my sisters night and day and destroying their provisions and lagging my Mother with an infant baby and those innocent men, but should follow me and my brother who was innocent of having anything to do with any stolen horses, into the wilds, where he had been quietly digging and doing well, neither molesting or interfering with anyone and I was not there long and on the 26th October I came on the tracks of police horses, between Table Top and the Bogs, I crossed there and went to Emu Swamp and returning home came on more police tracks making for our camp. I told my mates and me and my brother went out next morning and found police camped at the Shingle Hut with long fire arms and we came to the conclusion our doom was sealed unless we could take their fire-arms, as we had nothing but a gun and a rifle if they came on us at our work or camp. We had no chance only to die like dogs as we thought the country was woven with police and we might have a chance of fighting them if we had firearms, as it generally takes 40 to one. We approached the Spring as close as we could get to the camp, the intervening space being clear. We saw two men at the Log, they got up and one took a double barrel fowling piece and one drove the horses down and hobbled them against the tent and we thought there was more men in the tent, those being on sentry. We could have shot those two men, without speaking, but not wishing to take life we waited. McIntyre laid the gun against the stump and Lonigan sat on the log. I advanced, my brother Dan keeping McIntyre covered. I called on them to throw up their hands McIntyre obeyed and never attempted to reach for his gun or revolver, Lonigan ran to a battery of logs and put his head up to take aim at me, when I shot him, or he would have shot me, as I knew well, I asked who was in the tent, McIntyre replied no one. I

239

approached the camp and took possession of their revolvers and fowling piece which I loaded with bullets instead of shot. I told McIntyre I did not want to shoot him or any man that would surrender. I explained Fitzpatrick's falsehood which no policeman can be ignorant of. He said he knew Fitzpatrick had wronged us but he could not help it. He said he intended to leave the Force on account of his bad health, his life was insured, the other two men who had no firearms came up when they heard the shot fired and went back to our camp for fear the police might call there in our absence and surprise us on our arrival. My brother went back to the Spring and I stopped at the Log with McIntyre. Kennedy and Scanlan came up, McIntyre said he would get them to surrender if I spared their lives as well as his. I said I did not know either him Scanlan or Kennedy, and had nothing up against them, and would not shoot any of them, if they gave up their firearms and promised to leave the Force, as it was the meanest billet in the world. They are worse than cold-blooded murderers and hangmen. He said he was sure they would never follow me any more. I gave them my word that I would give them a chance. McIntyre went up to Kennedy, Scanlan behind with a rifle and a revolver. I called on them to throw up their hands. Scanlan slewed his horse around to gallop away, but turned again and as quick as thought fired at me with the rifle and was in the act of firing again, when I shot him. Kennedy alighted on the off side of his horse and got behind a tree and opened hot fire. McIntyre got on Kennedy's horse and galloped away. I could have shot him if I choose as he was right against me but rather than break my word I let him go. My brother advanced from the Spring, Kennedy fired at him and ran as he found neither of us was dead. I followed him, he got behind another tree and fired at me again. I shot him in the armpit as he was behind the tree, he dropped his revolver and ran again and slewed round and I fired with the gun again and shot him through the right chest as I did not know that he had dropped his revolver and was turning to surrender. He could not live or I would have let him go. Had they been my own brothers, I could not help shooting them or else lie down and let them shoot me, which they would have done had their bullets been directed as they intended them. But as for handcuffing Kennedy to a tree or cutting his ear off or brutally treating any of them, is a cruel falsehood. If Kennedy's ear was cut off, it has been done since I put his cloak over him and left him as honourable as I could and if they were my own brothers I could not be more sorry for them, with the exception of Lonigan I did not begrudge him what bit of lead he got as he was the beastliest meanest man that I had any

240

account against for him. Fitzpatrick, Sergeant Whelan, Constable Day and King, the Bootmaker, once tried to hand-cuff me at Benalla and when they could not Fitzpatrick tried to choke me, Lonigan caught me by the privates and would have killed me but was not able. Mr McInnes came up and I allowed him to put the hand-cuffs on when the police were bested. This cannot be called wilful murder for I was compelled to shoot them in my own defence or lie down like a cur and die. Certainly their wives and children are to be pitied, but those men came into the bush with the intention of shooting me down like a dog, yet they know and acknowledge I have been wronged. And is my Mother and infant baby and my poor little brothers and sisters not to be pitied more so, who has got no alternative only to put up with brutal and unmanly conduct of the police who have never had any relations or a Mother or must have forgot them. I was never convicted of horse stealing. I was once arrested by Constable Hall and 14 more men in Greta, and there was a subscription raised for Hall, by persons who had too much money about Greta, in honour of Hall arresting Wild Wright and Gunn, Wright and Gunn were potted and Hall could not pot me for horse stealing, but with the subscription money he gave £20 to James Murdoch, who has recently been hung in Wagga Wagga and on Murdoch's evidence, I was found guilty of receiving, knowing to be stolen, which I, Wright, W. Ambrose, J. Ambrose and W. Hatcher and W. Williamson and others can prove I was innocent of knowing the Mare to be stolen, and I was accused of taking a hawker by the name of McCormack's horse to pull another hawker named Ben Gould out of a bog. Mr Gould got up in the morning to feed his horses, seen Mr McCormack's horse, and knew he had strayed and sent his man with him about two miles to where McCormack was camped in Greta. Mr and Mrs McCormack came out and seen the waggons bogged and accused him of using the horse. I told Gould that was for his good nature. Mrs McCormack turned on me and accused me for catching the horse for Gould, as Gould knew that he was wicked and could not catch him himself. Me and my uncle was cutting and branding calves and Ben Gould wrapped up a pair of testicles, wrote a note and gave it to me to give to Mrs McCormack. McCormack said he would fight me I was then 14 years of age, I was getting off my horse and Mrs McCormack hit the horse, he jumped forward and my fist came in collision with Mr McCormack's nose who swore he was standing 10 yards away from another man and the one hit knocked the two men down. However ridiculous the evidence may seem, I received three months or £10, for hitting him and 3 months for delivering the parcel and bound to the peace for 12 months. At the time I was taken by Hall and his 14 assistants, therefore I dare not strike any of them as Hall was a great cur. And as for Dan he never was tried for assaulting a woman. Mr Butler, P.M., sentenced him to 3 months without the option of a fine and one month or two pounds fine for wilfully destroying property, a sentence which there is no law to uphold, and yet they had to do their sentence and other prosecutors. Mr D. Goodman since got 4 years for perjury concerning the same property. The Minister of Justice should enquire into this respecting their sentence and he will find a wrong jurisdiction given by Butler P.M. on the 19th of October 1877 at Benalla and these are the only charges was ever proved against either of us, therefore we are falsely represented. The reports of bullets having been fired into the bodies of the Troopers after death is false and the Coroner should be consulted. I have no intention of asking mercy for myself or any mortal man or apologising, but wish to give timely warning that if my people do not get justice and those innocents released from prison and the police wear their uniform, I shall be forced to seek revenge of everything of the human race for the future, I will not take innocent life, if justice is given, but as the police are afraid or ashamed to wear their uniforms, therefore every man's life is in danger. As I was outlawed without any cause and cannot be no worse, and have but once to die, and if the public do not see justice done, I will seek revenge for the name and character which has been given to me and my relations while God gives me strength to pull a trigger. The witness which can prove Fitzpatrick's falsehood can be found by advertisement and if this is not done immediately horrible disasters shall follow, Fitzpatrick shall be the cause of greater slaughter to the rising generation than St Patrick was to the snakes and frogs in Ireland, for had I robbed, plundered, ravished and murdered everything I met, my character could not be painted blacker than it is at present, but thank God my conscience is as clear as the snow in Peru, and as I hear a picked Jury amongst which was a discharged Sergeant of Police, was empanelled on the trial and David Lindsay who gave evidence for the Crown is a Shanty Keeper having no licence and is liable to a heavy fine and keeps a book of information for the police and his character needs no comment for he is capable of rendering Fitzpatrick any assistance he required for a conviction as he could be broke any time Fitzpatrick chose to inform on him.

I am really astonished to see Members of the Legislative Assembly led astray by such articles as the Police, for while an outlaw reigns their pocket swells, tis double pay and country girls —

by concluding, as I have no more paper unless I rob for it, if I get justice I will cry a go. For I need no lead or powder to revenge my cause. And if words be louder, I will oppose your laws with no offence. (Remember your Railroads), and a sweet good bye from
EDWARD KELLY
A Forced Outlaw

Appendix 2: The Jerilderie Letter

The text is from a copy of the original made in 1879 or 1880 by a government clerk and held by the Public Records Office of Victoria. It is published here with such spelling and punctuation as Kelly and Byrne or the clerk, or all three, possessed.

> THE QUEEN *v.* EDWARD KELLY
> WILFUL MURDER
> (copy of statement handed by
> defendant to Mr. Living)

Dear Sir,

I wish to acquaint you with some of the occurrences of the present past and future.

In or about the spring of 1870 the ground was very soft a hawker named Mr Gould got his waggon bogged between Greta and my mother's house on the eleven mile creek, the ground was that rotten it would bog a duck in places so Mr. Gould had abandon his waggon for fear of loosing his horses in the spewy ground he was stopping at my mothers awaiting finer or dryer weather Mr. McCormack and his wife hawkers also were camped in Greta the mosquitoes were very bad which they generally are in a wet spring and to help them Mr. Johns had a horse called ruila cruta although a gelding was as clever as old Wombat or any other stallion at running horses away and taking them on his beat which was from Greta swamp to the seven mile creek consequently he enticed McCormacks horse away from Greta.

Mr. Gould was up early feeding his horses heard a bell and seen McCormack horse for he knew the horse well he sent his boy to take him back to Greta.

When McCormack's got the horse they came straight out to Goold and accused him of working the horse; this was false and Goold was amazed at the idea I could not help laughing to hear Mrs. McCormack accusing him of using the horse after him being so kind as to send his boy to take him from the ruta cruta and take him back to them.

I pleaded Goulds innocence and Mrs McCormack turned on me and accused me of bringing the horse from Greta to Goold's waggon to pull him out of the bog I did not say much to the woman as my mother was present but the same day me and my uncle was cutting calves Gould wrapped up a note and a pair of the calves testicles and gave them to me to give them to Mrs McCormack. I did not see her and gave the parcel to a boy to give

244

to her when she would come instead of giving it to her he gave it to her husband consequently McCormack said he would summons me I told him neither me nor Goold used their horse.

he said I was a liar and he could welt me or any of my breed I was about 14 years of age but accepted the challenge and dismounting when Mrs McCormack struck my horse in the flank with a bullocks skin it jumped forward and my fist came in collision with McCormack's nose and caused him to loose his equilibrium and fall postrate I tied up my horse to finish the battle but McCormack got up and ran to the Police camp.

Constable Hall asked me what the row was about. I told him they accused me and Gould of using their horse and I hit him and would do the same to him if he challenged me McCormack pulled me and swore their lies against me

I was sentenced to three months for hitting. him and three months for the parcel and bound to keep the peace for 12 months.

Mrs McCormack gave good substantial evidence as she is well acquainted with that place called Tasmania better known as the Dervon or Vandiemans land and McCormack being a Police man over the convicts and women being scarce released from that land of bondage and tyranny, and they came to Victoria and are at present residents of Greta and on the 29th of March I was released from prison and came home Wild Wright came to the eleven mile to see Mr Gunn stopped all night and lost his mare both him and me looked all day for her and could not get her Wright who was a stranger to me was in a hurry to get back to Mansfield and I gave him another mare and he told me if I found his mare to keep her until he brought mine back.

I was going to Wangaratta and saw the mare and I caught her and took her with me all the Police and Detective Berrill seen her as Martins girls used to ride her about the town during several days that I stopped at Petre Martains Star Hotel in Wangaratta, she was a chestnut mare white face docked tail very remarkable branded (M) as plain as the hands on a town clock, the property of a Telegraph Master in Mansfield, he lost her on the 6th gazetted her on the 12th of March and I was a prisoner in Beechworth Gaol until the 29 of March therefore I could not have stole the mare.

I was riding the mare through Greta Constable Hall came to me and said he wanted me to sign some papers that I did not sign at Beechworth concerning my bail bonds I thought it was the truth he said the papers was at the Barracks and I had no idea he wanted to arrest me or I would have quietly rode away instead of going to the Barracks.

I was getting off when Hall caught hold of me and thought to throw me but made a mistake and came on the broad of his back himself in the dust the mare galloped away and instead of me putting my foot on Halls neck and taking his revolver and putting him in the lock up. I tried to catch the mare. Hall got up and snapped three or four caps at me and would have shot me but the colts patent refused.

This is well known in Greta Hall never told me he wanted to arrest me until after he tried to shoot me when I heard the caps snapping I stood until Hall came close he had me covered and was shaking with fear and I knew he would pull the trigger before he would be game to put his hand on me so I duped and jumped at him caught the revolver with one hand and Hall by the collar with the other.

I dare not strike him or my sureties would loose the bond money I used to trip him and let him take a mouth ful of dust now and again as he was as helpless as a big guano after leaving a dead bullock or horse.

I kept throwing him in the dust until I got him across the street the very spot where Mrs O'Briens Hotel stands now the cellar was just dug then there was some brush fencing where the post and rail was taking down and on this I threw the big cowardly Hall on his belly I straddled him and rooted both spurs into his thighs he roared like a big calf attacked by dogs and shifted several yards of fence I got his hands at the back of his neck and tried to make him let the revolver go but he stuck to it like grim death to a dead volunteer he called for assistance to a man named Cohen and Barnett, Lewis, Thompson, Jewitt two blacksmiths who was looking on I dare not strike any of them as I was bound to keep the peace or I could have spread those curs like dung in a paddock

they got ropes tied my hands and feet and Hall beat me over the head with his six chambered colts revolver nine stitches were put in some of the cuts by Dr Hastings And when Wild Wright and my mother came they could trace us across the street by the blood in the dust and which spoiled the lustre of the paint on the gate-post of the Barracks Hall sent for more Police and Doctor Hastings. Next morning I was handcuffed a rope tied from them to my legs and to the seat of the cart and taken to Wangaratta Hall was frightened I would throw him out of the cart so he tied me whilst Constable Arthur laughed at his cowardice for it was he who escorted me and Hall to Wangaratta.

I was tried and committed as Hall swore I claimed the mare the Doctor died or he would have proved Hall a perjurer Hall has been tried several times for perjury but got clear as this is no crime in the Police force it is a credit to a Policeman to convict an innocent man but any mutt can pot a guilty one Halls character is well known about El Dorado and Snowy Creek and Hall was considerably in debt to Mr L. O'Brien and he was going to leave Greta Mr O.Brien seen no other chance of getting his money so there was a subscription collected for Hall and with the aid of this money he got James Murdock who was recently hung in Wagga Wagga to give false evidence against me but I was acquitted on the charge of horsestealing and on Hall and Murdocks evidence I was found guilty of receiving and got 3 years experience in Beechworth Pentridges dungeons. this is the only charge ever proved against me Therefore I can say I never was convicted of horse or cattle stealing

My Brother Dan was never charged with assaulting a woman but he was sentenced to three months without the option of a fine and one month and two pound fine for damaging property by Mr. Butler P.M. a sentence that there is no law to uphold therefore the minister of Justice neglected his duty in that case, but there never was such a thing as justice in the English laws but any amount of injustice to be had. Out of over thirty head of the very best horses the land could produce I could only find one when I got my liberty.

Constable Flood stole and sold the most of them to the navvies on the railway line one bay cob he stole and sold four different times the line was completed and the men all gone when I came out and Flood was shifted to Oxley.

he carried on the same game there all the stray horses that was any time without an owner and not in the Police Gazette Flood used to claim He was doing a good trade at Oxley until Mr Brown of the Laceby Station got him shifted as he was always running his horses about.

Flood is different to Sergeant Steel, Strachan, Hall and the most of Police a they have got to hire cads and if they fail the police are quite helpless. But Flood can make a cheque single-handed he is the greatest horsestealer with the exception of myself and George King I know of.

I never worked on a farm a horse and saddle was never traced to me after leaving employment since February 1873 I worked as a faller at Mr J. Saunders and R Rules sawmills then for Heach and Dockendorf I never worked for less than two pound ten a week since I left Pentridge and in 1875 or 1876 I was overseer for Saunders and Rule. Bourkes water-holes sawmills in Victoria since then I was on the King river. during my stay there I ran in a wild bull which I gave to Lydicher a farmer he sold him to Carr a Publican and Butcher who killed him for beef, sometime afterwards I was blamed for stealing this bull from James Whitty Boggy Creek I asked Whitty Oxley racecourse why he blamed me for stealing his bull

he said he had found his bull and never blamed me but his son-in-law Farrell told him he heard I sold the bull to Carr not long afterwards I heard again I was blamed for stealing a mob of calves from Whitty and Farrell which I knew nothing about. I began to think they wanted me to give them something to talk about. Therefore I started wholesale and retail horse and cattle dealing Whitty and Burns not being satisfied with all the picked land on the Boggy Creek and King River and the run of their stock on certificate ground free and no one interfering with them paid heavy rent to the banks for all the open ground so as a poor man could keep no stock, and impounded every beast they could get. even off Government roads.

If a poor man happened to leave his horse or a bit of a poddy calf outside his paddock they would be impounded.

I have known over 60 head of horses impounded in one day by Whitty and Burns all belonging to poor farmers they would have to leave their ploughing or harvest or other employment to go to Oxley.

when they would get there perhaps not have money enough to release them and have to gave a bill of sale or borrow money which is no easy matter and along with this sort of work, Farrell the Policeman stole a horse from George King and had him in Whitty and Farrell's Paddocks until he left the force

and all this was the cause of me and my step-father George King taking their horses and selling them to Baumgarten and Kennedy.

the pick of them was taken to a good market and the culls were kept in Petersons paddock and their brands altered by me two was sold to Kennedy and the rest to Baumgarten who were strangers to me and I believe honest men.

They paid me full value for the horses and could not have known they were stolen.

no person had anything to do with the stealing and selling of the horses but me and George King.

William Cooke who was convicted for Whitty's horses was innocent he was not in my company at Petersons. But it is not the place of the Police to convict guilty men as it is by them they get their living had the right parties been convicted it would have been a bad job for the Police as Berry would have sacked a great many of them only I came to their aid and kept them in their bilits and good employment and got them double pay and yet the ungrateful articles convicted my mother and an infant my brother-in-law and another man who was innocent and still annoy my brothers and sisters and the ignorant unicorns even threaten to shoot myself But as soon as I am dead they will be heels up in the muroo. there will be no more police required they will be sacked and supplanted by soldiers on low pay in the towns and special constables made of some of the farmers to make up for this double pay and expense.

It will pay Government to give those people who are suffering innocence, justice and liberty. if not I will be compelled to show some colonial strategm which will open the eyes of not only the Victoria Police and inhabitants but also the whole British army and now doubt they will acknowledge their hounds were barking at the wrong stump and that Fitzpatrick will be the cause of greater slaughter to the Union Jack than Saint Patrick was to the snakes and toads in Ireland.

The Queen of England was as guilty as Baumgarten and Kennedy Williamson and Skillion of what they were convicted for when the horses were found on the Murray River I wrote a letter to Mr Swanhill of Lake Rowan to acquaint the Auctioneer and to advertize my horses for sale I brought some of them to that place but did not sell I sold some of them in Benalla Melbourne and other places and left the colony and became a rambling gambler soon after I left there was a warrant for me and the Police searched the place and watched night and day for two or three weeks and when they could not snare me they got a warrant against my brother Dan And on the 15th of April Fitzpatrick came to the eleven mile creek to arrest him he had some conversation with a horse dealer whom he swore was William Skillion this man was not called in Beechworth besides several other witnesses, who alone could have proved Fitzpatricks falsehood after leaving this man he went to the house asked was dan in Dan came out I hear previous to this Fitzpatrick had some conversation with Williamson on the hill. he asked Dan to come to Greta with him as he had a warrant for him for stealing Whitty's horses Dan said all right they both went inside Dan was having something to eat his mother asked Fitzpatrick what he wanted Dan for the trooper said he had a warrant for him Dan then asked him to produce it he said it was only a telegram sent from Chiltern but Sergeant Whelan ordered him to relieve Steel at Greta and call and arrest Dan and take him in to Wangaratta next morning and get him remanded Dans mother said Dan need not go without a warrant unless he liked and that the trooper had no business on her premises without some authority besides his own word.

The trooper pulled out his revolver and said he would blow her brains out if she interfered in the arrest she told him it was a good job for him Ned was not there or he would ram his revolver down his throat Dan looked out and said Ned is coming now, the trooper being off his guard looked out and when Dan got his attention drawn he dropped the knife and fork which showed he had no murderous intent and slapped Hennan's hug on him took his revolver and kept him there until Skillion and Ryan came with horses which Dan sold that night.

The trooper left and invented some scheme to say that he got shot which any man can see is false, he told Dan to clear out that Sergeant Steel and Detective Brown and Strachan would be there before morning Strachan had been over the Murray trying to get up a case against him and they would convict him if they caught him as the stock society offored an enticement for witnesses to swear anything and the germans over the Murray would swear to the wrong man as well as the right.

Next day Williamson and my mother was arrested and Skillion the day after who was not there at all at the time of the row which can be proved by 8 or 9 witnesses and the Police got great credit and praise in the papers for arresting the mother of 12 children one an infant on her breast and those two quiet hard working innocent men who would not know the difference a revolver and a saucepan handle and kept them six months awaiting trial and then convicted them on the evidence of the meanest article that ever the sun shone on it seems that the jury was well chosen by the Police as there was a discharged Sergeant amongst them which is contrary to law they thought it impossible for a Policeman to swear a lie but I can assure them it was by that means and hiring cads they get promoted I have heard from a trooper that he never knew Fitzpatrick to be one night sober and that he sold his sister to a chinaman but he looks a young strapping rather genteel more fit to be a starcher to a laundress than a policeman. For to a keen observer he has the wrong appearance for a manly heart the deceit and cowardice is too plain to be seen in the puny cabbage hearted looking face.

I heard nothing of this transaction until very close on the trial I being then over 400 miles from Greta when I heard I was outlawed and a hundred pound reward for me for shooting a trooper in Victoria and a hundred pound for any man that could prove a conviction of horsestealing against me so I came back to Victoria knew I would get no justice if I gave myself up I enquired after my brother Dan and found him digging on Bullock Creek heard how the Police used to be blowing that they would not ask me to stand they would shoot me first and then cry surrender and how they used to rush into the house upset all the milk dishes break tins of eggs empty the flour out of bags onto the ground and even the meat out of the cask and destroy all the provisions and shove the girls in front of them into the rooms like dogs so as if anyone was there they would shoot the girls first but they knew well I was not there or I would have scattered their blood and brains like rain I would manure the Eleven Mile with their bloated carcasses and yet remember there is not one drop of murderous blood in my veins

Superintendent Smith used to say to my sisters see all the men all I have out today I will have as many more tomorrow and we will blow him into pieces as small as paper that is in our guns Detective Ward and Constable Hayes took out their revolvers and threatened to shoot the girls and children in Mrs Skillions absence the greatest ruffians and murderers no matter how deprived would not be guilty of such a cowardly action, and this sort of cruelty and disgraceful and cowardly conduct to my brothers and sisters who had no protection coupled with the conviction of my mother and those men certainly made my blood boil and I don't thing there is a man born could have the patience to suffer it as long as I did or ever allow his blood to get cold while such insults as these were unavenged and yet in every paper that is printed I am called the blackest and coldest blooded murderer ever on record But if I hear any more of it I will not exactly show them what cold blooded murder is but wholesale and retail slaughter something different to shooting three troopers in self defence and robbing a bank. I would have been rather hot blooded to throw down my rifle and let them shoot me and my innocent brother. they were not satisfied with frightening my sisters night and day and destroying their provisions and lagging my mother and infant and those innocent men but should follow me and my brother into the wilds where he had been quietly digging neither molesting or interfering with anyone he was making good wages as the creek is very rich within half a mile from where I shot Kennedy. I was not there long and on the 25th of October I came on Police tracks between Table top and the bogs. I crossed them and returning in the evening I came on a different lot of tracks making for the shingle hut I went to our camp and told my brother and his two mates. me and my brother went and found their camp at the shingle hut about a mile from my brothers house. We saw they carried long firearms and we knew our doom was sealed if we could not beat those before the others would come as I knew the other party of Police would soon join them and if they came on us at our camp they would shoot us down like dogs at our work as we had only two guns we thought it best to try and bail those up, take their firearms and ammunition and horses and we could stand a chance with the rest We approached the spring as close as we could get to the camp as the intervening space being clear ground and no battery we saw two men at the logs they got up and one took a double barreled fowling piece and fetched a horse down and hobbled him at the tent we thought there were more men in the tent asleep those outside being on sentry we could have shot those two men without speaking but not wishing to take their lives we waited McIntyre laid his gun against a stump and Lonigan sat on the log I advanced, my brother Dan keeping McIntyre covered which he took to be Constable Flood and had he not obeyed my orders, or attempted to reach for the gun or draw his revolver he would have been shot dead, but when I called on them to throw up their hands McIntyre obeyed and Lonigan ran some six or seven yards to a battery of logs instead of dropping behind the one he was sitting on, he had just got to the logs and put his head up to take aim when I shot him that instant or he would have shot me as I took him for Strachan the man who said he would not ask me to stand he would shoot me first like a dog. But it happened to be Lonigan the man who in company with Sergeant Whelan Fitzpatrick and King the Bootmaker and Constable O'Day that tried to put a pair of handcuffs on me in Benalla but could not and had to allow McInnis the miller to put them on, previous to Fitzpatrick swearing he was shot, I was fined two pounds for hitting Fitzpatrick and two pounds for not allowing five curs like Sergeant Whelan O'Day Fitzpatrick King and Lonigan who caught me by the privates and would have sent me to Kingdom come only I was not ready and he is the man that blowed before he left Violet Town if Ned Kelly was to be shot he was the man would shoot him and no doubt he would shoot me even if I threw up my arms and laid down as he knew four of them could not arrest me single handed not to talk of the rest of my mates, also either he or me would have to die, this he knew well therefore he had a right to keep out of my road, Fitzpatrick is the only one I hit out of the five in Benalla, this shows my feeling towards him as he said we were good friends and even swore it but he was the biggest enemy I had in the country with the exception of Lonigan and he can be thankful I was not there when he took a revolver and threatened to shoot my mother in her own house it is not true I fire three shots and missed him at a yard and a half I don't think I would use a revolver to shoot a man like him when I was within a yard and a half of him or attempt to fire into a house where my mother brothers and sisters was according to Fitzpatricks statement all around him a man that is such a bad shot as to miss a man three times at a yard and a half would never attempt to fire into a house among a house full of women and children while I had a pair of arms and bunch of fives at the end of them they never failed to peg out anything they came in contact with and Fitzpatrick knew the weight of one of them only too well as it run up against him once in Benalla and cost me two pound odd as he is very subject to fainting. As soon as I shot Lonigan he jumped up and staggered some distance from the logs with his hands raised and then fell he surrendered but too late I asked McIntyre who was in the tent he replied no one. I advanced and took possession of their two revolvers and fowling piece which I loaded with bullets instead of shot.

I asked McIntyre where his mates was he said they had gone down the creek and he did not expect them that night he asked me was I going to shoot him and his mates. I told him no I would shoot no man if he gave up his arms and leave the force he said the police all knew Fitzpatrick had wronged us and he intended to leave the force as he had bad health and his life was insured he told me he intended going home and that Kennedy and Scanlon were out looking for our camp and also about the other Police he told me the N.S.W. Police had shot a man for shooting Sergeant Walling I told him if they did they had shot the wrong man and I expect your gang came to do the same with me he said no they did not come to shoot me they came to apprehend me I asked him what they carried spencer rifles and breech loading fowling pieces and so much ammunition for as the Police was only supposed to carry one revolver and 6 cartridges in the revolver but they had eighteen rounds of revolver cartridges each three dozen for the fowling piece and twenty one spencer rifle cartridges and God knows how many they had away with the rifle this looked as if they meant not only to shoot me but to riddle me but I don't know either Kennedy Scanlon or him and had nothing against them, he said he would get them to give up their arms if I would not shoot them as I could not blame them, they had to do their duty I said I did not blame them for doing honest duty but I could not suffer them blowing me to pieces in my own native land and they knew Fitzpatrick wronged us and why not make it public and convict him but no they would rather riddle poor unfortunate creoles. but they will rue the day ever Fitzpatrick got among them. Our two mates came over when they heard the shot fired but went back again for fear the Police might come to our camp while we were all away and manure bullock flat with us on our arrival I stopped at the logs and Dan went back to the spring for fear the troopers would come in that way but I soon heard them coming up the creek I told McIntyre to tell them to give up their arms, he spoke to Kennedy who was some distance in front of Scanlon he reached for his revolver and jumped off, on the offside of his horse and got behind a tree when I called on them to throw up their arms and Scanlan who carried the rifle slewed his horse around to gallop away but the horse would not go and as quick as thought fired at me with the rifle without unslinging it and was in the act of firing again when I had to shoot him and he fell from his horse.

I could have shot them without speaking but their lives was no good to me. McIntyre jumped on Kennedys horse and I allowed him to go as I did not like to shoot him after he surrendered or I would have shot him as he was between me and Kennedy therefore I could not shoot Kennedy without shooting him first. Kennedy kept firing from behind the tree my brother Dan advanced and Kennedy ran I followed him he stopped behind another tree and fired again. I shot him in the arm pit and he dropped his revolver and ran I fired again with the gun as he slewed around to surrender I did not know he had dropped his revolver, the bullet passed through the right side of his chest and he could not live or I would have let him go had they been my own brothers I could not help shooting them or else let them shoot me which they would have done had their bullets been directed as they intended them. But as for handcuffing Kennedy to a tree or cutting his ear off or brutally treating any of them is a falsehood if Kennedy's ear was cut off it was not done by me and none of my mates was near him after he was shot I put his cloak over him and left him as well as I could and were they my own brothers I could not have been more sorry for them this cannot be called wilful murder for I was compelled to shoot them, or lie down and let them shoot me it would not be wilful murder if they packed our remains in, shattered into a mass of animated gore to Mansfield, they would have got great praise and credit as well as promotion but I am reconed a horrid brute because I had not been cowardly enough to lie down for them under such trying circumstances and insults to my people certainly their wives and children are to be pitied but they must remember those men came into the bush with the intention of scattering pieces of me and my brother all over the bush and yet they know and acknowledge I have been wronged and my mother and four or five men lagged innocent and is my brothers and sisters and my mother not to be pitied also who has no alternative only to put up with the brutal and cowardly conduct of a parcel of big ugly fat-necked wombat headed big bellied magpie legged narrow hipped splay-footed sons of Irish Bailiffs or english landlords which is better known as offices of Justice or Victorian Police who some calls honest gentlemen but I would like to know what business an honest man would have in the Police as it is an old saying it takes a rogue to catch a rogue and a man that knows nothing about roguery would never enter the force and take an oath to arrest brother sister father or mother if required and to have a case and conviction if possible any man knows it is possible to swear a lie and if a policeman looses a conviction for the sake of swearing a lie he has broke his oath therefore he is a perjuror either ways, a Policeman is a disgrace to his country not alone to the mother that suckled him, in the first place he is a rogue in his heart but too cowardly to follow it up without having the force to disguise it. Next he is a traitor to his country ancestors and religion as they were all catholics before the Saxons and Cranmore yoke held sway since then they were persecuted massacred thrown into martyrdom and tortured beyond the ideas of the present generation. What would people say if they saw a strapping big lump of an Irishman shepherding sheep for fifteen bob a week or tailing turkeys in Tallarook ranges for a smile from Julia or even begging his tucker, they would say he ought to be ashamed of himself and tar-and-feather him. But he would be a king to a policeman who for a lazy loafing cowardly bilit left the ash corner deserted the shamrock, the emblem of true wit and beauty to serve under a flag and nation that has destroyed massacreed and murdered their fore-fathers by the greatest torture as rolling them down hill in spiked barrels pulling their toe and finger nails and on the wheel and every torture imaginable more was transported to Van Diemand's Land to pine their young lives away in starvation and misery among tyrants worse than the promised hell itself all of true blood bone and beauty, that was not murdered on their own soil, or had fled to America or other countries to bloom again another day were doomed to Port McQuarie Toweringabbie Norfolk island and Emu plains and in those places of tyrany and condemnation many a blooming Irishman rather than subdue to the Saxon yoke were flogged to death and bravely died in servile chains but true to the shamrock and a credit to Paddys land What would people say if I became a policeman and took an oath to arrest my brother and sisters and relations and convict them by fair or foul means after the conviction of my mother and the persecutions and insults offered to myself and people Would they say I was a decent gentleman and yet a policeman is still in worse and guilty of meaner actions than that The Queen must surely be proud of such herioc men as the Police and Irish soldiers as It takes eight or eleven of the biggest mud crushers in Melbourne to take one poor little half starved larrakin to a watchhouse. I have seen as many as eleven, big and ugly enough to lift Mount Macedon out of a crab hole more like the species of a baboon or Guerilla than a man actually come into a court house and swear they could not arrest one eight stone larrakin and them armed with battens and niddies without some civilians assistance and some of them going to the hospital from the effects of hits from the fists of the larrakin and the Magistrate would send the poor little larrakin into a dungeon for being a better man than such a parcel of armed curs. What would England do if America declared war and hoisted a green flag as it is all Irishman that has got command of her armies forts and batteries even her very life guards and beef tasters are Irish would they not slew around and fight her with their own arms for the sake of the colour they dare not wear for years and to reinstate it and rise old Erins isle once more from the pressure and tyrannism of the English yoke which has kept it in poverty and starvation and caused them to wear the enemy's coat. What else can England expect.

Is there not big fat-necked Unicorns enough paid to torment and drive me to do thing which I don't wish to do, without the public assisting them I have never interfered with any person unless they deserved it and yet there are civilians who take fire-arms against me, for what reason I do not know unless they want me to turn on them and exterminate them with out medicine. I shall be compelled to make an example of some of them if they cannot find no other employment If I had robbed and plundered ravished and murdered everything I met young and old rich and poor the public could not do any more than take firearms and assisting the police as they have done, but by the light that shines pegged on an ant-bed with their bellies opened their fat taken out rendered and poured down their throat boiling hot will be cool to what pleasure I will give some of them and any person aiding or harbouring or assisting the Police in any way whatever or employing any person whom they know to be a detective or cad or those who would be so deprived as to take blood money will be outlawed and declared unfit to be allowed human buriel their property either consumed or confiscated and them theirs and all belonging to them exterminated off the face of the earth, the enemy I cannot catch myself I shall give a payable reward for, I would like to know who put that article that reminds me of a poodle dog half clipped in the lion fashion called Brooke E. Smith Superintendent of Police he knows as much about commanding Police as Captain Standish does about mustering mosquitoes and boiling them down for their fat on the back blocks of the Lachlan for he has a head like a turnip a stiff neck as big as his shoulders narrow hipped and pointed towards the feet like a vine stake and if there is any one to be called a murderer regarding Kennedy, Scanlan and Lonigan it is that misplaced poodle he gets as much pay as a dozen good troopers if there is any *good* in them, and what does he do for it he cannot look behind him without turning his whole frame it takes three or four police to keep sentry while he sleeps in Wangaratta, for fear of body snatchers do they think he is a superior animal to the men that has to guard him if so why not send the men that gets big pay and reconed superior to the common police after me and you shall soon save the country of high salaries to men that is fit for nothing else but getting better men than himself shot and sending orphan children to the industrial school to make prostitutes and cads of them for the Detectives and other evil disposed persons send the high paid and men that received big salaries for year in a gang by themselves after me, As it makes no difference to them but it will give them a chance of showing whether they are worth more pay than a common trooper or not and I think the Public will soon find they are only in the road of good men and obtaining money under false pretences. I do not call McIntyre a coward for I reckon he is as game a man as wears the jacket as he had the presence of mind to know his position, directly as he was spoken to, and only foolishness to disobey, it was cowardice that made Lonigan and the others fight it is only foolhardiness to disobey an outlaw as any Policeman or other man who do not throw up their arms directly as I call on them knows the consequence which is a speedy dispatch to Kingdom come I wish those men who joined the stock protection society to withdraw their money and give it and as much more to the widows and orphans and poor of Greta district where I spent and will again spend many a happy day fearless free and bold as it only aids the police to procure false witnesses and go whacks with men to steal horses and lag innocent men it would suit them far better to subscribe a sum and give it to the poor of their district and there is no fear of anyone stealing their property for no man could steal their horses without the knowledge of the poor if any man was mean enough to steal their property the poor would rise out to a man and find them if they were on the face of the earth it will always pay a rich man to be liberal with the poor and make as little enemies as he can as he shall find if the poor is on his side he shall loose nothing by it. If they depend in the police they shall be drove to destruction, as they can not and will not protect them if duffing and bushranging were abolished the police would have to cadge for their living I speak from experience as I have sold horses and cattle innumerable and yet eight head of the culls is all ever was found I never was interfered with whilst I kept up this successful trade. I give fair warning to all those who has reason to fear me to sell out and give £10 out of every hundred towards the widow and orphan fund and do not attempt to reside in Victoria but as short a time as possible after reading this notice, neglect this and abide by the consequences, which shall be worse than the rust in the wheat in Victoria or the druth of a dry season to the grasshoppers in New South Wales I do not wish to give the order full force without giving timely warning, but I am a widows son outlawed and my orders *must be obeyed*.

EDWARD KELLY.

Index

44-5, 153, 203, 231

Squatters, 3-4, 7, 11, 12, 16, 20, 21, 23, 29, 37, 38, 41, 93, 94, 102, 121, 122, 232

Standish, Captain, background 89; command of hunt 94-137; Sebastopol 70, 71; Euroa 89-90; sympathisers' arrests 95, 122; cave parties 121, 143; Glenrowan 169-70; and Hare 90, 131, 136, 146; and McBean 25; and Nicolson 41, 90, 136, 142, 143-4, 145, 231; and Commission 228, 231, 234

views on — Fitzpatrick 45; — Mrs Kelly 142; — trackers and O'Connor 123, 136, 146, 150, 170, 228

Stanistreet, S. M., 158, 159, 160, 162, 172, 176

Steele, Sergeant A. L. M., 40, 41, 42, 43, 49, 50, 58, 177, 178, 179, 180, 181, 182, 183, 197, 200, 208, 227, 231

Stephens, George, 74, 77, 88, 203, 206

Stock Protection Societies, 38, 42, 46, 121, 123, 231, 232

Stock theft, 9, 10, 11, 16, 21, 23, 24, 29, 36, 37, 51, 73

Strahan, Senior Constable H., 41, 42, 44, 56, 58, 59, 71

Strathbogie Ranges, 19, 38, 72, 73, 81, 200

Stringybark Creek, police plans 52-4; attack at 55-62; search for bodies 63, 64

Sullivan (N.Z. murderer), 166-7, 168

Sympathisers, see Kelly sympathy

Tarleton, 105, 106, 107, 108, 112, 114, 115, 138, 208

Thom, Constable, 38, 39

Vandemonians, 2

Wallan, 4, 6, 15

Wallings, Sergeant, 57, 58

Wangaratta, 17, 19, 20, 27, 34, 41; and Kellys 30 passim

Warby Ranges, 19, 69, 88, 101, 133, 135, 201

Ward, Detective M. E., 43, 47, 52, 95, 100, 101, 118, 119, 120, 129, 141, 142, 147, 148, 149, 153, 206, 227, 231

Westwood, William, 5

Whelan, Sergeant J., 40, 41, 43, 46, 230

Whitty, James, 35, 36, 37, 40, 112

Wicks, Anton, 153, 154, 156

Williamson, William, 22, 31, 33, 42, 43, 44, 45, 153, 203, 231

Wodonga 15, 34, 69, 91, 139, 143

Wombat Ranges, 20, 47, 52, 53, 134

Woolshed, 20, 50; and Kellys 100 passim

Wright, Isaiah (Wild), 29, 30, 31, 35, 53, 66, 95, 97, 122, 189, 193, 220, 222

Wyatt, A. (Police Magistrate), 46, 82, 97; and Euroa 86-7, 88, 90

Yackandandah, 139, 151

Younghusbands' station, and Euroa 73-8, 82-4, 86-7